HUNTED AND DESPISED, BUT HEROIC in spirit and sense of mission. Such were the apostles after the resurrection of their Lord and Master. What was the secret of their remarkable strength and courage? How could a handful of very common men and women become the nucleus of a vigorous world church, even within the first century? These and other subjects of immense concern to the human family are discussed in this worldwide best seller—a book that will delight and reward the reader.

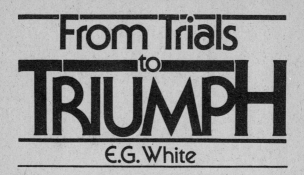

From Trials to TRIUMPH

E.G. White

A condensation of
The Acts of the Apostles

PACIFIC PRESS
PUBLISHING ASSOCIATION
Mountain View, California
Oshawa, Ontario

This condensation is not a paraphrase. The author's own words are retained throughout, except when it has been necessary to substitute a proper noun for a pronoun to avoid confusion, to change a verb tense to maintain meaning and continuity, or to supply a word or phrase to make a sentence read more smoothly.

ISBN 0-8163-0565-X   84 85 86 87 88 89 • 6 5 4 3 2 1

Why You Should Read This Book

The book of Acts was written by "the beloved physician," Luke, a Gentile convert. In the book God clearly indicates that the church in every age shall experience the presence of the same Spirit who came with power at Pentecost and fanned the gospel message into flame.

The abruptness with which Acts ends deliberately suggests that the thrilling narrative is unfinished. The acts recorded in this remarkable book are in the truest sense the acts of the Spirit. At Pentecost the praying disciples were filled with the Spirit and preached the gospel with power. When the church suffered intensely at the hands of Roman and Jewish persecutors, it was the Spirit who sustained the believers and kept them from error.

The future will witness a bestowal of spiritual power exceeding that of Pentecost. The work of the gospel is not to close with a lesser display of the Holy Spirit's power than marked its beginning.

It is our hope and prayer that you, the reader, may participate in this reenactment of the glorious scenes of the early church and be preserved from the subtle counterfeits of the enemy of souls.

The Publishers

Contents

1 / God's Purpose for His Church

The church is God's appointed agency for the salvation of men. Its mission is to carry the gospel to the world. Through the church will eventually be made manifest, even to "the principalities and powers in heavenly places," the final and full display of the love of God. Ephesians 3:10.

Many and wonderful are the promises in the Scriptures regarding the church. "Mine house shall be called an house of prayer for all people." "I will preserve thee, and give thee for a covenant of the people, to establish the earth, to cause to inherit the desolate heritages; that thou mayest say to the prisoners, Go forth; to them that are in darkness, Show yourselves." "Can a woman forget her sucking child, that she should not have compassion on the son of her womb? yea, they may forget, yet will I not forget thee." Isaiah 56: 7; 49:8, 9, 15.

The church is God's fortress, His city of refuge, which He holds in a revolted world. Any betrayal of the church is treachery to Him who has bought mankind with the blood of His only-begotten Son. From the beginning, faithful souls have constituted the church. In every age the Lord's watchmen have borne a faithful testimony to the generation in which they lived. God has sent forth His angels to minister to His church, and the gates of hell have not been able to prevail against His people. Not one opposing force has risen to counterwork His work that God has not foreseen. He has not left His church forsaken, but has traced in prophetic declarations what would occur. All His purposes will be fulfilled. Truth is inspired and guarded by God, and it will triumph over all opposition.

Enfeebled and defective as it may appear, the church is the one object on which God bestows His supreme regard. It is the theater of His grace, in which He delights to reveal His power to transform hearts.

Earthly kingdoms rule by physical power, but from Christ's kingdom every instrument of coercion is banished. This kingdom is to uplift and ennoble humanity. God's church is filled with varied gifts and endowed with the Holy Spirit.

From the beginning God has wrought through His people to bring blessing to the world. To the ancient Egyptian nation God made Joseph a fountain of life. Through him that whole people was preserved. Through Daniel God saved the life of all the wise men of Babylon. These deliverances illustrate the spiritual blessings offered the world through the God whom Joseph and Daniel worshiped. Everyone who will show forth Christ's love to the world is a worker with God for blessing humanity.

God desired Israel to be as wells of salvation in the world. The nations of the world had lost the knowledge of God. They had once known Him; but because "they glorified Him not as God, neither were thankful; but became vain in their imaginations, . . . their foolish heart was darkened." Romans 1:21. Yet God did not blot them out. He purposed to give them opportunity to become acquainted with Him through His chosen people. Through the sacrificial service, Christ was to be uplifted, and all who would look to Him should live. The whole system of types and symbols was a compacted prophecy of the gospel.

But the people of Israel forgot God and failed to fulfill their holy mission. All their advantages they appropriated for their own glorification. They shut themselves away from the world in order to escape temptation. They robbed God of service, and their fellowmen of a holy example.

Priests and rulers became satisfied with a legal religion. They thought their own righteousness all-sufficient. The good will of God to men they did not accept as something apart from themselves, but connected it with their own merit because of their good works. The faith that works by love could find no place in the religion of the Pharisees.

Of Israel God declared: "I had planted thee a noble vine, wholly a right seed: how then art thou turned into the degenerate plant of a strange vine?" Jeremiah 2:21.

"For the vineyard of the Lord of hosts is the house of Israel, and the men of Judah His pleasant plant: and He looked for judgment, but behold oppression; for righteousness, but behold a cry." "The diseased have ye not strengthened, neither have ye healed that which was sick, neither have ye bound up that which was broken, neither have ye brought again that which was driven away, neither have ye sought that which was lost; but with force and with cruelty have ye ruled them." Isaiah 5:7; Ezekiel 34:4.

The Saviour turned from the Jewish leaders to entrust to others the privileges they had abused and the work they had slighted. God's glory must be revealed; His kingdom must be established. The disciples were called to do the work that the Jewish leaders had failed to do.

2/ The Training of the Twelve

For the carrying on of His work, Christ chose humble, unlearned men. These men He purposed to train and educate. They in turn were to educate others and send them out with the gospel message. They were to be given the power of the Holy Spirit. Not by human wisdom was the gospel to be proclaimed, but by the power of God.

For three years and a half the disciples were under the instruction of the greatest Teacher the world has ever known. Day by day He taught them, sometimes sitting on the mountainside, sometimes beside the sea or walking by the way. He did not command the disciples to do this or that, but said, "Follow Me." On His journeys through country and cities, He took them with Him. They shared His frugal fare and like Him were sometimes hungry and often weary. They saw Him in every phase of life.

The ordination of the Twelve was the first step in the organization of the church. The record says, "He ordained twelve, that they should be with Him, and that He might send them forth to preach." Mark 3:14. By these feeble agencies, through His word and Spirit, He designed to place salvation within the reach of all. The words spoken by them as they witnessed would echo from generation to generation till the close of time.

The disciples' office was the most important to which human beings had ever been called, second only to that of Christ Himself. They were workers together with God for saving men. As the twelve patriarchs stood as representatives of Israel, so the twelve apostles stand as representatives of the gospel church.

No "Wall" Between Jews and Gentiles

Christ began to break down the "middle wall of partition" (Ephesians 2:14) between Jew and Gentile and to preach salvation to all mankind. He mingled freely with the despised Samaritans, setting at nought the customs of the Jews. He slept under their roofs, ate at their tables, and taught in their streets.

The Saviour longed to unfold to His disciples the truth that "the Gentiles should be fellow heirs" with the Jews and "partakers of His promise in Christ by the gospel." Ephesians 3:6. He rewarded the faith of the centurion at Capernaum; He preached to the inhabitants of Sychar; and on His visit to Phoenicia, He healed the daughter of the Canaanite woman. Among those whom many regarded as unworthy of salvation, there were souls hungering for truth.

Thus Christ sought to teach the disciples that in God's kingdom there are no territorial lines, no caste, no aristocracy. They must bear to all nations the message of a Saviour's love. But not until later did they realize in its fullness that God "made of one blood all nations of men for to dwell on all the face of the earth." Acts 17:26.

These first disciples represented widely varied types of character. Differing in natural characteristics, they needed to come into unity. To this end Christ sought to bring them into unity with Himself. His burden for them was expressed in His prayer to His Father, "That they all may be one; . . . that the world may know that Thou hast sent Me, and hast loved them, as Thou hast loved Me." John 17:21-23. He knew that truth would conquer in the battle with evil, and that the blood-stained banner would one day wave triumphantly over His followers.

As Christ realized that soon He must leave His disciples to carry on the work, He sought to prepare them for the future. He knew that they would suffer persecution, be cast out of the synagogues, and be thrown into prison. Some would suffer death. In speaking of their future, He was plain and definite, that in their coming trial they might remember His words and be strengthened to believe in Him as the Redeemer.

"Let not your heart be troubled," He said. "I go to prepare a place for you. And if I go and prepare a place for you, I will come again, and receive you unto Myself; that where I am, there ye may be also." John 14:1-3. When I go away I shall still work earnestly for you. I go to My Father and yours to cooperate with Him in your behalf.

"He that believeth on Me, the works that I do shall he do also; and greater works than these shall he do; because I go unto My Father." Verse 12. Christ did not mean that the disciples would make more exalted exertions than He had made, but that their work would have greater magnitude. He referred to all that would take place under the agency of the Holy Spirit.

What the Holy Spirit Accomplished

Wonderfully were these words fulfilled. After the descent of the Spirit, the disciples were so filled with love that hearts were melted by the words they spoke and the prayers they offered. Under the influence of the Spirit thousands were converted.

As Christ's representatives the apostles were to make a decided impression on the world. Their words of courage and trust would assure all that it was not in their own power that they worked, but in the power of Christ. They would declare that He whom the Jews had crucified was the Prince of life and that in His name they did the works that He had done.

On the night before the crucifixion the Saviour made no reference to the suffering He had endured and must yet endure. He sought to strengthen their faith, leading them to look forward to the joys that await the overcomer. He would do more for His followers than He had promised; from Him would flow love and compassion, making men like Him in character. His truth, armed with the power of the Spirit, would go forth conquering and to conquer.

Christ did not fail, neither was He discouraged; and the disciples were to show a faith of the same nature. They were to work as He worked. By His grace they were to go forward, despairing of nothing and hoping for everything.

Christ had finished the work given Him. He had gathered out those who were to continue His work. And He said: "Neither pray I for these alone, but for them also which shall believe on Me through their word; that they all may be one; . . . that the world may know that Thou hast sent Me, and hast loved them, as Thou hast loved Me." John 17:20-23.

3/ The Good News to Go Everywhere

After the death of Christ the disciples were well-nigh overcome by discouragement. The sun of their hope had set, and night settled down on their hearts. Lonely and sick at heart, they remembered Christ's words, "If they do these things in a green tree, what shall be done in the dry?" Luke 23:31.

Jesus had several times attempted to open the future to His disciples, but they had not cared to think about what He said. This left them in utter hopelessness at the time of His death. Their faith did not penetrate the shadow Satan cast athwart their horizon. If they had believed the Saviour's words, that He was to rise on the third day, how much sorrow they might have been spared!

Crushed by despondency and despair, the disciples met together in the upper chamber and fastened the doors, fearing that the fate of their beloved Teacher might be theirs. Here the Saviour, after His resurrection, appeared to them.

For forty days Christ remained on earth, preparing the disciples for the work before them. He spoke of the prophecies concerning His rejection by the Jews, and His death, showing that every specification had been fulfilled. "Then opened He their understanding," we read, "that they might understand the Scriptures." And He added, "Ye are witnesses of these things." Luke 24:45, 48.

As the disciples heard their Master explaining the Scriptures in the light of all that had happened, their faith in Him was fully established. They reached the place where they could say, "I know whom I have believed." 2 Timothy 1:12. The events of Christ's life, death, and resurrection, the prophecies pointing to these events, the plan of salvation, and the power of Jesus for remission of sins—to all these things they had been witnesses, and they were to make them known to the world.

Before ascending to heaven, Christ told His disciples that they were to be the executors of the will in which He bequeathed to the world the treasures of eternal life. Although priests and rulers have rejected Me, He said, they shall have still another opportunity of accepting the Son of God. To you, My disciples, I commit this message of mercy, to be given to Israel first, and then to all nations. All who believe are to be gathered into one church.

The gospel commission is the great missionary charter of Christ's kingdom. The disciples were to work earnestly for souls. They were to go to the people with their message. Their every word and act was to fasten attention on Christ's name, as possessing that vital power by which sinners may be saved. His name was to be their badge of distinction, the authority for their action, and the source of their success.

Successful Weapons in the Great Warfare

Christ plainly set before the disciples the necessity of maintaining simplicity. The less ostentation and show, the greater would be their influence for good. The disciples were to speak with the same simplicity with which Christ had spoken.

Christ did not tell His disciples that their work would be easy. They would have to fight "against principalities, against powers, against the rulers of the darkness of this world, against spiritual wickedness in high places." Ephesians 6:12. But they would not be left to fight alone. He would be with them. If they would go forth in faith, One mightier than angels would be in their ranks—the General of the armies of heaven. He took on Himself the responsibility of their success. So long as they worked in connection with Him, they could not fail. Go to the farthest part of the habitable globe and be assured that My presence will be with you even there.

Christ's sacrifice was full and complete. The condition of the atonement had been fulfilled. He had wrested the kingdom from Satan and become heir of all things. He was on His way to the throne of God, to be honored by the heavenly host. Clothed with boundless authority, He gave His disciples their commission: "Go ye therefore, and teach all nations, baptizing them in the name of the Father, and of the Son, and of the Holy Ghost: teaching them to observe all things whatsoever I have commanded you: and, lo, I am with you alway, even unto the end." Matthew 28:19, 20.

Just before leaving His disciples, Christ once more plainly stated that it was not His purpose to establish a temporal kingdom, to reign as an earthly monarch on David's throne. Their work was to proclaim the gospel message.

Christ's visible presence was about to be withdrawn, but a new endowment of power was to be theirs. The Holy Spirit was to be given them in its fullness. "I send the promise of My Father upon you," the Saviour said, "but tarry ye in the city of Jerusalem, until ye be endued with power from on high." "Ye shall receive power, after that the Holy Ghost is come upon you: and ye shall be witnesses unto Me both in Jerusalem, and in all Judea, and in Samaria, and unto the uttermost part of the earth." Luke 24:49; Acts 1:8.

The Saviour knew that His disciples must receive the heavenly endowment. A vigilant, determined leader was in command of the forces of darkness, and the followers of Christ could battle for the right only through the help that God, by His Spirit, would give them.

Christ's disciples were to begin their work at Jerusalem, the scene of His amazing sacrifice for the human race. In Jerusalem were many who secretly believed Jesus of Nazareth to be the Messiah, and many who had been deceived by priests and rulers. These were to be called to repentance. And it was while all Jerusalem was stirred by the thrilling events of the past few weeks that the preaching of the disciples would make the deepest impression.

During His ministry, Jesus had kept constantly before the disciples the fact that they were to be one with Him in the recovery of the world from the slavery of sin. And the last lesson He gave His followers was that they held in trust for the world the glad tidings of salvation.

When the time came for Christ to ascend to His Father, He led the disciples out as far as Bethany. Here He paused, and they gathered about Him. With His hands outstretched as if in assurance of His protecting care, He slowly ascended from among them. "While He blessed them, He was parted from them, and carried up into heaven." Luke 24:51.

While the disciples were gazing upward to catch the last glimpse of their ascending Lord, He was received into the ranks of heavenly angels and escorted to the courts above. The disciples were still looking toward heaven when "two men stood by them in white apparel; which also said, Ye men of Galilee, why stand ye gazing up into heaven? this same Jesus, which is taken up from you into heaven, shall so come in like manner as ye have seen Him go into heaven." Acts 1:10, 11.

Christ's Second Coming—the Hope of the Church

The promise of Christ's second coming was ever to be kept fresh in the minds of His disciples. The same Jesus would come again to take to Himself those who here below give themselves to His service; His voice would welcome them to His kingdom.

As in the typical service the high priest laid aside his pontifical robes and officiated in the white linen dress of an ordinary priest; so Christ laid aside His royal robes and garbed Himself with humanity and offered sacrifice, Himself the priest, Himself the victim. As the high priest, after performing his service in the holy of holies, came forth to the waiting congregation in his pontifical robes, so Christ will come the second time, clothed in His own glory and in the glory of His Father; and all the angelic host will escort Him on His way.

Thus will be fulfilled Christ's promise: "I will come again, and receive you unto Myself." John 14:3. The righteous dead will come from their graves, and those who are alive will be caught up with them, "to meet the Lord in the air" (1 Thessalonians 4:17). They will hear the voice of Jesus, sweeter than music, saying, "Come, ye blessed of My Father, inherit the kingdom prepared for you from the foundation of the world." Matthew 25:34.

Well might the disciples rejoice in the hope of their Lord's return.

4/ Pentecost: The Apostles Begin Their Work

As the disciples returned from Olivet to Jerusalem, the people expected to see on their faces confusion and defeat; but they saw gladness and triumph. The disciples had seen the risen Saviour, and His parting promise echoed in their ears.

In obedience to Christ's command, they waited in Jerusalem for the outpouring of the Spirit, "continually in the temple, praising and blessing God." Luke 24:53. They knew they had an Advocate at the throne of God. In awe they bowed in prayer, repeating the assurance, "Whatsoever ye shall ask the Father in My name, He will give it you." John 16:23. Higher and still higher they extended the hand of faith.

As the disciples waited, they humbled their hearts in repentance and confessed their unbelief. Truths which had passed from their memory were again brought to· their minds, and these they repeated to one another. Scene after scene of the Saviour's life passed before them. As they meditated on His pure life they felt that no toil would be too hard, no sacrifice too great, if only they could bear witness in their lives to the loveliness of Christ's character. If they could have the past three years to live over, they thought, how differently they would act! But they were comforted by the thought that they were forgiven, and they determined, so far as possible, to atone for their unbelief by bravely confessing Him before the world.

The disciples prayed with intense earnestness for a

This chapter is based on Acts 2:1-41.

21

fitness to meet men and speak words that would lead sinners to Christ. Putting away all differences, they came close together. And as they drew nearer to God, they realized what a privilege had been theirs to associate so closely with Christ.

The disciples did not ask for a blessing merely for themselves. They were weighted with the burden of the salvation of souls. In obedience to the word of the Saviour, they offered their supplications for the gift of the Holy Spirit, and in heaven Christ claimed the gift, that He might pour it upon His people.

How the Holy Spirit Came Upon the Apostles

"When the Day of Pentecost was fully come, they were all with one accord in one place. And suddenly there came a sound from heaven as of a rushing mighty wind, and it filled all the house where they were sitting." The Spirit came on the praying disciples with a fullness that reached every heart. Heaven rejoiced in being able to pour out the riches of the Spirit's grace. Words of penitence and confession mingled with songs of praise. Lost in wonder, the apostles grasped the imparted gift.

And what followed? The sword of the Spirit, newly edged with power and bathed in the lightnings of heaven, cut its way through unbelief. Thousands were converted in a day.

"When He, the Spirit of truth, is come," Christ had said, "He will guide you into all truth: for He shall not speak of Himself; but whatsoever He shall hear, that shall He speak: and He will show you things to come." John 16:13.

When Christ passed within the heavenly gates, He was enthroned amidst the adoration of the angels. The Holy Spirit descended on the disciples, and Christ was indeed glorified. The Pentecostal outpouring was Heaven's communication that the Redeemer's inauguration was accomplished. The Holy Spirit was sent as a token that He had, as Priest and King, received all authority in heaven and on earth and was the Anointed One.

"And there appeared unto them cloven tongues like as of fire, and it sat upon each of them. And they were all filled with the Holy Ghost, and began to speak with other tongues, as the Spirit gave them utterance." The gift of the Holy Spirit enabled the disciples to speak with fluency languages with which they had been unacquainted. The appearance of fire signified the power that would attend their work.

What the Genuine Gift of Tongues Accomplished

"There were dwelling at Jerusalem Jews, devout men, out of every nation under heaven." Scattered to almost every part of the world, they had learned to speak various languages. Many of these were in Jerusalem, attending the religious festivals. Every known tongue was represented. This diversity of languages would have been a great hindrance to the proclamation of the gospel. God therefore miraculously did for the apostles what they could not have accomplished for themselves in a lifetime. They could now speak with accuracy the languages of those for whom they were laboring—a strong evidence that their commission bore the signet of Heaven. From this time forth the language of the disciples was pure, simple, and accurate, whether in their native tongue or in a foreign language.

The multitude were "amazed and marveled, saying one to another, Behold, are not all these which speak Galileans? and how hear we every man in our own tongue?"

The priests and rulers were enraged. They had put the Nazarene to death, but here were His servants telling in all the languages then spoken, the story of His life and ministry. The priests declared that they were drunk from the new wine prepared for the feast. But those who understood the different languages testified to the accuracy with which these languages were used by the disciples.

In answer to the accusation, Peter showed that this was in fulfillment of the prophecy of Joel. He said, "These are not drunken, as ye suppose, seeing it is but the third hour of the day. But this is that which was spoken by the prophet Joel; And it shall come to pass in the last days, saith God, I will pour out of My Spirit upon all flesh: and your sons and your daughters shall prophesy, and your young men shall see visions, and your old men shall dream dreams: and on My servants and on My handmaidens I will pour out in those days of My Spirit; and they shall prophesy." See Joel 2:28, 29.

Conviction That Jesus Was the True Messiah

With power Peter bore witness of the death and resurrection of Christ: "Jesus of Nazareth, . . . ye have taken, and by wicked hands have crucified and slain: whom God hath raised up, having loosed the pains of death: because it was not possible that He should be holden of it."

Peter, knowing that the prejudice of his hearers was great, spoke of David, who was regarded by the Jews as one of the patriarchs. "David speaketh concerning Him," he declared. "I foresaw the Lord always before My face, for He is on My right hand, that I should not be moved. . . . Thou wilt not leave My soul in hell, neither wilt Thou suffer Thine Holy One to see corruption. . . .

"Let me freely speak unto you of the patriarch David, that he is both dead and buried, and his sepulcher is with us unto this day." "He . . . spake of the resurrection of Christ, that His soul was not left in hell, neither His flesh did see corruption. This Jesus hath God raised up, whereof we all are witnesses."

The people from all directions pressed in, crowding the temple. Priests and rulers were there, their hearts still filled with abiding hatred against Christ, their hands uncleansed from the blood shed when they crucified the world's Redeemer. They found the apostles lifted above all fear and filled with the Spirit, proclaiming the divinity of Jesus of Nazareth, declaring with boldness that the One so recently humiliated and crucified by cruel hands is the Prince of life exalted to the right hand of God.

Some who listened had taken part in the condemnation and death of Christ, their voices calling for His crucifixion. When Pilate asked, "Whom will ye that I release unto you?" they had shouted, 'Not this man, but Barabbas!" When Pilate delivered Christ to them, they had cried, "His blood be on us, and on our children." Matthew 27:17; John 18:40; Matthew 27:25.

Now they heard the disciples declaring that it was the Son of God who had been crucified. Priests and rulers trembled. Conviction and anguish seized the people. They said to Peter and the rest of the apostles, "Men and brethren, what shall we do?" The power that accompanied the speaker convinced them that Jesus was indeed the Messiah.

"Repent, and be baptized every one of you in the name of Jesus Christ for the remission of sins, and ye shall receive the gift of the Holy Ghost."

Thousands in Jerusalem Converted

Peter urged on the convicted people the fact that they had rejected Christ because they had been deceived by priests and rulers, and that if they continued to look to these men they would never accept Him. These powerful men were ambitious for earthly glory. They were not willing to come to Christ to receive light.

The scriptures that Christ had explained to the disciples stood out before them with the luster of perfect truth. The veil was now removed, and they comprehended with perfect clearness the object of Christ's mission and the nature of His kingdom. As they unfolded to their hearers the plan of salvation, many were convicted and convinced. Traditions and superstitions were swept away, and the teachings of the Saviour were accepted.

"Then they that gladly received his word were baptized: and the same day there were added unto them about three thousand souls." In Jerusalem, the stronghold of Judaism, thousands openly declared their faith in Jesus as the Messiah.

The disciples were astonished and overjoyed. They did not regard this as the result of their own efforts; they realized that they were entering into other men's labors. Christ had sown the seed of truth and watered it with His blood. The conversions on the Day of Pentecost were the harvest of His work.

The arguments of the apostles alone would not have removed prejudice. But the Holy Spirit sent the words of the apostles home as sharp arrows of the Almighty, convicting men of their terrible guilt in rejecting the Lord of glory.

No longer were the disciples ignorant and uncultured; no longer a collection of independent, conflicting elements. They were of "one accord," "of one heart and of one soul." In mind and character they had become like their Master, and men recognized that "they had been with Jesus." Acts 2:46; 4:32, 13. The truths they could not understand while Christ was with them were now unfolded. No longer was it a matter of faith with them that Christ was the Son of God. They knew He was indeed the Messiah, and they told their experience with a confidence which carried with it the conviction that God was with them.

Brought into close communion with Christ, the disciples sat with Him "in heavenly places." Benevolence full, deep, and far-reaching, impelled them to go to the ends of the earth, filled with an intense longing to carry forward the work He had begun. The Spirit animated them and spoke through them. The peace of Christ shone from their faces. They had consecrated their lives to Him, and their very features bore evidence to the surrender they had made.

5 / The Gift of the Spirit Is for Us

Christ was standing in the shadow of the cross, with a full realization of the load of guilt that was to rest upon Him as the Sin Bearer, when He instructed His disciples regarding a most essential gift He was to bestow on His followers. "I will pray the Father," He said, "and He shall give you another Comforter, that He may abide with you forever; even the Spirit of truth; . . . for He dwelleth with you, and shall be in you." John 14:16, 17. The evil that had been accumulating for centuries was to be resisted by the divine power of the Holy Spirit.

What was the result of the outpouring of the Spirit on the Day of Pentecost? The glad tidings of a risen Saviour were carried to the uttermost parts of the world. Converts flocked to the church from all directions. Some who had been the bitterest opponents of the gospel became its champions. One interest prevailed—to reveal the likeness of Christ's character and to labor for the enlargement of His kingdom.

"With great power gave the apostles witness of the resurrection of the Lord Jesus: and great grace was upon them all." Acts 4:33. Chosen men consecrated their lives to the work of giving to others the hope that filled their hearts with peace and joy. They could not be restrained or intimidated. As they went from place to place, the poor had the gospel preached to them, and miracles of divine grace were wrought.

From the Day of Pentecost to the present, the Comforter has been sent to all who have yielded themselves to the Lord and to His service. The Holy Spirit has come as a counselor, sanctifier, guide, and witness. The men and women who through the long centuries of persecution enjoyed the presence of the Spirit in their lives, have stood as signs and wonders in the world. They have revealed the transforming power of redeeming love.

Those who at Pentecost were endued with power, were not thereby freed from further temptation. They were repeatedly assailed by the enemy, who sought to rob them of their Christian experience. They were compelled to strive with all their God-given powers to reach the stature of men and women in Christ. Daily they prayed that they might reach still higher toward perfection. Even the weakest learned to improve their entrusted powers and to become sanctified, refined, and ennobled. As in humility they submitted to the molding influence of the Holy Spirit, they were fashioned in the likeness of the divine.

God Has Not Restricted His Gift

The lapse of time has made no change in Christ's promise to send the Holy Spirit. If the fulfillment is not seen, it is because the promise is not appreciated as it should be. Wherever the Holy Spirit is little thought of, there is seen spiritual drought, spiritual darkness, and spiritual death. When minor matters occupy the attention, the divine power necessary for the growth and prosperity of the church is lacking.

Why do we not hunger and thirst for the Spirit? The Lord is more willing to give the Spirit than parents are to give good gifts to their children. For the daily baptism of the Spirit every worker should petition God. The presence of the Spirit with God's workers will give the proclamation of truth a power that not all the glory of the world could give.

The words spoken to the disciples are spoken also to us. The Comforter is ours as well as theirs. The Spirit furnishes the strength that sustains wrestling souls in every emergency, amidst the hatred of the world and the realization of their own failures. When the outlook seems dark and the future perplexing, and we feel helpless and alone, the Holy Spirit brings comfort to the heart.

Holiness is living by every word that proceeds from the mouth of God. It is trusting God in darkness as well as in the light, walking by faith and not by sight.

The nature of the Holy Spirit is a mystery. Men may bring together passages of Scripture and put a human construction on them, but the acceptance of fanciful views will not strengthen the church. Regarding mysteries which are too deep for human understanding, silence is golden.

The Holy Spirit convicts of sin. See John 16:8. If the sinner responds, he will be brought to repentance and aroused to the importance of obeying the divine requirements. To the repentant sinner, the Holy Spirit reveals the Lamb of God that takes away the sin of the world. Christ said, "He shall teach you all things, and bring all things to your remembrance, whatsoever I have said unto you." John 14:26.

The Spirit is given as a regenerating agency, to make effectual the salvation wrought by the death of our Redeemer. The Spirit is constantly seeking to draw attention to the cross of Calvary, to unfold the love of God, and to open to the convicted soul the precious things of the Scriptures. Having brought conviction of sin, the Holy Spirit withdraws the affections from the things of this earth and fills the soul with a desire for holiness. "He will guide you into all truth." John 16:13. The Spirit will take the things of God and stamp them on the soul.

From the beginning, God has been working by His Holy Spirit through human instrumentalities. In the days of the apostles He worked mightily for His church through the Holy Spirit. The same power that sustained the patriarchs, that gave Caleb and Joshua faith and courage, and that made the work of the apostolic church effective has upheld God's faithful children in every succeeding age. Through the Holy Spirit during the Dark Ages the Waldensian Christians helped prepare the way for the Reformation. The same power made successful the efforts of noble men and women who pioneered the way for modern missions and for the translation of the Bible into the languages of all nations.

And today the heralds of the cross are going from land to land, preparing the way for the second advent of Christ. God's law is being exalted. The Spirit is moving on men's hearts, and those who respond become witnesses for God's truth. Consecrated men and women communicate the light that has made plain the way of salvation through Christ. And as they continue to let their light shine, they receive still more of the Spirit's power. Thus the earth is to be lightened with the glory of God.

On the other hand, some are idly waiting for some spiritual refreshing by which their ability to enlighten others will be greatly increased. They allow their light to burn dim, while they look to a time when, without any effort on their part, they will be transformed and fitted for service.

The Early Rain and the Latter Rain

It is true that when God's work in the earth is closing, earnest efforts by consecrated believers are to be accompanied by special tokens of divine favor. Under the figure of the early and latter rains that fall in Eastern lands at seedtime and harvest, the prophets foretold the outpouring of the Spirit. The outpouring in the days of the apostles was the early, or former, rain, and glorious was the result.

But near the close of earth's harvest a special bestowal is promised to prepare the church for the coming of the Son of man. This outpouring is the latter rain, and for this added power Christians are to send their petitions to the Lord of the harvest "in the time of the latter rain." In response, "the Lord shall . . . give them showers of rain." "He will cause to come down . . . the rain, the former rain, and the latter rain." Zechariah 10:1; Joel 2:23. But only those who constantly receive fresh supplies of grace will have ability ot use that power. Daily they are improving the opportunities for service that lie within their reach, witnessing wherever they may be, in the home or in a public field of usefulness.

Even Christ during His life on earth sought His Father daily for fresh supplies of grace. The Son of God bowed in prayer to His Father! He strengthened His faith by prayer and gathered to Himself power to resist evil and to minister to men.

The Elder Brother of our race knows the necessities of those who live in a world of sin and temptation. The messengers whom He sees fit to send are weak and erring, but to all who give themselves to His service He promises divine aid. His own example is an assurance that faith and unreserved consecration to His work will bring the Holy Spirit's aid in the battle against sin.

Morning by morning, as the heralds of the gospel renew their vows of consecration to the Lord, He will grant them His Spirit, with its reviving, sanctifying power. As they go forth to the day's duties, the unseen agency of the Holy Spirit enables them to be "laborers together with God."

6/ Peter and John Forbidden to Do Christ's Work

A short time after the descent of the Holy Spirit, Peter and John, going up to the temple, saw at the gate Beautiful a cripple, forty years of age, whose life from birth had been one of pain. This unfortunate man had long desired to be healed but was far removed from the scene of Jesus' labors. His pleadings at last induced some friends to bear him to the gate of the temple, but he found that the One on whom his hopes were centered had been put to death.

Those who knew how long he had eagerly hoped to be healed by Jesus brought him to the temple daily, in order that passers-by might give him a trifle to relieve his wants. As Peter and John passed, he asked alms from them. Peter said, "Look on us. And he gave heed unto them, expecting to receive something of them. Then Peter said, Silver and gold have I none." The countenance of the cripple fell, but the apostle continued: "But such as I have give I thee: In the name of Jesus Christ of Nazareth rise up and walk.

"And he took him by the right hand, and lifted him up: and immediately his feet and ankle bones received strength. And he leaping up stood, and walked, and entered with them into the temple, walking, and leaping, and praising God. And all the people saw him walking and praising God: and they knew that it was he which sat for alms at the Beautiful Gate of the temple."

And "all the people ran together unto them in the

This chapter is based on Acts 3; 4:1-31.

porch that is called Solomon's, greatly wondering." Here was this man, for forty years a helpless cripple, rejoicing in the full use of his limbs and happy in believing in Jesus.

Peter assured the people that the cure had been wrought through the merits of Jesus of Nazareth, whom God had raised from the dead. "His name through faith in His name, hath made this man strong, whom ye see and know: yea, the faith which is by Him hath given him this perfect soundness in the presence of you all."

The True Guilt of the Jews Revealed

The apostles spoke plainly of the great sin of the Jews in putting to death the Prince of life, but they were careful not to drive their hearers to despair. "Ye denied the Holy One and the Just," Peter said, "and desired a murderer to be granted unto you; and killed the Prince of life, whom God hath raised from the dead; whereof we are witnesses." "And now, brethren, I wot that through ignorance ye did it, as did also your rulers." RSV. He declared that the Holy Spirit was calling them to repent. Only by faith in the One whom they had crucified could their sins be forgiven.

"Repent ye therefore, and be converted," Peter cried, "that your sins may be blotted out, when the times of refreshing shall come from the presence of the Lord." "God, having raised up His Son Jesus, sent Him to bless you, in turning away every one of you from his iniquities."

Many were waiting for this testimony, and when they heard it they believed and took their stand in the ranks of those who accepted the gospel.

While the disciples were speaking, "the priests, and the captain of the temple, and the Sadducees, came upon them, being grieved that they taught the people, and preached through Jesus the resurrection from the dead."

The priests had spread the report that Christ's body

had been stolen by the disciples while the Roman guard slept. It is not surprising that they were displeased when they heard Peter and John preaching the resurrection of the One they had murdered. The Sadducees felt that their most cherished doctrine was in danger.

Pharisees and Sadducees agreed that if these new teachers were to go unchecked, their own influence would be in greater danger than when Jesus was on earth. Accordingly, the captain of the temple, with the help of a number of Sadducees, arrested Peter and John and put them in prison.

Abundant evidence that the apostles were speaking and acting under divine inspiration had been given the Jewish rulers, but they firmly resisted the truth. Though at times they had been convinced that Christ was the Son of God, they had stifled conviction and crucified Him. Now another opportunity was granted them to turn to Him. But the Jewish teachers refused to admit that the men charging them with crucifying Christ were speaking by direction of the Holy Spirit.

Their obstinacy became more determined. It was not that they could not yield; they could, but would not. They persistently rejected light and stifled the convictions of the Spirit, their rebellion intensified by each successive act of resistance against the message God had given His servants to declare.

A Sin Worse Than the Original Crucifixion of Christ

The wrath of God is not declared against unrepentant sinners merely because of the sins they have committed, but because, when called to repent, they choose to continue in defiance of light. If the Jewish leaders had submitted to the convicting power of the Holy Spirit, they would have been pardoned; but they were determined not to yield.

On the day following the healing of the cripple, Annas and Caiaphas met for the trial, and the prisoners were brought before them. In that very room, before some of those men, Peter had shamefully denied his

Lord. He now had an opportunity of redeeming his cowardice. The Peter who denied Christ was impulsive and self-confident; but since his fall he had been converted. He was modest and self-distrustful, filled with the Holy Spirit, and was resolved to remove the stain of his apostasy by honoring the name he had once disowned.

The priests were forced to inquire of the accused how the cure of the crippled man had been accomplished. With holy boldness Peter declared: "Be it known unto you all, and to all the people of Israel, that by the name of Jesus Christ of Nazareth, whom ye crucified, whom God raised from the dead, even by Him doth this man stand here before you whole."

The Jewish leaders had supposed the disciples would be overcome with fear and confusion when brought before the Sanhedrin. Instead, these witnesses spoke with a convincing power that silenced their adversaries. There was no trace of fear in Peter's voice as he declared of Christ, "This is the stone which was set at naught of you builders, which is become the head of the corner."

As the priests listened to the apostles' fearless words, "they took knowledge of them, that they had been with Jesus." When the disciples first heard the words of Christ, they felt their need of Him. They sought, they found, they followed Him, in the temple, at the table, on the mountainside, in the field. They were as pupils with a teacher, daily receiving from Him lessons of eternal truth.

Jesus, the Saviour, who had walked and talked and prayed with them, had ascended to heaven in the form of humanity. They knew that He was before the throne of God, their Friend and Saviour still, forever identified with suffering humanity. Their union with Him was stronger now than when He was with them in person. An indwelling Christ shone out through them, so that men, beholding, marveled.

Close beside Peter as a convincing witness stood the

man who had been miraculously healed. The appearance of this man added weight to Peter's words. Priests and rulers were silent, unable to refute Peter's statement, but they were nonetheless determined to put a stop to the teaching of the disciples.

The priests had crucified Jesus, but here was convincing proof that they had not put a stop to the working of miracles in His name, nor to the proclamation of the truth He taught. The healing of the cripple and the preaching of the apostles had filled Jerusalem with excitement!

The priests and rulers ordered the apostles to be taken away, that they might counsel among themselves. It would be useless to deny that the man had been healed. To cover up the miracle by falsehoods was impossible, for it had been wrought before a multitude of people. They felt that the work of the disciples must be stopped, or their own disgrace would follow.

Calling them again before the Sanhedrin, the priests commanded them not to speak or teach in the name of Jesus. But Peter and John answered: "Whether it be right in the sight of God to hearken unto you more than unto God, judge ye. For we cannot but speak the things which we have seen and heard." So, with repeated threats and injunctions, the apostles were set at liberty.

The Divine Gift of Holy Boldness

While Peter and John were prisoners, the other disciples prayed unceasingly for their brethren, fearing that the cruelty shown to Christ might be repeated. As soon as the two apostles were released, they reported the result of the examination. Great was the joy of the believers. "They lifted their voices together to God and said, Sovereign Lord, . . . look upon their threats, and grant to Thy servants to speak Thy word with all boldness, while Thou stretchest out Thy hand to heal, and signs and wonders are performed through the name of Thy Holy Servant Jesus." RSV.

The disciples saw that they would meet the same determined opposition that Christ had encountered. While their united prayers were ascending in faith to heaven, the answer came. They were endowed anew with the Holy Spirit. Filled with courage, they again went forth to proclaim the word of God. "With great power gave the apostles witness of the resurrection of the Lord Jesus." And God blessed their efforts.

The principle for which the disciples stood so fearlessly is the same that adherents of the gospel maintained in the days of the Reformation. At the Diet of Spires, in 1529, there was presented to the German princes the emperor's decree restricting religious liberty and prohibiting further dissemination of the reformed doctrines. Would the princes accept the decree? Should the light of the gospel be shut out from multitudes still in darkness? Those who had accepted the reformed faith met together, and their unanimous decision was, "Let us reject this decree. In matters of conscience the majority has no power."

The banner of religious liberty held aloft by the founders of the gospel church and by God's witnesses during the centuries since then, has, in this last conflict, been committed to our hands. We are to recognize human government as of divine appointment and teach obedience to it as a sacred duty, within its legitimate sphere; but when its claims conflict with the claims of God, we must obey God rather than men. A "Thus saith the Lord" is not to be set aside for a "Thus saith the church" or a "Thus saith the state."

We are not to defy authorities. Our words should be carefully considered, lest we appear antagonistic to law and order. We are not to say or do anything that would unnecessarily close up our way of advocating the truths committed to us. If we are forbidden by men to do this work, then we may say, as did the apostles, "Whether it be right in the sight of God to hearken unto you more than unto God, judge ye. For we cannot but speak the things which we have seen and heard."

7 / A Dishonest Husband and Wife Punished

As the disciples proclaimed the gospel, a multitude believed. Many of these early believers were immediately cut off from family and friends, and it was necessary to provide them with food and shelter.

Those among the believers who had money and possessions cheerfully sacrificed to meet the emergency. Selling their houses or lands, they brought the money and laid it at the apostles' feet. Their love for their brethren and the cause they had espoused was greater than their love of money and possessions. They accounted souls of higher value than earthly wealth.

In sharp contrast was the conduct of Ananias and Sapphira. These professed disciples had heard the gospel preached by the apostles. They had been present when "the place was shaken where they were assembled together; and they were all filled with the Holy Ghost." Acts 4:31. Under the direct influence of the Spirit of God, Ananias and Sapphira had made a pledge to give to the Lord the proceeds from the sale of a certain property.

Afterward, they began to regret their promise and yielded to feelings of covetousness. They thought they had been too hasty and decided not to fulfill their pledge. Ashamed to have their brethren know that their selfish souls grudged that which they had solemnly dedicated to God, they deliberately decided to sell their property and pretend to give all into the gen-

This chapter is based on Acts 4:32 to 5:11.

eral fund, but to keep a large share for themselves. Thus they would secure their living from the common store and at the same time gain the esteem of their brethren. But God notes hypocrisy and falsehood. Ananias and Sapphira lied to the Holy Spirit, and their sin was visited with swift judgment. When Ananias came with his offering, Peter said: "Ananias, why hath Satan filled thine heart to lie to the Holy Ghost, and to keep back part of the price of the land? Whiles it remained, was it not thine own? and after it was sold, was it not in thine own power? why hast thou conceived this thing in thine heart? thou hast not lied unto men, but unto God."

"Ananias hearing these words fell down, and gave up the ghost: and great fear came on all them that heard these things."

No undue influence had been brought to bear on Ananias to compel him to sacrifice his possessions. He had acted from choice. But in attempting to deceive the disciples, he had lied to the Almighty.

"After an interval of about three hours his wife came in, not knowing what had happened. And Peter said to her, 'Tell me whether you sold the land for so much.' And she said, 'Yes, for so much.' But Peter said to her, 'How is it that you have agreed together to tempt the Spirit of the Lord? Hark, the feet of those that have buried your husband are at the door, and they will carry you out.' Immediately she fell down at his feet and died. When the young men came in they found her dead, and they carried her out and buried her beside her husband. And great fear came upon the whole church, and upon all who heard of these things." RSV.

Why This Manifestation of God's Wrath

Infinite Wisdom saw that this manifestation of the wrath of God was necessary to guard the young church from becoming demoralized. The church would have been endangered if, in the rapid increase of converts, men and women had been added who were worshiping mammon. This judgment was a warning to the church to avoid pretense and hypocrisy and to beware of robbing God.

God has made the proclamation of the gospel dependent on the labors and gifts of His people—voluntary offerings and the tithe. God claims the tenth; He leaves all free to say whether to give more than this. But when the heart is stirred by the Holy Spirit and a vow is made to give a certain amount, the one who vows has no longer any right to the consecrated portion. Are promises made to God less binding than written agreements of men?

When divine light is shining into the heart with unusual clearness, habitual selfishness relaxes its grasp and there is a disposition to give to God. But Satan is not pleased to see the Redeemer's kingdom on earth built up. He suggests that the pledge was too much, that it may cripple their efforts to acquire property or gratify the desires of their families.

God blesses men and women with property that they may be able to give to His cause. He gives them health and the ability to acquire means. In turn, He would have them show their gratitude by returning tithes and offerings. Should means flow into the treasury in accordance with this divinely appointed plan, there would be an abundance for the advancement of the Lord's work.

But hearts become hardened through selfishness. Like Ananias and Sapphira, many spend money lavishly in self-gratification while they bring to God almost unwillingly a stinted offering. They forget that God will no more accept the pittance they hand into the treasury than He accepted the offering of Ananias and Sapphira.

God would have us learn how deep is His hatred for hypocrisy and deception. Ananias and Sapphira lied to the Holy Spirit and lost this life and the life that is to come. God declares that into the Holy City "there shall in no wise enter . . . anything that defileth, neither whatsoever worketh abomination, or maketh a lie." Revelation 21:27. Let truth telling become a part of the life! Playing fast and loose with truth means shipwreck of faith. "Stand therefore, having your loins girt about with truth." Ephesians 6:14. He who utters untruths sells his soul in a cheap market. He may seem to make business advancement that he could not gain by fair dealing; but finally he can trust no one. Himself a falsifier, he has no confidence in the word of others.

In the case of Ananias and Sapphira, fraud against God was speedily punished. The same sin is committed by many in our time. It is no less heinous in His sight now than in the apostles' time. The warning has been given; all who give themselves up to hyprocrisy and covetousness are destroying their own souls.

8/ Peter and John Freed From Prison

In Christ's strength the disciples went forth to tell the story of the manger and the cross, and to triumph over all opposition. From their lips came words of divine eloquence that shook the world.

In Jerusalem, where deep prejudice and confused ideas prevailed in regard to Him who had been crucified as a malefactor, the disciples set before the Jews the mission of Christ, His crucifixion, resurrection, and ascension. Priests and rulers heard with amazement the bold testimony. The power of the risen Saviour had indeed fallen on the disciples. Along the streets where they were to pass, the people laid their sick "on beds and pallets, that as Peter came by at least his shadow might fall on some of them." RSV. Crowds gathered around them, and those who were healed glorified the name of the Redeemer.

As the Sadducees, who did not believe in a resurrection, heard the apostles declare that Christ had risen from the dead, they were enraged. If the apostles were allowed to preach a risen Saviour, the sect of the Sadducees would soon become extinct. The Pharisees perceived that the tendency of the disciples' teaching was to undermine the Jewish ceremonies. Now both Sadducees and Pharisees determined that the disciples should be stopped. Filled with indignation, the priests put Peter and John in prison.

This chapter is based on Acts 5:12-42.

Those whom the Lord had made the depositaries of truth had proved unfaithful, and God chose others to do His work. These leaders would not even admit the possibility that they did not rightly understand the Word or had misinterpreted the Scriptures. What right have these teachers, they said, some of them mere fishermen, to present ideas contrary to the doctrines that we have taught the people?

The disciples were not intimidated. The Holy Spirit brought to their minds the words spoken by Christ: "If they have persecuted Me, they will also persecute you." "The time cometh, that whosoever killeth you will think that he doeth God service." "These things have I told you, that when the time shall come, ye may remember that I told you of them." John 15:20; 16:2, 4.

God's Command Comes First

The mighty Ruler of the universe took the imprisonment of the disciples into His own hands, for men were warring against His work. By night the angel of the Lord opened the prison doors and said to the disciples, "Go, stand and speak in the temple to the people all the words of this life." Did the apostles say, We cannot do this until we have received permission from the magistrates? No. God had said, "Go," and they obeyed. "They entered into the temple early in the morning, and taught."

When Peter and John appeared among the believers and recounted how the angel had led them through the band of soldiers guarding the prison, bidding them resume the work that had been interrupted, the brethren were filled with joy.

In the meantime the high priest had "called the council together." The priests and rulers had decided to fix on the disciples the charge of insurrection, to accuse them of murdering Ananias and Sapphira, and of conspiring to deprive the priests of their authority. They hoped to excite the mob to deal with the disciples as it had dealt with Jesus. The priests feared that if people acknowledged Jesus as the Messiah, their anger would be raised against the religious leaders, who would then be made to answer for the murder of Christ. They decided to take strong measures to prevent this.

When they sent for the prisoners, great was their amazement at the word brought back: the prison doors were securely bolted and the guard stationed before them, but the prisoners were nowhere to be found.

Soon the report came, "The men whom ye put in prison are standing in the temple, and teaching the people. Then went the captain with the officers, and brought them without violence: for they feared the people, lest they should have been stoned."

Although the apostles were delivered from prison, they were not safe from punishment. By sending an angel to deliver them, God had given them a token of His presence. It was now their part to suffer for the One whose gospel they were preaching.

Peter's Amazing Boldness

The record left by Peter and John is heroic. As they stood for the second time before the men bent on their destruction, no fear or hesitation could be discerned in their words or attitude. And when the high priest said, "Did not we straitly command you that ye should not teach in this name? and, behold, ye have filled Jerusalem with your doctrine, and intend to bring this Man's blood upon us." Peter answered, "We ought to obey God rather than men." It was an angel from heaven who delivered them from prison, and in following his directions they were obeying the divine command.

Then the Spirit came upon the disciples; the accused became the accusers, charging the murder of Christ on those who composed the council. "The God of our fathers raised up Jesus whom ye slew and hanged on a tree. Him hath God exalted with His right hand to be a Prince and a Saviour, for to give repentance to Israel, and forgiveness of sins. And we are His witnesses of these things; and so is also the Holy Ghost, whom God hath given to them that obey Him.''

So enraged were the Jews at these words that they decided without further trial, or without authority from the Roman officers, to put the prisoners to death. Already guilty of the blood of Christ, they were now eager to stain their hands with the blood of His disciples.

But in the council one man recognized the voice of God in the words spoken by the disciples. Gamaliel, a Pharisee of learning and high position, saw clearly that the violent step contemplated by the priests would lead to terrible consequences. Before addressing those present, he requested that the prisoners be removed. He well knew that the murderers of Christ would hesitate at nothing to carry out their purpose.

He then spoke with great deliberation: ''Men of Israel, take care what you do with these men. . . . I tell you, keep away from these men and let them alone; for if this plan or this undertaking is of men, it will fail; but if it is of God, you will not be able to overthrow them. You might even be found opposing God!'' RSV.

The priests were obliged to agree with Gamaliel. Very reluctantly, after beating the disciples and charging them again to preach no more in the name of Jesus, they released them. ''And they departed from the presence of the council, rejoicing that they were counted worthy to suffer shame for His name. And daily in the temple, and in every house, they ceased not to teach and preach Jesus Christ.''

In the World We Have Trouble

Christ said of Himself, ''Think not that I am come to send peace on earth: I came not to send peace, but a sword.'' Matthew 10:34. The Prince of Peace, He was yet the cause of division. He who came to proclaim glad tidings opened a controversy that burns deep and arouses intense passion in the human heart. And He warns His followers, ''Ye shall be betrayed both by parents, and brethren, and kinsfolks, and friends; and some of you shall they cause to be put to death." Luke 21:16.

Every reproach and cruelty that Satan could instigate human hearts to devise has been visited on the followers of Jesus. The carnal heart is still at enmity with the law of God. The world is no more in harmony with the principles of Christ today than in the days of the apostles. The same hatred that prompted the cry, "Crucify Him! crucify Him!" still works in the children of disobedience. The same spirit which in the Dark Ages consigned men and women to prison, to exile, and to death, which conceived the torture of the Inquisition, which planned and executed the Massacre of St. Bartholomew, and which kindled the fires of Smithfield, is still at work. The proclamation of the gospel has ever been carried forward in the face of opposition, peril, and suffering.

Reproach and persecution have separated many from earthly friends, but never from the love of Christ. Never is the tempest-tried soul more dearly loved by His Saviour than when he is suffering reproach for the truth's sake. Christ stands by his side. When he is confined within prison walls, Christ cheers his heart with His love. When he suffers death for Christ's sake, the Saviour says to him, They may kill the body, but they cannot hurt the soul. "Fear thou not; for I am with thee: be not dismayed; for I am thy God: I will strengthen thee; yea, I will help thee; yea, I will uphold thee with the right hand of My righteousness." Isaiah 41:10.

"From oppression and violence He redeems their life; and precious is their blood in His sight." Psalm 72:14, RSV.

9 / Why the Seven Deacons Were Chosen

"In those days, when the number of the disciples was multiplied, there arose a murmuring of the Grecians against the Hebrews, because their widows were neglected in the daily ministration."

The early church was made up of many classes of people, of various nationalities. At the time of Pentecost, "there were dwelling at Jerusalem Jews, devout men, out of every nation under heaven." Acts 2:5. Among those of the Hebrew faith were some known as Grecians. Between them and the Jews of Palestine there had long existed distrust.

Those who had been converted were united by Christian love. Despite former prejudices, all were in harmony with one another. But Satan sought to take advantage of former habits of thought, thereby to introduce disunion into the church.

The enemy succeeded in arousing the suspicions of some who had been in the habit of finding fault with their spiritual leaders, and so "there arose a murmuring of the Grecians against the Hebrews." The cause of complaint was an alleged neglect of the Greek widows in the daily distribution of assistance. Prompt measures must be taken to remove all occasion for dissatisfaction, lest the enemy bring division among the believers.

Under the wise leadership of the apostles, the church was continually enlarging, and this growth

This chapter is based on Acts 6:1-7.

brought increasingly heavy burdens on those in charge. There was necessity for a distribution of the responsibilities borne faithfully by a few during the earlier days. The apostles must lay on others some of the burdens thus far borne by themselves.

Summoning the believers, the apostles stated that the spiritual leaders should be relieved from the task of distributing to the poor and from similar burdens. They must be free to preach the gospel. "Wherefore, brethren, look ye out among you seven men of honest report, full of the Holy Ghost and wisdom, whom we may appoint over this business. But we will give ourselves continually to prayer, and to the ministry of the word." This advice was followed, and by prayer and laying on of hands, seven chosen men were set apart as deacons.

The Results of This New Plan

The appointment of the seven proved a great blessing to the church. These officers gave careful consideration to individual needs, as well as to the general financial interests of the church and were an important aid in binding together the various interests of the church.

"And the word of God increased; and the number of the disciples multiplied in Jerusalem greatly; and a great company of the priests were obedient to the faith." This was due both to the greater freedom secured by the apostles and the zeal shown by the seven deacons. These brethren ordained for looking after the needs of the poor were also fully qualified to instruct others in the truth and they engaged in the work with earnestness.

The proclamation of the gospel was to be worldwide, and the messengers of the cross should remain united, and thus reveal to the world that they were one with Christ in God. See John 17:11, 14, 21, 23. Their power was dependent on a close connection with the One who had commissioned them to preach the gospel.

As they should continue to labor unitedly, heavenly messengers would open the way before them, hearts would be prepared for the truth, and many would be won to Christ. The church would go forth "fair as the moon, clear as the sun, and terrible as an army with banners" (Song of Solomon 6:10), gloriously fulfilling her divine mission.

The church at Jerusalem was to serve as a model for the organization of churches in every place. Those given the responsibility of the general oversight of the church were, as wise shepherds, to "feed the flock of God, . . . being ensamples to the flock" (1 Peter 5:2, 3), and the deacons were to be "men of honest report, full of the Holy Ghost and wisdom."

When in various parts of the world many believers had been formed into churches, the organization was further perfected. Every member was to make a wise use of the talents entrusted to him. Some were endowed with special gifts—"first apostles, second prophets, third teachers, then workers of miracles, then healers, helpers, administrators, speakers in various kinds of tongues." 1 Corinthians 12:28, RSV. But all were to labor in haromony.

Each Believer Has a Special Gift of the Spirit

"To each is given the manifestation of the Spirit for the common good. To one is given through the Spirit the utterance of wisdom, and to another the utterance of knowledge according to the same Spirit, to another faith by the same Spirit, to another gifts of healing by the one Spirit, to another the working of miracles, to another prophecy, to another the ability to distinguish between spirits, to another various kinds of tongues, to another the interpretation of tongues. All these are inspired by one and the same Spirit, who apportions to each one individually as He wills. For just as the body is one and has many members, and all the members of the body, though many, are one body, so it is with Christ." Verses 7-12, RSV.

When Moses was endeavoring to carry burdens so heavy that he would soon have worn away, he was counseled by Jethro to plan for a wise distribution of responsibilities. "Represent the people before God," Jethro advised, "and bring their cases to God." Jethro further advised that men be appointed to act as "rulers of thousands, of hundreds, of fifties, and of tens," thus relieving Moses of many minor matters that could be dealt with by consecrated helpers. Exodus 18:19, 21, RSV.

Those in leading positions of responsibility in the church should deal with the weightier matters demanding special wisdom and largeness of heart. Such men should not adjust minor matters that others are well qualified to handle.

"Moses chose able men out of all Israel. . . . Hard cases they brought to Moses, but any small matter they decided themselves." Verses 25, 26, RSV. Moses was careful to select men possessing dignity, sound judgment, and experience.

To Solomon, called to occupy a position of leading responsibility, David gave a special charge: "Thou, Solomon my son, know thou the God of thy father, and serve Him with a perfect heart and with a willing mind: for the Lord searcheth all hearts, and understandeth all the imaginations of the thoughts: if thou seek Him, He will be found of thee." 1 Chronicles 28:9.

A Beautiful Plan of Organization

The same principles of piety and justice that were to guide God's people in the time of Moses and David were to be followed by those given the oversight of the newly organized church in the gospel dispensation. In setting things in order and ordaining men to act as officers, the apostles held to the standards of leadership outlined in the Old Testament. He who is called to leading responsibility in the church "must be blameless; he must not be arrogant or quick-tempered or a drunkard or violent or greedy for gain, but hospitable, a lover of goodness, master of himself, upright, holy, and self-controlled; he must hold firm to the sure word as taught, so that he may be able to give instruction in sound doctrine and also to confute those who contradict it.'' Titus 1:7-9, RSV.

The order maintained in the early Christian church made it possible for them to move forward as a well-disciplined army. Believers, though scattered over a large territory, were all one body; all moved in concert and in harmony. When dissension arose in a local church, matters were not permitted to create division, but were referred to a general council of appointed delegates from the various churches, with the apostles and elders in positions of leading responsibility. Thus the plans of the enemy to disrupt and destroy were thwarted.

''God is not the author of confusion, but of peace.'' 1 Corinthians 14:33. He requires that order and system be observed today. Christian is to be united with Christian, church with church, every agency subordinate to the Holy Spirit, and all combined in giving the world the good tidings of the grace of God.

10 / Stephen, the First Martyr for Christ

Stephen, foremost of the seven deacons, spoke the Greek language and was familiar with the customs of the Greeks. He therefore found opportunity to preach the gospel in the synagogues of the Greek Jews and boldly proclaimed his faith. Learned rabbis and doctors of the law engaged him in public discussion, "but they were not able to resist the wisdom and the spirit by which he spake." He utterly defeated his opponents. To him was the promise fulfilled, "I will give you a mouth and wisdom, which all your adversaries shall not be able to gainsay nor resist." Luke 21:15.

The priests and rulers were filled with bitter hatred. They determined to silence his voice. On several occasions they had bribed the Roman authorities to pass over instances where the Jews had tried, condemned, and executed prisoners. The enemies of Stephen did not doubt that they could again pursue such a course; therefore they brought him before the Sanhedrin council for trial.

Learned Jews were summoned for the purpose of refuting the arguments of the prisoner. Saul of Tarsus was present and brought eloquence and logic to bear on the case to convince the people that Stephen was preaching dangerous doctrines; but in Stephen he met one who had a full understanding of the purpose of God in spreading the gospel to other nations.

The priests and rulers determined to make an exam-

This chapter is based on Acts 6:5-15; 7.

ple of Stephen. While satisfying their revengeful hatred, they would prevent others from adopting his belief. Witnesses were hired to bear false testimony. "We have heard him say," they declared, "that this Jesus of Nazareth shall destroy this place, and shall change the customs which Moses delivered us."

A Holy Radiance Shines on Stephen's Face

As Stephen stood to answer the charges, "all that sat in the council, . . . saw his face as it had been the face of an angel." Many trembled and veiled their faces, but the stubborn unbelief and prejudice of the rulers did not waver.

Stephen began his defense in a clear, thrilling voice which rang through the council hall. In words that held the assembly spellbound, he rehearsed the history of the chosen people. He showed a thorough knowledge of the Jewish economy and the spiritual interpretation of it now made manifest through Christ. He made plain his loyalty to God and to the Jewish faith, while he connected Jesus Christ with all the Jewish history.

When Stephen connected Christ with the prophecies, the priest, pretending to be horror-stricken, rent his robe. To Stephen this was a signal that he was giving his last testimony. He abruptly concluded his sermon.

Turning on his infuriated judges, he cried: "Ye stiffnecked and uncircumcised in heart and ears, ye do always resist the Holy Ghost: as your fathers did, so do ye. Which of the prophets have not your fathers persecuted? and they have slain them which showed before of the coming of the Just One; of whom ye have been now the betrayers and murderers: who have received the law by the disposition of angels, and have not kept it."

Priests and rulers were beside themselves with anger. In their cruel faces the prisoner read his fate, but he did not waver. For him the fear of death was gone. The scene before him faded from his vision. To him the gates of heaven were ajar, and, looking in, he saw Christ, as if just risen from His throne, standing ready to sustain His servant. Stephen exclaimed, "I see the heavens opened, and the Son of man standing on the right hand of God."

As he described the glorious scene, it was more than his persecutors could endure. Stopping their ears, they ran furiously on him with one accord and "cast him out of the city." "And as they were stoning Stephen, he prayed, 'Lord Jesus, receive my spirit.' And he knelt down and cried with a loud voice, 'Lord, do not hold this sin against them.' And when he had said this, he fell asleep." RSV.

The Roman authorities were bribed by large sums of money to make no investigation.

Stephen's Martyrdom Makes a Deep Impression

The memory of Stephen's face and his words which touched the souls of those who heard them, remained in the minds of the beholders and testified to the truth of that which he had proclaimed. His death was a sore trial to the church, but it resulted in the conviction of Saul, who could not efface from his memory the glory that had rested on the martyr's countenance.

Saul was angered by his secret conviction that Stephen had been honored by God when dishonored by men. He continued to persecute the followers of Christ, seizing them in their houses and delivering them to the priests and rulers for imprisonment and death. His zeal brought terror to the Christians at Jerusalem. The Roman authorities secretly aided the Jews in order to conciliate them and secure their favor.

After the death of Stephen, Saul was elected a member of the Sanhedrin council in consideration of the part he had acted. He was a mighty instrument in the hands of Satan to carry out his rebellion against the Son of God. But a Mightier than Satan had chosen Saul to take the place of the martyred Stephen, to spread far and wide the tidings of salvation through His blood.

11 / The Gospel Reaches Samaria and Ethiopia

After the death of Stephen there arose against the believers in Jerusalem a relentless persecution. "They were all scattered abroad throughout the regions of Judea and Samaria." Saul "laid waste the church, and entering house after house, he dragged off men and women and committed them to prison." RSV. Of this cruel work he said at a later day: "I myself was convinced that I ought to do many things in opposing the name of Jesus of Nazareth. . . . I not only shut up many of the saints in prison, . . . I punished them often in all the synagogues and tried to make them blaspheme." "When they were put to death I cast my vote against them." Acts 26:9-11, RSV.

At this time of peril Nicodemus came forward in fearless avowal of his faith in the Saviour. Nicodemus was a member of the Sanhedrin. As he had witnessed Christ's wonderful works, the conviction had fastened on his mind that this was the Sent of God. Too proud to acknowledge openly his sympathy with the Galilean Teacher, he had sought a secret interview. Jesus unfolded to him His mission to the world, yet still Nicodemus had hesitated. For three years there was little apparent fruit. But in the Sanhedrin council he had repeatedly thwarted schemes to destroy Christ. When at last Christ had been lifted up on the cross, Nicodemus remembered the words spoken to him in the night interview. "As Moses lifted up the serpent in

This chapter is based on Acts 8.

the wilderness, even so must the Son of man be lifted up'' (John 3:14); and he saw in Jesus the world's Redeemer.

With Joseph of Arimathea, Nicodemus had borne the expense of the burial of Jesus. The disciples had been afraid to show themselves openly as Christ's followers, but Nicodemus and Joseph, rich and honored men, had come boldly to do for their dead Master what it would have been impossible for the poor disciples to do. Their wealth and influence had protected them, in a great measure, from the malice of the priests and rulers.

Nicodemus No Longer Cautious and Questioning

Now Nicodemus came forward in defense of the infant church. He encouraged the faith of the disciples and used his wealth in helping to sustain the church at Jerusalem and advance the work. Those who had paid him reverence now scorned him, and he became poor; yet he faltered not in the defense of his faith.

The persecution gave great impetus to the work of the gospel. Success had attended the ministry in Jerusalem, and there was danger that the disciples would linger there too long, unmindful of the Saviour's commission to go to all the world. Instead of educating new converts to carry the gospel to those who had not heard it, they were in danger of taking a course that would lead all to be satisfied with what had been accomplished. To scatter His representatives where they could work for others, God permitted persecution to come. Driven from Jerusalem, the believers ''went everywhere preaching the word.''

When they were scattered by persecution they went forth filled with missionary zeal. They knew they held in their hands the bread of life for a famishing world, and they were constrained by the love of Christ to break this bread to all who were in need. Wherever they went, the sick were healed and the poor had the gospel preached unto them.

Philip, one of the seven deacons, was among those driven from Jerusalem. He "went down to the city of Samaria, and preached Christ unto them. And the people with one accord gave heed unto those things which Philip spoke, hearing and seeing the miracles which he did. . . . There was great joy in that city."

Christ's message to the Samaritan woman at Jacob's well had borne fruit. The woman had gone to the men of the city, saying, "Is not this the Christ?" They went with her, heard Jesus, and believed on Him. For two days Jesus stayed with them, "and many more believed because of His own word." John 4:29, 41.

When His disciples were driven from Jerusalem, the Samaritans welcomed them, and the Jewish converts gathered a precious harvest from among those who had once been their bitterest enemies.

While Philip was in Samaria, he was directed by a heavenly messenger to "go toward the south unto the way that goeth down from Jerusalem unto Gaza. . . . And he arose and went." He did not hesitate to obey, for he had learned the lesson of conformity to God's will.

The Baptism of the First Person From Africa

"And, behold, a man of Ethiopia, an eunuch of great authority under Candace queen of the Ethiopians, who had the charge of all her treasure, had come to Jerusalem for to worship, was returning, and sitting in his chariot read Esaias the prophet." God saw that this Ethiopian of good standing and wide influence would give others the light he had received and would exert a strong influence in favor of the gospel. Angels were attending this seeker for light, and the Holy Spirit brought him in touch with one who could lead him to the Saviour.

Philip was directed to go to the Ethiopian and explain the prophecy he was reading. "Go near," the Spirit said, "and join thyself to this chariot." Philip asked the eunuch, " 'Do you understand what you are reading?' And he said, 'How can I, unless some one guides me?' And he invited Philip to come up and sit with him.'' RSV. The scripture he was reading was the prophecy of Isaiah relating to Christ: ''He was led as a sheep to the slaughter; and like a lamb dumb before his shearer, so opened He not His mouth: in His humiliation His judgment was taken away: and who shall declare His generation? for His life is taken from the earth.''

''Of whom speaketh the prophet this?'' the eunuch asked, ''of himself, or of some other man?'' Then Philip, beginning at the same scripture, ''preached unto him Jesus.''

The man's heart thrilled, and he was ready to accept the light. He did not make his high position an excuse for refusing the gospel. ''As they went on their way, they came unto a certain water: and the eunuch said, See, here is water; what doth hinder me to be baptized? And Philip said, If thou believest with all thine heart, thou mayest. And he answered and said, I believe that Jesus Christ is the son of God. And he commanded the chariot to stand still: and they went down both into the water, both Philip and the eunuch; and he baptized him.

''And when they were come up out of the water, the Spirit of the Lord caught away Philip, that the eunuch saw him no more: and he went on his way rejoicing.''

Angels Still Guide the Footsteps of People

This Ethiopian represented a large class who need to be taught by such missionaries as Philip—men who will hear the voice of God and go where He sends them. Many who are reading the Scriptures cannot understand their true import. All over the world men and women are looking wistfully to heaven. Prayers and tears and inquiries go up from souls longing for light. Many are on the verge of the kingdom, waiting only to be gathered in.

An angel guided Philip to one who was seeking light,

and today angels will guide workers who will allow the Holy Spirit to sanctify their tongues and ennoble their hearts. The angel could himself have done the work for the Ethiopian, but this is not God's way of working. It is His plan that men are to work for their fellowmen.

In every age everyone who has received the gospel has been given sacred truth to impart to the world. God's faithful people have always been aggressive, wisely using their talents in His service.

The members of God's church are to be zealous, separating from worldly ambition and walking in the footsteps of Him who went about doing good. They are to minister to those in need of help, bringing to sinners a knowledge of the Saviour's love. Such work brings a rich reward. Those who engage in it will see souls won to the Saviour. Everyone who has received Christ is called to work for the salvation of his fellowmen. "The Spirit and the bride say, Come. And let him that heareth say, Come." Revelation 22:17. The charge to give this invitation includes everyone who has heard the invitation!

Thousands who have heard the message are still idlers in the market place, when they might be engaged in active service. To these Christ is saying, "Why stand ye here all the day idle?" And He adds, "Go ye also into the vineyard." Matthew 20:6, 7.

Long has God waited for the spirit of service to take possession of the whole church. When the members do their appointed work in fulfillment of the gospel commission, the whole world will be warned and the Lord Jesus will return to this earth with power and great glory. "This gospel of the kingdom shall be preached in all the world for a witness unto all nations; and then shall the end come." Matthew 24:14.

12 / From Saul to Paul: Persecutor to Disciple

Saul of Tarsus, a Roman citizen by birth, was a Jew by descent and had been educated by eminent rabbis. He was "a Hebrew of the Hebrews; as touching the law, a Pharisee; concerning zeal, persecuting the church; touching the righteousness which is in the law, blameless." Philippians 3:5, 6. High hopes were cherished concerning him as an able and zealous defender of the ancient faith. His elevation to the Sanhedrin council placed him in a position of power.

Saul had taken part in the conviction of Stephen, and the striking evidence of God's presence with the martyr had led him to doubt the cause he had espoused against the followers of Jesus. But the arguments of the priests finally convinced him that Stephen was a blasphemer, that Christ was an impostor, and that those in holy office must be right.

Saul's education and prejudice, his respect for his teachers, and his pride, braced him to rebel against the voice of conscience. And having decided that the priests and scribes were right, he became bitter in his opposition to the disciples of Jesus. His activity in causing holy men and women to be condemned to imprisonment and even to death brought gloom to the newly organized church and caused many to seek safety in flight.

Those who were driven from Jerusalem "went everywhere preaching the word." Acts 8:4. In Damascus the new faith gained many converts.

This chapter is based on Acts 9:1-18.

The priests and rulers had hoped that by stern persecution the heresy might be suppressed. Now they must carry forward in other places the decided measures taken in Jerusalem against the new teaching. For the special work at Damascus, Saul offered his services. "Breathing out threatenings and slaughter against the disciples of the Lord," he "went unto the high priest, and desired of him letters to Damascus to the synagogues, that if he found any of this way, whether they were men or women, he might bring them bound unto Jerusalem." thus "with authority and commission from the chief priests" (Acts 26:12), Saul of Tarsus, in the vigor of manhood and fired with mistaken zeal, set out on that memorable journey.

A Light Too Glorious for Mortal Eyes to Bear

As the weary travelers neared Damascus, "at midday" they came within view of fertile lands, beautiful gardens, and fruitful orchards, watered by cool streams from the mountains. While Saul gazed with admiration on the fair city below, "suddenly," as he afterward declared, there shone "round about me and them which journeyed with me" "a light from heaven, above the brightness of the sun." Blinded, Saul fell prostrate to the ground. He heard "a voice speaking . . . in the Hebrew tongue, Saul, Saul, why persecutest thou Me? . . . I am Jesus whom thou persecutest." Acts 22:6; 26:13-15.

Almost blinded by the light, the companions of Saul heard a voice, but saw no man. But Saul understood the words spoken, and in the glorious Being who stood before him he saw the Crucified One. On the soul of the stricken Jew the image of the Saviour's countenance was imprinted forever. Into the darkened chambers of his mind there poured a flood of light, revealing the error of his former life and his need of the Holy Spirit.

Saul now saw that he had been doing the work of Satan. He had believed the priests and rulers when they told him that the story of the resurrection was an artful fabrication of the disciples. Now that Jesus Himself stood revealed, he was convinced of the claims made by the disciples.

In that hour the prophetic records were opened to Saul's understanding He saw that the crucifixion, resurrection, and ascension of Jesus had been foretold by the prophets and proved Him to be the Messiah. Stephen's sermon was brought forcibly to his mind, and he realized that the martyr had indeed beheld "the glory of God, and Jesus standing on the right hand of God." Acts 7:55.

Saul Under Conviction

In that moment of divine revelation Saul remembered with terror that Stephen had been sacrificed by his consent and that many other followers of Jesus had met death through his instrumentality. Stephen's clear reasoning could not be controverted. The learned Jew had seen the face of the martyr as if it had been "the face of an angel." Acts 6:15. He had witnessed Stephen's forgiveness of his enemies. He also had witnessed the fortitude and cheerful resignation of many whom he had caused to be tormented. He had seen some yield up even their lives with rejoicing for their faith.

All these things had at times thrust upon Saul's mind an almost overwhelming conviction that Jesus was the promised Messiah. At such times he had struggled for entire nights against this conviction. Now Christ had spoken with His own voice, saying, "Saul, Saul, why persecutest thou Me?" And the question, "Who art Thou, Lord?" was answered by the same voice, "I am Jesus whom thou persecutest." Christ here identifies Himself with His people. In persecuting the followers of Jesus, Saul had struck directly against the Lord of heaven.

"Trembling and astonished," he inquired, "Lord, what wilt Thou have me to do? And the Lord said unto him, Arise, and go into the city, and it shall be told thee what thou must do.'' When Saul arose from the ground, he found himself totally deprived of sight. He believed that this blindness was a punishment from God. In terrible darkness he groped about, and his companions in fear "led him by the hand, and brought him into Damascus.''

On the morning of that day, Saul had neared Damascus with feelings of self-satisfaction because of the confidence placed in him by the chief priest. He was to check the spread of the new faith in Damascus and had looked forward with anticipation to the experiences before him.

But how unlike his anticipations was his entrance into the city! Blind, tortured by remorse, knowing not what judgment might be in store for him, he sought out the home of the disciple Judas, where, in solitude, he had ample opportunity for reflection and prayer.

For three days Saul was "without sight, and neither did eat nor drink.'' Again and again he recalled with anguish his guilt in allowing himself to be controlled by the malice of the priests and rulers, even when the face of Stephen had been lighted up with the radiance of heaven. He recounted the many times he had closed his eyes against evidence and had urged the persecution of believers in Jesus.

In Lonely Seclusion

These days of self-examination and humiliation were spent in lonely seclusion. The believers feared that he might be acting a part, in order to deceive them; and they refused him sympathy. He had no desire to appeal to the unconverted Jews, for he knew they would not even listen to his story. Thus his only hope of help was in a merciful God, and to Him he appealed in brokenness of heart. Shut in with God alone, Saul recalled many passages of Scripture referring to the first advent of Christ. As he reflected on the meaning of these prophecies, he was astonished at his former blindness and the blindness of the Jews in general. Prejudice and unbelief had prevented him from discerning in Jesus the Messiah of prophecy.

As Saul yielded to the Holy Spirit, he saw the mistakes of his life and recognized the far-reaching claims of the law of God. He who had been a proud Pharisee, confident that he was justified by his good works, now bowed before God with humility, confessing his unworthiness and pleading the merits of a crucified Saviour. Saul longed to come into full harmony with the Father and the Son; and in intensity he offered fervent supplications to the throne of grace.

His prayers were not in vain. The inmost thoughts of his heart were transformed, and his nobler faculties were brought into harmony with the purposes of God. Christ and His righteousness became to Saul more than the whole world.

He had believed that Jesus had disregarded the law of God and taught His disciples that it was of no effect; but after conversion Saul recognized Jesus as the one who had come into the world for the purpose of vindicating His Father's law. He was convinced that Jesus was the originator of the Jewish system of sacrifices and that at the crucifixion type had met antitype.

Saul was one whom Christ intended for a most important work, yet the Lord did not at once tell him of the work that had been assigned him. When Saul asked, "What wilt Thou have me to do?" the Saviour placed him in connection with His church, to obtain God's will for him. Christ had performed the work of revelation and conviction; now the penitent was to learn from those whom God had ordained to teach His truth.

While Saul in solitude continued in prayer, the Lord appeared in vision to "a certain disciple at Damascus, named Ananias." "Arise, and go into the street which is called Straight, and inquire in the house of Judas for one called Saul of Tarsus: for, behold, he prayeth, and hath seen in a vision a man named Ananias coming in, and putting his hand on him, that he might receive his sight.''

Ananias could scarcely credit the words of the angel. ''Lord, I have heard by many of this man, how much evil he hath done to Thy saints at Jerusalem: and here he hath authority from the chief priests to bind all that call on Thy name.'' But the command was imperative: ''Go thy way: for he is a chosen vessel unto Me, to bear My name before the Gentiles, and kings, and the children of Israel.''

Obedient, Ananias sought out the man who had breathed out threatenings against all who believed in Jesus; and putting his hands on the head of the penitent sufferer, he said, ''Brother Saul, the Lord . . . hath sent me, that thou mightest receive thy sight, and be filled with the Holy Ghost.

''And immediately there fell from his eyes as it had been scales: and he received sight forthwith, and arose, and was baptized.''

Thus Jesus placed Saul in connection with His appointed agencies on earth. To the organized church belonged the work of directing the repentant sinner in the way of life.

Many have an idea that they are responsible to Christ alone, independent of His recognized followers on earth. Jesus is the friend of sinners and has all power, but He respects the means He has ordained for the salvation of men. He directs sinners to the church, which He has made a channel of light to the world.

When Saul was given a revelation of Christ, he was placed in direct communication with the church. In this case Ananias represented Christ and also Christ's ministers, who are appointed to act in His stead. In Christ's stead Ananias touched the eyes of Saul. In Christ's stead he placed his hands on him, and as he prayed in Christ's name, Saul received the Holy Spirit. All was done in the name of and by the authority of Christ. Christ is the fountain; the church is the channel of communication.

13/ How God Educated Paul

Paul remained "certain days with the disciples which were at Damascus. And straightway he preached Christ in the synagogues, that He is the Son of God," who "died for our sins according to the Scriptures; . . . was buried, and . . . rose again the third day." 1 Corinthians 15:3, 4. His arguments from prophecy were so conclusive that the Jews were confounded and unable to answer him.

He who had journeyed to Damascus to persecute the believers was now preaching the gospel, strengthening its disciples, and bringing in new converts! Formerly known as a zealous defender of the Jewish religion, Paul could reason with extraordinary clearness, and by his withering sarcasm could place an opponent in no enviable light. Now the Jews saw this young man of unusual promise fearlessly preaching in the name of Jesus.

A general slain in battle is lost to his army, but his death gives no strength to the enemy. But when a man of prominence joins the opposing forces, they gain a decided advantage. Saul might easily have been struck dead by the Lord, and much strength would have been withdrawn from the persecuting power. But God not only spared Saul's life but converted him, transferring a champion from the side of the enemy to the side of Christ. An eloquent speaker and a severe critic, Paul, with stern purpose and undaunted courage, possessed the very qualifications needed in the early church.

This chapter is based on Acts 9:19-30.

All who heard him in Damascus were amazed. He declared that his change of faith had not been prompted by impulse, but by overwhelming evidence. He showed that the prophecies relating to the first advent of Christ had been literally fulfilled in Jesus of Nazareth.

Paul "increased the more in strength, and confounded the Jews which dwelt at Damascus, proving that this is very Christ." But many hardened their hearts, and soon their astonishment at his conversion was changed into intense hatred.

The opposition grew so fierce that Paul was not allowed to continue at Damascus. He "went into Arabia" (Galatians 1:17), where he found a safe retreat.

Paul's "University" in the Desert

In the solitude of the desert Paul had opportunity for study and meditation. He calmly reviewed his past experience and sought God with all his heart, resting not until he knew for certain that his repentance was accepted and his sin pardoned. Jesus communed with him and established him in the faith, bestowing upon him a rich measure of wisdom and grace. When the mind is brought into communion with the mind of God, the effect on body, mind, and soul is beyond estimate.

Ananias under the inspiration of the Holy Spirit had said to Paul: "The God of our fathers hath chosen thee, that thou shouldest know His will, and see that Just One, and shouldest hear the voice of His mouth. For thou shalt be His witness unto all men of what thou hast seen and heard. And now why tarriest thou? Arise, and be baptized, and wash away thy sins, calling on the name of the Lord." Acts 22:14-16.

Jesus Himself, when He arrested Saul on the journey to Damascus, declared: "I have appeared unto thee for this purpose, to make thee a minister and a witness both of these things which thou hast seen, and of those things in the which I will appear unto thee; delivering thee from the people, and from the Gentiles, unto whom now I send thee, to open their eyes, and to turn them from darkness to light, and from the power of Satan unto God, that they may receive forgiveness of sins, and inheritance among them which are sanctified by faith that is in Me." Acts 26:16-18.

As he pondered these things Paul understood more clearly his call "to be an apostle of Christ Jesus," 1 Corinthians 1:1. His call had come "not from men nor through man, but through Jesus Christ and God the Father." Galatians 1:1, RSV. He gave much study to the Scriptures, that he might preach "not with eloquent wisdom, lest the cross of Christ be emptied of its power," "but in demonstration of the Spirit and power," that the faith of all who heard "might not rest in the wisdom of men but in the power of God." 1 Corinthians 1:17; 2:4, 5, RSV. Viewing the wisdom of the world in the light of the cross, Paul "decided to know nothing . . . except Jesus Christ and Him crucified." 1 Corinthians 2:2, RSV.

Paul never lost sight of the Source of wisdom and strength. Hear him declare, "For to me to live is Christ." Philippians 1:21. "I count everything as loss because of the surpassing worth of knowing Christ Jesus my Lord. For His sake I have suffered the loss of all things." Philippians 3:8, RSV.

The Former Persecutor Is Persecuted

From Arabia Paul "returned again unto Damascus" (Galatians 1:17), and "preached boldly . . . in the name of Jesus." Unable to withstand his arguments, "the Jews took counsel to kill him." The gates of the city were guarded day and night to cut off his escape. Finally, the disciples "took him by night and let him down over the wall, lowering him in a basket." RSV.

After his escape he went to Jerusalem, about three years having passed since his conversion. His chief object was to visit Peter. Galatians 1:18. Upon arriving "he assayed to join himself to the disciples: but they were all afraid of him, and believed not that he was a disciple." Could so bigoted a Pharisee become a sincere follower of Jesus? "But Barnabas took him, and brought him to the apostles, and declared unto them how he had seen the Lord in the way, and that He had spoken to him, and how he had preached boldly at Damascus in the name of Jesus."

Soon the disciples had abundant evidence as to the genuineness of his experience. The future apostle to the Gentiles was now where his former associates lived, and he longed to make plain to these leaders the prophecies concerning the Messiah. Paul felt sure that these teachers in Israel were as sincere and honest as he had been. But he had miscalculated. Those at the head of the Jewish church refused to believe, but "went about to slay him."

Sorrow filled his heart. With shame he thought of the part he had taken in the martyrdom of Stephen, and now he sought to vindicate the truth for which Stephen had given his life.

Burdened for those who refused to believe, Paul was praying in the temple when a heavenly messenger appeared and said, "Make haste, and get thee quickly out of Jerusalem: for they will not receive thy testimony concerning Me." Acts 22:18. To Paul it seemed an act of cowardice to flee. And so he answered: "Lord, they themselves know that in every synagogue I imprisoned and beat those who believed in Thee. And when the blood of Stephen Thy witness was shed, I also was standing by and approving, and keeping the garments of those who killed him." But it was not the purpose of God that His servant should needlessly expose his life, and the heavenly messenger replied, "Depart; for I will send you far away to the Gentiles." Verses 19-21, RSV.

Learning of this vision, the brethren hastened Paul's secret escape. They "brought him down to Caesarea, and sent him forth to Tarsus." The departure of Paul suspended for a time the violent opposition of the Jews, and many were added to the number of believers.

14 / The Gospel Goes to the Gentiles

In his ministry at Lydda, Peter healed Aeneas, who for eight years had been confined to his bed with palsy. "Aeneas, Jesus Christ maketh thee whole," the apostle said; "arise, and make thy bed." "He arose immediately. And all that dwelt of Lydda and Saron saw him, and turned to the Lord."

At Joppa, near Lydda, there lived a woman named Dorcas, a worthy disciple of Jesus. Her life was filled with acts of kindness. She knew who needed comfortable clothing and who needed sympathy, and she freely ministered to the poor and sorrowful. Her skillful fingers were more active than her tongue.

"And it came to pass in those days, that she was sick, and died." Hearing that Peter was at Lydda, the believers sent messengers to him, "desiring him that he would not delay to come. . . . When he was come, they brought him into the upper chamber: and all the widows stood by him weeping, and showing the coats and garments which Dorcas made, while she was with them."

The apostle's heart was touched with sympathy. Then, directing that the weeping friends be sent from the room, he kneeled down and prayed God to restore Dorcas to life. Turning to the body, he said, "Tabitha, arise. And she opened her eyes: and when she saw Peter, she sat up." God saw fit to bring her back from the land of the enemy, that her skill and energy might still be a blessing to others.

This chapter is based on Acts 9:32 to 11:18.

While Peter was still at Joppa he was called by God to take the gospel to Cornelius, in Caesarea. This Roman centurion was a man of noble birth, and his position was one of honor. Through the Jews he had gained a knowledge of God and worshiped Him with a true heart. He was known far and near for his beneficence and righteous life. The inspired record describes him as "a devout man, and one that feared God with all his house, which gave much alms to the people, and prayed to God alway." He had erected the altar of God in his home, for he dared not attempt to carry out his plans or to bear his responsibilities without the help of God.

Though Cornelius believed the prophecies, he had no knowledge of the gospel as revealed in the life and death of Christ. But the same Holy Watcher who said of Abraham, "I know him," knew Cornelius and sent a message direct from heaven to him.

The angel appeared to him while he was at prayer. As the centurion heard himself addressed by name, he said, "What is it, Lord?" The angel answered, "Send men to Joppa, and call for one Simon, whose surname is Peter: he lodgeth with one Simon a tanner, whose house is by the seaside." Even the occupation of the man with whom Peter was staying was named! Heaven is acquainted with the history and business of men, with the experience and work of the humble laborer as well as with that of the king on his throne.

Frail, Tempted Humans Are the Messengers

The angel was not commissioned to tell Cornelius the story of the cross. A man subject to human frailties and temptations was to tell him of the crucified and risen Saviour. As His representatives God does not choose angels, but human beings, men of like passions with those they seek to save. Christ took humanity that He might reach humanity. A divine-human Saviour was needed to bring salvation to the world. And to men and women has been committed the sacred trust of

making known "the unsearchable riches of Christ."
Ephesians 3:8. The Lord brings those who are seeking
for truth into touch with fellow beings who know the
truth. Those who have received light are to impart it to
those in darkness. Humanity is made the working
agency through which the gospel exercises its transforming power.

Cornelius was gladly obedient. When the angel had
gone, he "called two of his household servants, and a
devout soldier of them that waited on him continually;
and when he had declared all these things unto them,
he sent them to Joppa."

After his interview with Cornelius, the angel went to
Peter. At the time, he was praying on the housetop of
his lodging, and "became very hungry, and would
have eaten: but while they made ready, he fell into a
trance." It was not for physical food alone that Peter
hungered; he hungered for the salvation of his countrymen. He had an intense desire to point out to them the
prophecies relating to Christ.

In the vision Peter saw "a great sheet. . . . In it were
all kinds of animals and reptiles and birds of the air.
And there came a voice to him, 'Rise, Peter; kill and
eat.' But Peter said, 'No, Lord; for I have never eaten
anything that is common or unclean.' And the voice
came to him again a second time, 'What God has
cleansed, you must not call common.' This happened
three times, and the thing was taken up at once to
heaven." RSV.

This vision revealed to Peter the purpose of God—
that the Gentiles should be fellow heirs with the Jews
to the blessings of salvation. As yet none of the disciples had preached the gospel to Gentiles. In their
minds the Gentiles were excluded from the blessings of
the gospel. Now the Lord was seeking to teach Peter
the world-wide extent of the divine plan.

Many Gentiles had listened to the preaching of Peter
and the other apostles, and many Greek Jews had become believers in Christ, but the conversion of

Cornelius was to be the first of importance among Gentiles. The door that many Jewish converts had closed against Gentiles was now to be thrown open. Gentiles who accepted the gospel were to be equal with Jewish disciples, without the necessity of circumcision.

How carefully the Lord worked to overcome the prejudice in Peter's mind! By the vision He sought to teach that in heaven there is no respect of persons. Through Christ the heathen may be made partakers of the privileges of the gospel.

While Peter was meditating on the vision, the men sent from Cornelius arrived and stood before his lodginghouse. Then the Spirit said to him, "Three men are looking for you. Rise and go down, and accompany them without hesitation; for I have sent them." RSV.

Peter Finds This a Trying Command

It was with reluctance that Peter undertook the duty laid on him, but he dared not disobey. He went down and said, "I am he whom ye seek: what is the cause wherefore ye are come?" They told him, "Cornelius the centurion, a just man, and one that feareth God, and of good report among all the nation of the Jews, was warned from God by a holy angel to send for thee into his house, and to hear words of thee."

In obedience to God, on the following morning the apostle set out, accompanied by six of his brethren. These were to be witnesses of all that he should say or do, for Peter knew he would be called to account for so direct a violation of Jewish teachings.

As Peter entered the house of the Gentile, Cornelius saluted him as one honored of Heaven. Overwhelmed with reverence for the one sent by God to teach him, he fell at the apostle's feet and worshiped him. Peter was horror-stricken and lifted the centurion up, saying, "Stand up; I myself also am a man."

To the large company of Cornelius's "kinsmen and near friends" Peter said: "Ye know how that it is an unlawful thing for a Jew to keep company, or come unto one of another nation; but God hath showed me that I should not call any man common or unclean. Therefore came I . . . as soon as I was sent for. I ask therefore for what intent ye have sent for me?''

Cornelius then related his experience, saying in conclusion: We are "all here present before God, to hear all things that are commanded thee of God.''

Peter said, "I perceive that God is no respecter of persons: but in every nation he that feareth Him, and worketh righteousness, is accepted with Him.''

Then to that company of attentive hearers the apostle preached Christ. As Peter pointed those present to Him as the sinner's only hope, he himself understood more fully the vision he had seen, and his heart glowed with the spirit of the truth he was presenting.

Suddenly, "While Peter yet spake these words, the Holy Ghost fell on all them which heard the word. And they of the circumcision which believed were astonished, as many as came with Peter, because that on the Gentiles also was poured out the gift of the Holy Ghost. For they heard them speak with tongues, and magnify God.''

"Then answered Peter, Can any man forbid water, that these should not be baptized, which have received the Holy Ghost as well as we? And he commanded them to be baptized in the name of the Lord.''

Thus was the gospel brought to those who had been "strangers and foreigners," making them members of the household of God. From the household of Cornelius a widespread work of grace was carried on in that heathen city.

Today there are many like Cornelius whom the Lord desires to connect with His work. Their sympathies are with the Lord's people, but the ties that bind them to the world hold them firmly. Special efforts should be made for these souls.

God calls for earnest, humble workers who will carry the gospel to the higher class. The greatest men of this earth are not beyond the power of a wonder-working God. If workers will do their duty, God will convert men who occupy responsible positions, men of intellect and influence. Converted, they will have a special burden for other souls of this neglected class. Time and money will be consecrated to the work, and new efficiency and power will be added to the church.

Many in the world are nearer the kingdom than we suppose. Everywhere are those who will take their stand for Christ. Constrained by love, they will constrain others to come to Him.

Peter Lays the Matter Before His Associates

When the brethren in Judea heard that Peter had preached to Gentiles, they were surprised and offended. When they next saw Peter they met him with severe censure: "Thou wentest in to men uncircumcised, and didst eat with them."

Peter related his experience—the vision, the command to go to the Gentiles, the coming of the messengers, his journey to Caesarea, and the meeting with Cornelius. He recounted his interview with the centurion, who had told him of the vision by which he had been directed to send for Peter.

"As I began to speak," he said, "the Holy Ghost fell on them, as on us at the beginning. Then remembered I the word of the Lord, how that He said, John indeed baptized with water; but ye shall be baptized with the Holy Ghost. Forasmuch then as God gave them the like gift as He did unto us, who believed on the Lord Jesus Christ; what was I, that I could withstand God?"

The brethren were silenced. Convinced that their prejudice and exclusiveness were utterly contrary to the gospel, they said, "Then hath God also to the Gentiles granted repentance unto life."

Thus, prejudice was broken down, exclusiveness was abandoned, and the way was opened for the gospel to be proclaimed to the Gentiles.

15 / An Angel Delivers Peter From Prison

"About that time Herod the king laid violent hands upon some who belonged to the church." Herod Agrippa, subject to Claudius the Roman emperor, was professedly a proselyte to the Jewish faith. Desirous of obtaining the favor of the Jews, hoping thus to make secure his offices and honors, he proceeded to persecute the church of Christ. He cast James, the brother of John, into prison, and sent an executioner to kill him. Seeing that the Jews were well pleased, he imprisoned Peter also.

The death of James caused consternation among the believers. When Peter also was imprisoned, the entire church engaged in fasting and prayer.

Herod's act in putting James to death was applauded by the Jews, though some maintained that a public execution would have more thoroughly intimidated the believers. Herod therefore meant to gratify the Jews still further by the public spectacle of Peter's death, but not before all the people then assembled in Jerusalem. It was feared that the sight of him being led out to die might excite the pity of the multitude.

The priests and elders also feared lest Peter make one of those powerful appeals to study the life and character of Jesus—appeals which they had been unable to controvert. Peter's zeal had led many to take their stand for the gospel, and the rulers feared that should he be given an opportunity to defend his faith,

This chapter is based on Acts 12:1-23, RSV.

the multitude who had come to the city to worship would demand his release.

While, upon various pretexts, the execution of Peter was being delayed until after Passover, the church had time for searching of heart. They prayed without ceasing for Peter, for they felt that he could not be spared from the cause.

Meanwhile worshipers from every nation sought the temple, a glittering vision of beauty and grandeur. But Jehovah was no longer to be found in that place of loveliness. When Christ looked for the last time on the interior of the temple, He said, "Behold, your house is forsaken and desolate." Matthew 23:38, RSV. God's presence was withdrawn forever.

God Answers the Unceasing Prayers of His People

The day of Peter's execution was at last appointed, but still the prayers of the believers ascended to heaven. Angels were watching over the imprisoned apostle.

To prevent all possibility of release, Peter had been put under the charge of sixteen soldiers who guarded him day and night. In a rock-hewn cell he was placed between two soldiers and was bound by two chains, each fastened to one of the soldiers. He was unable to move without their knowledge. With the prison doors fastened and a guard before them, all chance of rescue or escape was cut off. But man's extremity is God's opportunity. The bolts and bars and the Roman guard were to make complete the triumph of God in the deliverance of Peter. Herod, lifting his hand against Omnipotence, was to be utterly defeated.

The last night before the execution a mighty angel was sent from heaven. The strong gates opened without the aid of human hands. The angel passed through, and the gates closed noiselessly behind him. He entered the cell, and there lay Peter, sleeping the peaceful sleep of perfect trust.

Not until the apostle felt the touch of the angel's

hand and heard a voice saying, "Get up quickly," did he awaken sufficiently to see his cell illuminated by an angel of glory standing before him. Mechanically he obeyed, and in rising lifted his hands, dimly conscious that the chains had fallen from his wrists.

Again the voice bade him, "Dress yourself and put on your sandals." Peter mechanically obeyed, believing himself to be dreaming.

Once more the angel commanded, "Wrap your mantle around you and follow me." He moved toward the door, the usually talkative Peter now dumb from amazement. They stepped over the guard. The heavily bolted door of its own accord swung open and closed again immediately, while the guards were motionless at their post.

The second door opened as did the first, with no creaking of hinges or rattling of bolts. They passed through, and it closed again as noiselessly. In the same way they passed through the third gate and found themselves in the open street. No word was spoken. The angel passed on in front, encircled by dazzling brightness, and Peter, still believing himself in a dream, followed. They passed on through one street; then, the mission of the angel accomplished, he disappeared.

Peter Finally Realizes He Is Free

Peter felt himself to be in profound darkness, but as his eyes gradually became accustomed to the darkness, it seemed to lessen, and he found himself alone in the silent street, the cool night air blowing on his brow. He was free, in a familiar part of the city; he recognized the place as one he had often frequented and had expected to pass on the morrow for the last time.

He remembered falling asleep, bound between two soldiers, with his sandals and outer garments removed. He examined his person and found himself fully dressed. His swollen wrists were free from the manacles. He realized that his freedom was no dream or vision, but a reality. An angel had delivered him from prison and death! "And Peter came to himself, and said, 'Now I am sure that the Lord has sent His angel and rescued me from the hand of Herod.' "

The apostle made his way at once to the house where his brethren were at that moment engaged in earnest prayer for him. "When he knocked at the door of the gateway, a maid named Rhoda came to answer. Recognizing Peter's voice, in her joy she did not open the gate but ran in and told that Peter was standing at the gate. They said to her, 'You are mad.' But she insisted that it was so. They said, 'It is his angel!'

"But Peter continued knocking; and when they opened, they saw him and were amazed. But motioning to them with his hand to be silent, he described to them how the Lord had brought him out of the prison." And Peter "departed . . . to another place." God had heard their prayers and delivered him from the hands of Herod.

In the morning, a large concourse of people gathered to witness the execution of the apostle. Herod sent officers to the prison for Peter, who was to be brought with a great display of arms, not only to ensure against his escape but to intimidate all sympathizers.

When the keepers found that Peter had escaped, they were seized with terror. It had been expressly stated that their lives would be required for the life of their charge, and they had been especially vigilant. When the officers came for Peter at the prison, the bolts and bars were still fast, the chains were still secured to the wrists of the two soldiers; but the prisoner was gone.

When the report of Peter's escape was brought to Herod, he was enraged. He ordered the prison guard to be put to death. Herod was determined not to acknowledge that divine power had frustrated his design, and he set himself in bold defiance against God.

Not long after, Herod went to a great festival in Caesarea designed to gain the applause of the people.

There was much feasting and wine drinking. With pomp and ceremony he addressed the people in an eloquent oration. Clad in a robe sparkling with silver and gold, which caught the rays of the sun in its glittering folds, he was a gorgeous figure. The majesty of his appearance and the force of his well-chosen language swayed the assembly. Wild with enthusiasm they showered adulation on him, declaring that no mortal could present such an appearance or command such eloquence. They declared that henceforth they would worship him as a god.

Some whose voices were now glorifying a vile sinner had a few years before raised the frenzied cry, Away with Jesus! Crucify Him! The Jews could not discern, under the humble exterior, the Lord of life and glory. But they were ready to worship as a god the king whose splendid garments of silver and gold covered a corrupt, cruel heart.

King Herod Stricken by an Angel

Herod accepted the idolatry of the people as his due. A glow of gratified pride overspread his countenance as he heard the shout, "It is the voice of a god, and not of man!"

But suddenly his face became pallid as death and distorted with agony. Great drops of sweat started from his pores. He stood for a moment transfixed with pain and terror; then turning his livid face to his horror-stricken friends, he cried in hollow tones, He whom you have exalted as a god is stricken with death.

Suffering excruciating anguish, he was borne from the scene of revelry. A moment before, he had been the proud recipient of the worship of that vast throng; now he realized he was in the hands of a Ruler mightier than himself.

He remembered his persecution of the followers of Christ, his command to slay James, his design to put to death the apostle Peter. He remembered how in mortification and rage he had wreaked vengeance on the prison guards. He felt that God was now dealing with him. He found no relief from pain of body or anguish of mind, and he expected none. Herod knew that in accepting the worship of the people he had filled up the measure of his iniquity.

The same angel who had come to rescue Peter had been the messenger of judgment to Herod, laying low his pride and bringing on him the punishment of the Almighty. Herod died in great agony of mind and body.

The tidings that the apostle of Christ had been delivered from prison and death, while his persecutor had been stricken by the curse of God, were borne to all lands, leading many to a belief in Christ.

What Angels Are Doing Today

Today, as in the days of the apostles, heavenly messengers are seeking to comfort the sorrowing, protect the impenitent, and win hearts to Christ. Angels are constantly bearing the prayers of the needy and distressed to the Father above and bringing hope and courage to the children of men. These angels create a heavenly atmosphere about the soul, lifting us toward the unseen and the eternal.

Only by spiritual vision can we discern heavenly things. The spiritual ear alone can hear the harmony of heavenly voices. "The angel of the Lord encampeth round about them that fear Him, and delivereth them." Psalm 34:7. God commissions angels to guard His chosen ones from "the pestilence that walketh in darkness" and "the destruction that wasteth at noonday." Psalm 91:6.

Angels have talked with men as a man speaks with a friend and have led them to places of security. Again and again have the encouraging words of angels renewed the drooping spirits of the faithful.

Angels labor untiringly in behalf of those for whom Christ died. "Joy shall be in heaven over one sinner that repenteth, more than over ninety and nine just persons, which need no repentance." Luke 15:7. A report is borne to heaven of every effort to dispel darkness and spread abroad the knowledge of Christ.

The powers of heaven are watching the warfare which God's servants are carrying on. All the heavenly angels are at the service of the humble, believing people of God.

Remember that every true child of God has the cooperation of heavenly beings. Invisible armies attend the meek and lowly ones who believe and claim the promises of God. Angels that excel in strength stand at God's right hand, "all ministering spirits, sent forth to minister for them who shall be heirs of salvation." Hebrews 1:14.

16 / Dramatic Success at Antioch

After the disciples had been driven from Jerusalem by persecution, the gospel message spread rapidly. Many small companies of believers were formed in important centers. Some disciples "traveled as far as Phenice, and Cyprus, and Antioch, preaching the word," their labors usually confined to Hebrew and Greek Jews found in nearly all the cities of the world.

The gospel was gladly received in Antioch, the metropolis of Syria. Extensive commerce brought to the city many people of various nationalities. Antioch was favorably known for its healthful situation, beautiful surroundings, wealth, culture, and refinement. It had become a city of luxury and vice.

The gospel was publicly taught in Antioch by disciples from Cyprus and Cyrene. Their earnest labors were productive. "A great number believed, and turned unto the Lord."

News of this came to the church in Jerusalem, and "they sent forth Barnabas, that he should go as far as Antioch." Barnabas saw the work that had already been accomplished, and he "was glad, and exhorted them all, that with purpose of heart they would cleave unto the Lord." Many were added to the believers there. As the work developed, Barnabas felt the need of help, and went to Tarsus to seek for Paul who had been laboring in "the regions of Syria and Cilicia," proclaiming "the faith which once he destroyed." Ga-

This chapter is based on Acts 11:19-26; 13:1-3.

latians 1:21, 23. Barnabas persuaded him to return with him.

In the populous city of Antioch, Paul's learning and zeal exerted a powerful influence, and he proved just the help that Barnabas needed. For a year the two labored unitedly, bringing to many a knowledge of the world's Redeemer.

In Antioch the disciples were first called Christians. The name was given them because Christ was the theme of their preaching and their conversation. Continually they dwelt upon His teachings and miracles of healing. With quivering lips and tearful eyes they spoke of His betrayal, trial, and execution, the torture imposed on Him by His enemies, and the Godlike pity with which He had prayed for those who persecuted Him. His resurrection, ascension, and work as Mediator for fallen man were topics on which they rejoiced to dwell. Well might the heathen call them Christians!

The Beautiful Name God Gave the Believers

God gave them the name of Christian, a royal name given to all who join themselves to Christ. Of this name James wrote later, "Do not rich men . . . blaspheme that worthy name by the which ye are called?" James 2:6, 7. And Peter declared, "If ye be reproached for the name of Christ, happy are ye." 1 Peter 4:14.

Living in the midst of a people who seemed to care little for things of eternal value, the believers at Antioch sought to arrest the attention of the honest in heart. In their humble ministry in the various walks of life, they daily bore testimony of their faith in Christ.

It is in the order of God today that chosen workers of talent be stationed in important centers of population; it also is His purpose that church members living in these cities shall use their God-given talents in working for souls. Such workers will find that many who never could have been reached in any other way are ready to respond to intelligent personal effort.

God is calling on ministers, physicians, nurses,

colporteurs, and other consecrated laymen of talent who know the Word of God and the power of His grace to consider the needs of the unwarned cities. Every agency must be set in operation, that present opportunities may be wisely improved.

Paul's labors with Barnabas strengthened his conviction that the Lord had called him to work for the Gentile world. At his conversion the Lord had declared that he was to minister to the Gentiles, "to open their eyes, and to turn them from darkness to light, and from the power of Satan unto God, that they may receive forgiveness of sins, and inheritance among them which are sanctified by faith that is in Me." Acts 26:18. The angel had said to Ananias, "He is a chosen vessel unto Me, to bear My name before the Gentiles, and kings, and the children of Israel." Acts 9:15.

Thus the Lord had given Paul his commission to enter the missionary field of the Gentile world, to make known "the mystery" which had been "kept secret since the world began" (Romans 16:25), "that the Gentiles should be fellow heirs, and of the same body, and partakers of His promise in Christ by the gospel: whereof," declares Paul, "I was made a minister. . . . Unto me, who am less than the least of all saints, is this grace given, that I should preach among the Gentiles the unsearchable riches of Christ." Ephesians 3:6-8.

Neither Paul nor Barnabas had as yet been formally ordained to gospel ministry, but God was about to entrust them with a difficult enterprise in which they would need every advantage that could be obtained through the church.

The Meaning of Gospel Ordination

"Now in the church at Antioch there were prophets and teachers, Barnabas, Simeon who was called Niger, Lucius of Cyrene, Manaen, . . . and Saul. While they were worshiping the Lord and fasting, the Holy Spirit said, 'Set apart for Me Barnabas and Saul for the work to which I have called them.' '' Acts 13:1, 2, RSV. These apostles, solemnly dedicated to God by fasting and prayer and laying on of hands, were authorized not only to teach the truth but to perform the rite of baptism and to organize churches.

Proclaiming the gospel among the Gentiles was now to be prosecuted with vigor, and the church was to be strengthened by a great ingathering of souls. The apostles' teaching concerning breaking down of "the middle wall of partition" (Ephesians 2:14) that had separated the Jewish and the Gentile world, would naturally subject them to the charge of heresy, and their authority as ministers of the gospel would be questioned by many believing Jews. In order that their work should be above challenge, God instructed the church to set them apart publicly to the work of the ministry, a recognition of their divine appointment to bear to the Gentiles the glad tidings of the gospel.

Both Paul and Barnabas had already received their commission from God Himself, and laying on of hands added no new qualification. It was an acknowledged form of designation to an appointed office. By it the seal of the church was set upon the work of God.

To the Jew this form was significant. When a father blessed his children, he laid his hands reverently on their heads. When an animal was devoted to sacrifice, the hand of the priest was laid on the head of the victim. When the ministers in Antioch laid their hands on Paul and Barnabas, by that action they asked God to bestow His blessing on the chosen apostles in their appointed work.

At a later date unwarrantable importance was attached to laying on of hands, as if a power came at once on those who received such ordination. But in the setting apart of these two apostles, there is no record that virtue was imparted by the mere laying on of hands.

Years before, when the divine purpose concerning Paul was first revealed to him, Paul was brought in contact with the newly organized church. Furthermore, the church at Damascus was not left in darkness as to the converted Pharisee. And now the Holy Spirit again laid on the church the work of ordaining Paul and his fellow laborer.

God Recognizes and Honors Church Organization

God has made His church a channel of light. He does not give to one of His servants an experience contrary to the experience of the church itself. Neither does He give one man a knowledge of His will for the entire church while the church is left in darkness. He places His servants in close connection with His church, that they may have less confidence in themselves and greater confidence in others whom He is leading.

Those constantly inclined toward individual independence seem unable to realize that independence of spirit is liable to lead the human agent to have too much confidence in himself, rather than to respect the counsel and judgment of his brethren, especially of those in the offices God has appointed for leadership. God has invested His church with special authority which no one can be justified in disregarding, for he who does this despises the voice of God.

It is Satan's effort to separate such ones from those through whom God had built up and extended His work. For any worker in the Lord's cause to pass these by and to think that his light must come through no other channel than directly from God is to place himself where he is liable to be deceived by the enemy and overthrown. The Lord has arranged that close relationship should be maintained by all believers; Christian shall be united to Christian and church to church, every agency subordinate to the Holy Spirit. All believers will be united in an organized effort to give to the world the glad tidings of the grace of God.

Paul regarded his ordination as marking a new epoch in his life. From this time he afterward dated the beginning of his apostleship.

While the light was shining brightly at Antioch, important work was continued by the apostles in Jerusalem. Every year, many Jews from all lands came to worship at the temple. Some of these fervent pilgrims were earnest students of the prophecies, longing for the advent of the Messiah. The apostles preached Christ with unflinching courage, though they knew they were placing their lives in jeopardy. Many converts to the faith were made, and these, returning home, scattered seeds of truth through all nations and among all classes.

Peter, James, and John felt confident that God had appointed them to preach Christ among their countrymen at home. Faithfully and wisely they testified of what they had seen and heard, appealing to the "more sure word of prophecy" (2 Peter 1:19) to persuade "the house of Israel . . . that God hath made that same Jesus . . . both Lord and Christ" (Acts 2:36).

17 / Heralds of the Gospel

After their ordination Paul and Barnabas "went down to Seleucia; and from there they sailed to Cyprus." Barnabas was "a native of Cyprus" (Acts 4:36, RSV), and now he and Paul, accompanied by John Mark, a relative of Barnabas, visited this island. Cyprus was one of the places to which believers had fled because of persecution following the death of Stephen.

Mark's mother was a convert, and the apostles were always sure of a welcome and rest in her home at Jerusalem. During one of these visits to his mother's home, Mark proposed to Paul and Barnabas that he accompany them on their missionary tour. He longed to devote himself to the work of the gospel.

When the apostles "had gone through the whole island as far as Paphos, they came upon a certain magician, a Jewish false prophet, named Bar-Jesus. He was with the proconsul, Sergius Paulus, a man of intelligence, who summoned Barnabas and Saul and sought to hear the word of God. But Elymas the magician (for that is the meaning of his name) withstood them, seeking to turn away the proconsul from the faith."

When Sergius Paulus was listening to the apostles, the forces of evil, working through the sorcerer Elymas, sought to turn him from the faith and so thwart the purpose of God. Thus the fallen foe works to keep in his ranks men of influence who might render effective service in God's cause.

This chapter is based on Acts 13:4-52, RSV.

Paul had the courage to rebuke the one through whom the enemy was working. "Filled with the Holy Spirit," he said, " 'You son of the devil, you enemy of all righteousness, full of all deceit and villainy, will you not stop making crooked the straight paths of the Lord? And now, behold, the hand of the Lord is upon you, and you shall be blind and unable to see the sun for a time.' Immediately mist and darkness fell upon him and he went about seeking people to lead him by the hand."

The sorcerer had closed his eyes to gospel truth, and the Lord, in righteous anger, caused his natural eyes to be closed. This blindness was only for a season, that he might repent and seek pardon of the God whom he had offended. The fact that he was obliged to grope about in blindness proved to all that the apostles' miracles, which Elymas had denounced as sleight of hand, were wrought by the power of God. The deputy, convinced, accepted the gospel.

Those who preach the truth will meet Satan in many forms. It is the duty of the minister of Christ to stand faithful at his post, in the fear of God. Thus he may put to confusion the hosts of Satan and triumph in the name of the Lord.

Paul and his company continued their journey, going to Perga in Pamphylia. They encountered hardships and privations, and in the towns and cities and along lonely highways they were surrounded by dangers seen and unseen. But Paul and Barnabas had learned to trust God's power. As faithful shepherds in search of lost sheep, forgetful of self, they faltered not when weary, hungry, and cold.

Here Mark, overwhelmed with fear and discouragement, unused to hardships, was disheartened. Amidst opposition and perils, he failed to endure hardness as a good soldier of the cross. He had yet to learn to face danger, persecution, and adversity with a brave heart. Losing all courage, he returned to Jerusalem.

This caused Paul to judge Mark severely for a time.

Barnabas was inclined to excuse him. He saw in him qualifications that would fit him to be a useful worker. In after years the young man gave himself unreservedly to proclaiming the gospel in difficult fields. Under the wise training of Barnabas, he developed into a valuable worker.

Paul and Mark Later Reconciled

Paul was afterward reconciled to Mark, and recommended him to the Colossians as a fellow worker "for the kingdom of God" and "a comfort to me." He spoke of Mark as profitable, "very useful." Colossians 4:11; 2 Timothy 4:11, RSV.

At Antioch in Pisidia Paul and Barnabas on the Sabbath went to the Jewish synagogue. "After the reading of the law and the prophets, the rulers of the synagogue sent to them saying, 'Brethren, if you have any word of exhortation for the people, say it.' " Being invited to speak, "Paul stood up, and motioning with his hand said: 'Men of Israel, and you that fear God, listen.' " Then he proceeded to give a history of how the Lord had dealt with the Jews and how a Saviour had been promised, and he boldly declared that " 'God has brought to Israel a Savior, Jesus, as He promised. Before His coming John had preached a baptism of repentance to all the people of Israel. And as John was finishing his course, he said, "What do you suppose that I am? I am not He. No, but after me One is coming, the sandals of whose feet I am not worthy to untie." ' " Thus with power he preached Jesus as the Messiah of prophecy.

Paul Speaks Plainly

Paul said, " 'Brethren, . . . those who live in Jerusalem and their rulers, because they did not recognize Him nor understand the utterances of the prophets which are read every Sabbath, fulfilled these [prophecies] by condemning Him.' "

Paul did not hesitate to speak the truth concerning the

Jewish leaders. " 'Though they could charge Him with nothing deserving death,' " the apostle declared, " 'yet they asked Pilate to have Him killed. And when they had fulfilled all that was written of Him, they took Him down from the tree, and laid Him in a tomb. But God raised Him from the dead; and for many days He appeared to those who came up with Him from Galilee to Jerusalem, who are now His witnesses to the people.' "

" 'And we bring you the good news,' " the apostle continued. " 'God raised Him from the dead.' "

And now Paul preached repentance and remission of sin through the merits of Jesus their Saviour: " 'By Him every one that believes is freed from everything from which you could not be freed by the law of Moses.' "

The apostle's appeal to Old Testament prophecies and his declaration that these had been fulfilled in Jesus of Nazareth carried conviction. And the speaker's assurance that the "glad tidings" were for Jew and Gentile alike brought hope and joy.

"As they went out, the people begged that these things might be told them the next Sabbath." "Many Jews and devout converts to Judaism" accepted the good news that day. Paul and Barnabas "urged them to continue in the grace of God."

The interest aroused by Paul's discourse brought together the next Sabbath "almost the whole city . . . to hear the word of God. But when the Jews saw the multitudes, they were filled with jealousy, and contradicted what was spoken by Paul, and reviled him.

"And Paul and Barnabas spoke out boldly, saying, 'It was necessary that the word of God should be spoken first to you. Since you thrust it from you, and judge yourselves unworthy of eternal life, behold, we turn to the Gentiles.' "

"When the Gentiles heard this, they were glad and glorified the word of God; and as many as were ordained to eternal life believed." Thus "the word of the Lord spread throughout all the region."

Centuries before, the pen of inspiration had traced this ingathering of the Gentiles. See Hosea 1:10; 2:23. The Saviour Himself foretold the spread of the gospel among them. See Matthew 21:43. And after His resurrection He commissioned His disciples to go "into all the world" and "make disciples of all nations." Mark 16:15; Matthew 28:19, RSV.

The Gentiles See the Light

Later, in important centers, Paul and his companions preached the gospel to both Jews and Gentiles. But their chief energies were henceforth directed toward heathen peoples who had little or no knowledge of the true God and of His Son. Through the untiring ministrations of the apostles to the Gentiles, those "separated from Christ" who "once were far off" learned that they had been "brought near in the blood of Christ," and through faith they might become "members of the household of God." Ephesians 2:12, 13, 19, RSV.

To those who believe, Christ is a sure foundation. This living stone is broad enough and strong enough to sustain the weight and burden of the whole world. The apostle wrote: "You are . . . built upon the foundation of the apostles and prophets, Christ Jesus Himself being the cornerstone." Ephesians 2:19, 20, RSV.

As the gospel spread in Pisidia, the unbelieving Jews in their blind prejudice "incited the devout women of high standing and the leading men of the city, and stirred up persecution against Paul and Barnabas, and drove them out" from that district.

The apostles were not discouraged. They remembered the words of their Master: "Rejoice and be glad, for your reward is great in heaven, for so men persecuted the prophets who were before you." Matthew 5:12, RSV.

The gospel message was advancing!

18 / The Apostles Are Both Persecuted and Adored

In Iconium as at Antioch, Paul and Barnabas began their labors in the synagogue of their own people. "A great company believed, both of Jews and of Greeks." But as in other places, "the unbelieving Jews stirred up the Gentiles and poisoned their minds against the brethren."

However, in the face of opposition and prejudice the apostles went on, "speaking boldly for the Lord," and God "bore witness to the word of His grace, granting signs and wonders to be done by their hands." Converts multiplied.

The popularity of the message filled the unbelieving Jews with envy, and they determined to stop Paul and Barnabas. By false reports they led the authorities to fear that the city would be incited to insurrection. They suggested that it was for secret and dangerous designs that large numbers were attaching themselves to the apostles.

The disciples were repeatedly brought before the authorities, but their defense was so clear and sensible that the magistrates dared not condemn them. They could not but acknowledge that the teachings of Paul and Barnabas, if accepted, would improve the morals and order of the city.

Through opposition the message of truth gained publicity; the Jews' efforts to thwart the work resulted only in adding greater numbers to the new faith. "The

This chapter is based on Acts 14:1-26, RSV.

people of the city were divided; some sided with the Jews, and some with the apostles.''

So enraged were the Jews that they determined to gain their ends by violence. Arousing the ignorant, noisy mob, they created a tumult, which they attributed to the disciples. They determined that the mob should stone Paul and Barnabas.

Friends of the apostles, though unbelievers, urged them not to expose themselves needlessly to the mob, but to escape. Paul and Barnabas accordingly departed in secret from Iconium, leaving the believers to carry on alone. But they purposed to return after the excitement had abated.

In every age and land, God's messengers have met opposition from those who reject light. Often, by misrepresentation and falsehood, enemies of the gospel have seemingly triumphed, closing doors by which God's messengers might gain access to the people. But these doors cannot remain forever closed!

Excitement at Lystra

Driven from Iconium, the apostles went to Lystra and Derbe, in Lycaonia. Among these largely heathen, superstitious people were some who were willing to accept the gospel. In these places the apostles decided to labor.

In Lystra there was no synagogue, though a few Jews were living in the town. Many of the inhabitants worshiped Jupiter. When Paul and Barnabas explained the simple truths of the gospel, many sought to connect these doctrines with the worship of Jupiter.

The apostles endeavored to impart a knowledge of the Creator and His Son. They first directed attention to the works of God—the sun, moon, and stars, the order of the recurring seasons, the mighty snow-capped mountains, and other varied wonders of nature, which showed a skill beyond human comprehension. Through these, the apostles led the minds of the heathen to contemplate the Ruler of the universe.

Having made plain these fundamental truths, the apostles told the Lystrians of the Son of God, who came from heaven because He loved the children of men. They spoke of His life, His rejection, His trial and crucifixion, His resurrection, and His ascension to heaven to act as man's advocate.

While Paul was telling of Christ's work as a healer, he saw a cripple whose eyes were fastened on him and who believed his words. Paul's heart went out in sympathy toward the afflicted man, in whom he discerned one who "had faith to be made well." Paul commanded the cripple to stand. The sufferer had been able to sit only, but now he instantly obeyed, and for the first time in his life stood on his feet. Strength came with faith, and he "sprang up and walked."

"When the crowds saw what Paul had done, they lifted up their voices, saying in Lycaonian, 'The gods have come down to us in the likeness of men!' " Their tradition was that the gods occasionally visited the earth. Barnabas they called Jupiter, the father of gods, because of his venerable, dignified bearing, mildness, and benevolence. Paul they believed to be Mercury, "because he was the chief speaker," active and eloquent.

The Lystrians prevailed on the priest of Jupiter to honor the apostles, and he "brought oxen and garlands to the gates and wanted to offer sacrifice with the people." Unaware of these preparations, Paul and Barnabas had sought rest. Soon, however, their attention was attracted by music and the shouting of a large crowd who had come where they were staying.

The apostles "tore their garments and rushed out among the multitude" in the hope of preventing further proceedings. In a loud voice which rose above the shouting, Paul said: " 'Men, why are you doing this? We also are men, of like nature with you, and bring you good news, that you should turn from these vain things to a living God who made the heaven and the earth and the sea and all that is in them.' "

Notwithstanding Paul's endeavors to direct the people to God as the only object worthy of adoration, so firm had been their belief that these men were indeed gods and so great their enthusiasm, that they were "scarcely restrained." The Lystrians had seen a cripple who had never been able to walk, rejoice in perfect health and strength. Only after much careful explanation on the part of Paul and Barnabas regarding their mission as representatives of the God of heaven and of His Son, the great Healer, did the people give up their purpose.

Jews Incite the Crowd to Stone Paul

The labors of Paul and Barnabas were suddenly checked. "Jews came there from Antioch and Iconium," and on learning of the success of the apostles, determined to persecute them. On arriving at Lystra, these Jews inspired the people with the same bitterness that actuated their own minds. Those who had recently regarded Paul and Barnabas as divine were persuaded that in reality the apostles were deserving of death.

The Lystrians turned against Paul and Barnabas with an enthusiasm approaching that with which they had hailed them as gods. They planned to attack the apostles by force. The Jews charged them not to allow Paul to speak, alleging that he would bewitch the people.

The Lystrians became possessed with a satanic fury, and, seizing Paul, stoned him. The apostle thought his end had come. The cruel part he himself had acted at the martyrdom of Stephen came vividly to his mind. Covered with bruises and faint with pain, he fell to the ground, and the infuriated mob "dragged him out of the city, supposing that he was dead."

In this trying hour the Lystrian believers who had been converted to the faith of Jesus remained loyal and true. Cruel persecution by their enemies only confirmed the faith of these devoted brethren; and now, in the face of danger, they showed their loyalty by gathering about the form of him whom they believed to be dead.

In the midst of their lamentations the apostle suddenly rose to his feet with the praise of God on his lips. This unexpected miracle seemed to set the signet of Heaven on their change of belief. They praised God with renewed faith.

Among those who had been converted at Lystra was one who was to share with the apostle the trials and joys of pioneer service in difficult fields. This was Timothy. This youth was among the number who took their stand beside Paul's apparently lifeless body and saw him arise, bruised and covered with blood, but with praises on his lips because he had been permitted to suffer for Christ.

The day following, the apostles departed for Derbe, where many were led to receive the Saviour. But neither Paul nor Barnabas was content to take up work elsewhere without confirming the faith of the converts where they had recently labored. So, undaunted by danger, "they returned to Lystra and to Iconium and to Antioch, strengthening the souls of the disciples, exhorting them to continue in the faith." Many had accepted the gospel. These the apostles sought to establish in the faith.

Instruction and Organization Essential to Success

The apostles were careful to surround the new converts with the safeguards of gospel order. Churches were organized in all places where there were believers. Officers were appointed, and proper order and system was established for the spiritual welfare of the believers.

Paul was careful to follow throughout his ministry the gospel plan of uniting in one body all believers in Christ. Even when believers were but few in number, they were, at the proper time, organized into a church and taught to help one another, remembering the promise, "Where two or three are gathered in My name, there am I in the midst of them." Matthew 18:20, RSV.

The care of these churches rested on Paul's mind as an ever-increasing burden. However small a company might be, it was the object of his constant solicitude. He watched over the smaller churches tenderly, that the members might be established in the truth and taught to put forth unselfish efforts for those around them.

Paul and Barnabas sought to follow Christ's example of willing sacrifice. Wide-awake, untiring, they did not consult personal ease, but with prayerful anxiety they sowed the seed of truth and gave to all who took their stand for the gospel practical instruction of untold value. This spirit of earnestness made a lasting impression on the minds of the new disciples.

When men of ability were converted, as in the case of Timothy, Paul and Barnabas sought to show them the necessity of laboring in the vineyard. When the apostles left, the faith of these men did not fail, but increased. They had been faithfully instructed how to labor unselfishly, perseveringly for their fellowmen. This careful training of new converts was an important factor in the remarkable success that attended Paul and Barnabas.

The first missionary journey was drawing to a close. Commending the newly organized churches to the Lord, the apostles "went down to Attalia; and from there they sailed to Antioch."

19 / Thorny Problems Settled by the Holy Spirit

On reaching Antioch in Syria, Paul and Barnabas assembled the believers and rehearsed "all that God had done with them, and how He had opened the door of faith unto the Gentiles." Acts 14:27. The large, growing church at Antioch was a center of missionary activity and was made up of both Jews and Gentiles.

While the apostles united with lay members to win souls, certain Jewish believers from Judea "of the sect of the Pharisees" (KJV), suçceeded in introducing a question that brought consternation to the believing Gentiles. These Judaizing teachers asserted that in order to be saved, one must be circumcised and keep the ceremonial law.

Paul and Barnabas opposed this false doctrine, but many of the believing Jews of Antioch favored the position of the brethren recently come from Judea. Many of the Jews who had been converted to Christ still felt that since God had once outlined the Hebrew manner of worship, it was improbable that He would ever authorize a change in it. They insisted that the Jewish ceremonies be incorporated into the Christian religion. They were slow to discern that the sacrificial offerings had prefigured the death of the Son of God, in which type met antitype, and were no longer binding.

Paul had gained a clear conception of the mission of the Saviour as the Redeemer of Gentile as well as Jew and had learned the difference between a living faith

This chapter is based on Acts 15:1-35, RSV.

THORNY PROBLEMS SETTLED BY THE HOLY SPIRIT / 101

and a dead formalism. In the light of the gospel, the ceremonies committed to Israel had gained a new significance. That which they foreshadowed had come to pass, and those who were living under the gospel dispensation had been freed from their observance. God's unchangeable law of Ten Commandments, however, Paul still kept in spirit as well as in letter.

The question of circumcision resulted in much discussion and contention. Finally, the members of the church decided to send Paul and Barnabas, with some responsible men from the church, to Jerusalem to lay the matter before the apostles and elders. A final decision given in general council was to be universally accepted by the different churches.

The First General Church Council

At Jerusalem the delegates from Antioch related the success that had attended their ministry among the Gentiles. They then gave a clear outline of the confusion that had resulted because certain converted Pharisees had declared that the Gentile converts must be circumcised and keep the law of Moses.

This question was warmly discussed in the assembly, also the problem of meats offered to idols. Many Gentile converts were living among superstitious people who made frequent sacrifices and offerings to idols. The Jews feared that Gentile converts would bring Christianity into disrepute by purchasing that which had been offered to idols, thereby sanctioning idolatrous customs.

Again, the Gentiles were accustomed to eat the flesh of animals that had been strangled; the Jews had been divinely instructed that when beasts were killed for food, the blood should flow from the body. God had given these injunctions for preserving health. The Jews regarded it as sinful to use blood as an article of diet. The Gentiles, on the contrary, practiced catching the blood from the sacrificial victim and using it in the preparation of food. Therefore, if Jew and Gentile should eat at the same table, the former would be shocked and outraged by the latter.

The Gentiles, especially Greeks, were licentious, and there was danger that some would make a profession of faith without renouncing their evil practices. The Jewish Christians could not tolerate the immorality that was not even regarded as criminal by the heathen. The Jews therefore held that circumcision and the observance of the ceremonial law should be enjoined on Gentile converts as a test of their sincerity. This, they believed, would prevent the addition to the church of those who afterward might bring reproach on the cause by immorality.

The various points involved seemed to present before the council insurmountable difficulties. "After there had been much debate, Peter rose and said to them, 'Brethren, you know that in the early days God made choice among you, that by my mouth the Gentiles should hear the word of the gospel and believe.' " He reasoned that the Holy Spirit had decided the matter under dispute by descending with equal power on Gentiles and Jews. He recounted his vision and related his summons to go to the centurion and instruct him in the faith of Christ. This message showed that God accepted all who feared Him. Peter told of his astonishment when he witnessed the Holy Spirit taking possession of Gentiles as well as Jews. Light and glory shone also on the faces of the uncircumcised Gentiles. This was God's warning that Peter was not to regard one as inferior to the other, for the blood of Christ could cleanse from all uncleanness.

Once before, Peter had related how the Holy Spirit fell on the Gentiles. He declared: "If then God gave the same gift to them as He gave to us when we believed in the Lord Jesus Christ, who was I that I could withstand God?" Acts 11:17, RSV. Now, with equal force, he said: "God who knows the heart bore witness to them, giving them the Holy Spirit just as He did to us; and He made no distinction between us and them, but cleansed their hearts by faith. Now therefore why do you make trial of God by putting a yoke upon the neck of the disciples which neither our fathers nor we have been able to bear?'' This yoke was not the Ten Commandments. Peter here referred to the law of ceremonies, which was made void by the crucifixion of Christ.

''All the assembly kept silence; and they listened to Barnabas and Paul as they related what signs and wonders God had done through them among the Gentiles.''

How the Holy Spirit Led the Council

The Holy Spirit saw good not to impose the ceremonial law on Gentile converts, and the mind of the apostles on this was as the mind of the Spirit of God. James presided at the council, and his decision was, ''We should not trouble those of the Gentiles who turn to God.''

This ended the discussion. In this instance we have a refutation of the doctrine that Peter was the head of the church. Those who have claimed to be his successors have no Scriptural foundation for their claim that Peter was elevated above his brethren as the vicegerent of the Most High. If those who are declared the successors of Peter, had followed his example, they would always remain on an equality with their brethren.

James sought to impress his brethren that the Gentiles had made a great change in their lives and should not be troubled with questions of minor importance, lest they be discouraged in following Christ.

The Gentile converts, however, were to give up customs inconsistent with Christianity. They were to abstain from meats offered to idols, from fornication, from things strangled, and from blood. They were to keep the commandments and lead holy lives.

Judas and Silas were sent with Paul and Barnabas to declare to the Gentiles by word of mouth the decision of the council. The message that was to put an end to all controversy was the voice of the highest authority on earth.

The council which decided this case was composed of apostles and teachers prominent in raising up Jewish and Gentile Christian churches, with delegates from various places. The most influential churches were represented. The council moved with the dignity of a church established by the divine will. As a result of their deliberations, they all saw that God Himself had answered the question at issue by bestowing on the Gentiles the Holy Spirit. It was their part to follow the guidance of the Spirit.

The entire body of Christians was not called to vote on the question. The "apostles and the elders" framed and issued the decree, which was thereupon generally accepted by the churches. Not all, however, were pleased. A faction of self-confident brethren indulged in murmuring and faultfinding, seeking to pull down the work of the men whom God had ordained to teach the gospel. The church will have such obstacles to meet till the close of time.

Trouble in Jerusalem

It was at Jerusalem that the greatest exclusiveness and bigotry were found. When Jewish Christians living within sight of the temple saw the Christian church departing from the ceremonies of Judaism and perceived that Jewish customs would soon be lost sight of in the new faith, many grew indignant with Paul. Even the disciples were not all prepared to accept willingly the decision of the council. Some, zealous for the ceremonial law, regarded Paul with disfavor. They thought his principles in regard to the Jewish law were lax.

The far-reaching decisions of the general council brought confidence to the Gentile believers, and the cause of God prospered. In Antioch Judas and Silas "exhorted the brethren with many words and strengthened them."

Later, when Peter visited Antioch, he won confidence by his prudent conduct toward the Gentile converts. In accordance with the light from heaven, he sat at table with the Gentile converts. But when certain Jews, zealous for the ceremonial law, came from Jerusalem, Peter injudiciously changed. A number of the Jews "acted insincerely, so that even Barnabas was carried away by their insincerity." This weakness on the part of those who had been respected as leaders left a painful impression on the Gentile believers. The church was threatened with division. But Paul, who saw the subverting influence of the wrong done through the double part acted by Peter, openly rebuked him. In the presence of the church, Paul inquired of Peter, "If you, though a Jew, live like a Gentile and not like a Jew, how can you compel the Gentiles to live like Jews." Galatians 2:13, 14, RSV.

Peter saw his error and immediately set about repairing the evil, so far as was in his power. God permitted Peter to reveal this weakness in order that he might see there was nothing in himself whereof to boast. Even the best of men, if left to themselves, will err. God also saw that in time to come some would claim for Peter and his pretended successors the exalted prerogatives that belong to God alone. This record of the apostle's weakness was proof of his fallibility and that he stood in no way above the other apostles.

The greater the responsibilities placed on the human agent and the larger his opportunities to dictate and control, the more harm he is sure to do if he does not carefully follow the way of the Lord and labor in harmony with decisions arrived at by the general body of believers in united council.

After Peter's fall and restoration, his intimate acquaintance with Christ, after all the knowledge and influence he had gained by teaching the Word—is it not strange that he should dissemble and evade the principles of the gospel in order to gain esteem? May God give every man a realization of his helplessness, his inability to steer his own vessel straight and safe into the harbor.

Paul was often compelled to stand alone. He dared

make no concessions that would involve principle. At times the burden was heavy. The traditions of men must not take the place of revealed truth. He realized the church must never be brought under the control of human power.

Paul had received the gospel direct from heaven, and he maintained a vital connection with heavenly agencies. He had been taught by God regarding the binding of unnecessary burdens on the Gentile Christians. Thus he knew the mind of the Spirit and took a firm, unyielding position which brought to the churches freedom from Jewish rites.

Notwithstanding the fact that Paul was personally taught by God, he was ever ready to recognize the authority vested in the body of believers united in church fellowship. When matters of importance arose, he was glad to unite with his brethren in seeking God for wisdom to make right decisions. "God is not the author of confusion, but of peace, as in all churches of the saints." 1 Corinthians 14:33. All united in church capacity should be "subject one to another." 1 Peter 5:5.

20 / Paul's Secret: Exalt the Cross

After spending some time at Antioch, Paul proposed to his fellow worker Barnabas, "Come, let us return and visit the brethren in every city where we proclaimed the word of the Lord, and see how they are."

Both Paul and Barnabas had a tender regard for those who had accepted the gospel under their ministry, and they longed to see them once more. Even when far from the scene of his earlier labors, Paul tried to help these converts become strong in faith and wholehearted in their consecration to God.

Barnabas was ready to go, but wished to take Mark with them. Paul objected. He "thought best not to take with them" one who had left them during their first missionary journey for the safety and comforts of home. He urged that one with so little stamina was unfitted for a work requiring self-denial, bravery, faith, and a willingness to sacrifice even life itself. So sharp was the contention that "Barnabas took Mark with him and sailed away to Cyprus, but Paul chose Silas and departed."

Paul and Silas at length reached Derbe and Lystra. It was at Lystra that Paul had been stoned, yet he was anxious to see how those who had accepted the gospel were enduring trial. He was not disappointed, for the Lystrian believers had remained firm in the face of violent opposition.

Here Paul again met Timothy, who was convinced

This chapter is based on Acts 15:36-41; 16:1-6, RSV.

that it was his duty to give himself fully to the work of the ministry. He longed to share the apostle's labors. Silas, Paul's companion, was a tried worker, gifted with the spirit of prophecy; but the work was so great that there was need of more laborers. In Timothy Paul saw one who appreciated the sacredness of the work and was not appalled at the prospect of persecution. Yet the apostle did not venture to take Timothy, an untried youth, without fully satisfying himself in regard to his character and past life.

How Two Women Trained a Man of God

From a child Timothy had known the Scriptures. The faith of his mother and grandmother was a constant reminder of the blessing in doing God's will. The lessons he had received from them kept him pure in speech and unsullied by the evil influences which surrounded him. Thus his home instructors had cooperated with God in preparing him to bear burdens.

Paul saw that Timothy was steadfast, and he chose him as a companion in labor and travel. Those who had taught Timothy in childhood were rewarded by seeing him linked with the great apostle. Timothy was a mere youth, but he was fitted to take his place as Paul's helper. Though young, he bore his responsibilities with Christian meekness.

Paul wisely advised Timothy to be circumcised in order to remove from the minds of the Jews that which might be an objection to Timothy's ministry. If it should be known that one of his companions was uncircumcised, his work might be hindered by prejudice and bigotry. He desired to bring to his Jewish brethren, as well as to Gentiles, a knowledge of the gospel and sought to remove every pretext for opposition. Yet while he conceded this much to Jewish prejudice, he believed and taught circumcision or uncircumcision to be nothing, and the gospel of Christ everything.

Paul loved Timothy, "my own son in the faith." 1 Timothy 1:2. As they traveled, he carefully taught him how to do successful work, to deepen the impression already made on his mind of the sacred nature of the work of the gospel minister.

Timothy constantly sought Paul's advice and instruction. He exercised consideration and calm thought, inquiring at every step, Is this the way of the Lord? The Holy Spirit found in him one who could be molded and fashioned as a temple for the indwelling of the divine Presence.

Timothy had no specially brilliant talents, but his knowledge of experimental piety gave him influence. Those who labor for souls must throw all their energies into the work; they must lay firm hold on God, daily receiving grace and power.

Before pressing into new territory, Paul and his companions visited the churches in Pisidia and regions round about. "They delivered to them for observance the decisions which had been reached by the apostles and elders who were at Jerusalem. So the churches were strengthened in the faith, and they increased in numbers daily."

The apostle Paul felt a deep responsibility for those converted under his labors. He knew that preaching alone would not suffice to educate the believers to hold forth the word of life. He knew that line upon line, here a little and there a little, they must be taught to advance in the work of Christ.

Whenever one refuses to use his God-given powers, these powers decay. Truth that is not lived, that is not imparted, loses its life-giving power, its healing virtue. Paul's knowledge, his eloquence, his miracles—all would be unavailing if through unfaithfulness in his work those for whom he labored should fail of the grace of God. And so he pleaded with those who had accepted Christ to be "blameless and innocent, children of God without blemish in the midst of a crooked and perverse generation, . . .holding fast the word of life." Philippians 2:15, 16, RSV.

Every true minister feels a heavy responsibility for

the believers entrusted to his care, that they shall be laborers together with God. Upon his work depends in a large degree the well-being of the church. Earnestly he seeks to inspire believers to win souls, remembering that every addition to the church should be one more agency for carrying out the plan of redemption.

The Cross and Righteousness by Faith

Having visited the chuches in Pisidia, Paul and Silas, with Timothy, pressed on into Phrygia and Galatia, where they proclaimed the glad tidings. The Galatians were given up to the worship of idols, but they rejoiced in the message that promised freedom from the thralldom of sin. Paul and his fellow workers proclaimed the doctrine of righteousness by faith in the atoning sacrifice of Christ. Seeing the helpless condition of the fallen race, Christ came to redeem men and women by living a life of obedience to God's law and by paying the penalty of disobedience. In the light of the cross many began to comprehend the greatness of the Father's love. "By the hearing of faith," they received the Spirit of God and became "the children of God, by faith in Christ." Galatians 3:2, 26.

Paul's life among the Galatians was such that he could afterward say, "I beseech you, be as I am." Galatians 4:12. He was enabled to rise above bodily infirmities and present Jesus as the sinner's only hope. Those who heard him knew he had been with Jesus. He was able to tear down the strongholds of Satan. Hearts were broken by his presentation of the love of God revealed in the sacrifice of His only-begotten Son.

Throughout his ministry among the Gentiles, the apostle kept before them the cross of Calvary. The consecrated messengers who carried to a perishing world the glad tidings of salvation allowed no self-exaltation to mar their presentation of Christ and Him crucified. They coveted neither authority nor preeminence. Christ, the same yesterday, today, and forever, was the burden of their teaching.

If those who today teach the Word of God would uplift the cross of Christ higher, their ministry would be far more successful. Christ's death proves God's love for man. It is our pledge of salvation. To remove the cross from the Christian would be like blotting the sun from the sky. The cross brings us near to God, reconciling us to Him.

From the cross shines the light of the Saviour's love, and when the sinner looks up to the One who died to save him, he may rejoice, for his sins are pardoned. Kneeling in faith at the cross, he has reached the highest place to which man can attain.

Can we wonder that Paul exclaimed, "God forbid that I should glory, save in the cross of our Lord Jesus Christ?" Galatians 6:14. It is our privilege also to glory in the cross. Then with the light that streams from Calvary shining in our faces, we may go forth to reveal this light to those in darkness.

21 / Angels Open a Philippian Prison

The time had come for the gospel to be proclaimed in Europe. At Troas "a vision appeared to Paul in the night: a man of Macedonia was standing beseeching him and saying, 'Come over to Macedonia and help us.' "

The call was imperative. "When he had seen the vision," declares Luke, who accompanied Paul, Silas, and Timothy to Europe, "immediately we sought to go on into Macdeonia, concluding that God had called us to preach the gospel to them. . . . Therefore . . . we made . . . voyage . . . to Philippi."

"On the Sabbath," Luke continues, "we went outside the gate to the riverside, where we supposed there was a place of prayer; and we sat down and spoke to the women who had come together. One who heard us was a woman named Lydia, from the city of Thyatira, a seller of purple goods, who was a worshiper of God. The Lord opened her heart." Lydia and her household received the truth gladly and were baptized.

As the messengers of the cross went about their work, a woman followed them, crying, " 'These men are servants of the Most High God, who proclaim to you the way of salvation.' And this she did for many days." This woman was a special agent of Satan and had brought her masters much gain by soothsaying. Satan knew his kingdom was invaded, and he hoped to mingle his sophistry with the truths taught by those

This chapter is based on Acts 16:7-40, RSV.

112

proclaiming the gospel. The words of recommendation uttered by this woman were an injury to the cause of truth, bringing disrepute on the gospel; and by them many were led to believe that the apostles were actuated by the same spirit as this emissary of Satan.

For some time the apostles endured this. Then Paul commanded the evil spirit to leave the woman. Her immediate silence testified that the demon acknowledged the apostles to be the servants of God. Dispossessed of the evil spirit and restored to her right mind, the woman chose to follow Christ. Then her masters were alarmed. All hope of receiving money from her divinations was at an end. Their income would soon be entirely cut off if the apostles were allowed to continue.

Many others in the city were interested in gaining money through satanic delusions, and these brought the servants of God before the magistrates with the charge: "These men are Jews and they are disturbing our city. They advocate customs which it is not lawful for us Romans to accept or practice."

A Frenzied Multitude

A mob spirit prevailed, and the authorities commanded that the apostles should be scourged. "They threw them into prison, charging the jailer to keep them safely. Having received this charge, he put them into the inner prison and fastened their feet in the stocks."

The apostles suffered extreme torture, but they did not murmur. Instead, in the darkness of the dungeon, they encouraged each other and sang praises to God. Their hearts were cheered by a deep love for their Redeemer. Paul thought of the persecution he had brought on the disciples of Christ and rejoiced that his heart had been opened to feel the power of the glorious truths which once he despised.

With astonishment the other prisoners heard the sound of prayer and singing from the inner prison. They had been accustomed to hear shrieks, moans, and swearing, but never words of prayer and praise from the gloomy cell. Guards and prisoners marveled. Who could these men be, who, cold, hungry, and tortured, could yet rejoice?

On the way to their homes the magistrates heard further particulars concerning the men they had sentenced to scourging and imprisonment. They saw the woman who had been freed from satanic influence and were struck by the change in her countenance and demeanor. Now she was quiet and peaceable. They were indignant with themselves and decided that in the morning they would command that the apostles be privately released and escorted from the city, beyond danger from the mob.

But while men were criminally negligent of their solemn responsibilities, God had not forgotten His servants who were suffering for Christ's sake. Angels were sent to the prison. At their tread the earth trembled. The heavily bolted prison doors were thrown open, the chains and fetters fell from the prisoners, and a bright light flooded the prison.

The keeper of the jail had heard the prayers and songs of the imprisoned apostles. He had seen their swollen, bleeding wounds, and had himself caused their feet to be fastened in the stocks. He had expected to hear bitter groans and imprecations, but heard instead songs of joy. With these sounds in his ears the jailer had fallen asleep.

He was awakened by the earthquake and the shaking of prison walls. In alarm he saw that all the prison doors were open, and the fear flashed on him that the prisoners had escaped. Paul and Silas had been entrusted to his care the night before, and he was certain that death would be the penalty of his apparent unfaithfulness. It was better to die by his own hand than submit to a disgraceful execution.

He was about to kill himself when Paul's voice was heard, "Do not harm yourself, for we are all here." Every man was in place, restrained by the power of

God. The apostles had not resented the severe treatment by the jailer. Filled with the love of the Saviour, they had no room for malice.

A Cruel Jailer Is Converted

The jailer, calling for lights, hastened into the inner dungeon. What manner of men were these who repaid cruelty with kindness? Casting himself before the apostles, he asked their forgiveness. Then, bringing them out into the open court, he inquired, "Men, what must I do to be saved?"

All things seemed of little consequence compared with his desire to possess the tranquillity and cheerfulness shown by the apostles under abuse. He saw in their countenances the light of heaven, and with peculiar force the words of the woman came to his mind: "These men are servants of the Most High God, who proclaim to you the way of salvation." He asked the disciples to show him the way of life.

"Believe on the Lord Jesus, and you will be saved, you and your household," the apostles answered. And "they spoke the word of the Lord to him and to all that were in his house." The jailer then washed the wounds of the apostles and was baptized by them, with all his household. The minds of the inmates of the prison were opened to listen to the apostles. The God whom these men served had miraculously released them from bondage.

The Authorities Apologize

The citizens of Philippi had been terrified by the earthquake, and when in the morning the officers of the prison told the magistrates of what had occurred during the night, they sent the sergeants to liberate the apostles. But Paul declared, "They have beaten us publicly, uncondemned, men who are Roman citizens, and have thrown us into prison; and do they now cast us out secretly? No! let them come themselves and take us out."

It was unlawful to scourge a Roman, save for flagrant crime, or to deprive him of liberty without a trial. Paul and Silas, publicly imprisoned, now refused to be privately released without proper explanation on the part of the magistrates.

The authorities were alarmed. Would the apostles complain to the emperor? Going at once to the prison, they apologized to Paul and Silas and personally conducted them out of the prison. They feared the apostles' influence over the people, and they also feared the Power that had interposed in their behalf.

The apostles would not urge their presence where it was not desired. "They went out of the prison, and visited Lydia; and when they had seen the brethren, they exhorted them and departed."

The apostles had met opposition and persecution in Philippi, but the conversion of the jailer and his household more than atoned for the disgrace and suffering they had endured. The news of their unjust imprisonment and miraculous deliverance became known through all that region and brought the work of the apostles to the notice of a large number who otherwise would not have been reached.

Paul's Example Became a Lasting Influence

Paul's labors at Philippi resulted in a church whose membership steadily increased. His willingness to suffer for Christ exerted a lasting influence on the converts. They gave themselves with wholehearted devotion to the cause of their Redeemer. Such was their steadfastness in the faith that Paul declared, "I thank my God upon every remembrance of you, always in every prayer of mine for you all making request with joy, for your fellowship in the gospel from the first day until now." Philippians 1:3-5.

Terrible is the struggle that takes place between the forces of good and evil. "We are not contending against flesh and blood," declares Paul, "but against the principalities, against the powers, against the world rulers of this present darkness." Ephesians 6:12, RSV. Till the close of time there will be conflict between the church and those who are under the control of evil angels.

The early Christians were often called to meet the powers of darkness face to face. At the present time, when the end of all things earthly is rapidly approaching, Satan is devising many plans to occupy minds and divert attention from the truths essential to salvation. In every city his agencies are busily organizing those opposed to the law of God. The archdeceiver is at work to introduce elements of confusion and rebellion.

Wickedness is reaching a height never before attained, and yet many ministers of the gospel are crying, "Peace and safety." But clothed with the panoply of heaven, God's faithful messengers are to advance fearlessly and victoriously, never ceasing their warfare until every soul within their reach shall have received the message of truth for this time.

22/ A Revival and a Riot at Thessalonica

After leaving Philippi, Paul and Silas made their way to Thessalonica. Here they addressed large congregations in the Jewish synagogue. Their appearance bore evidence of shameful treatment and necessitated an explanation. Without exalting themselves, they magnified the One who had wrought their deliverance.

In preaching, Paul appealed to the Old Testament prophecies foretelling the birth, sufferings, death, resurrection, and ascension of Christ. He clearly proved the identity of Jesus of Nazareth with the Messiah, and showed that it was the voice of Christ which had been speaking through patriarchs and prophets:

1. The sentence pronounced on Satan, "I will put enmity between thee and the woman, and between thy seed and her seed; it shall bruise thy head, and thou shalt bruise his heel" (Genesis 3:15), was to our first parents a promise of the redemption through Christ.

2. To Abraham was given the promise that the Saviour should come: "In thy seed shall all the nations of the earth be blessed." "Thy seed, which is Christ." Genesis 22:18; Galatians 3:16.

3. Moses prophesied of the Messiah to come: "The Lord thy God will raise up unto thee a Prophet from the midst of thee, of thy brethren, like unto Me; unto Him ye shall hearken." Deuteronomy 18:15.

4. The Messiah was to be of the royal line, for Jacob said: "The scepter shall not depart from Judah, nor a lawgiver from between his feet, until Shiloh come;

This chapter is based on Acts 17:1-10, RSV.

and unto Him shall the gathering of the people be.'' Genesis 49:10.

5. Isaiah prophesied: "There shall come forth a shoot from the stump of Jesse, and a Branch shall grow out of his roots." Isaiah 11:1, RSV.

6. Jeremiah also bore witness of the coming Redeemer: "The days are coming, says the Lord, when I will raise up for David a righteous Branch, and He shall reign as king and deal wisely, and shall execute justice and righteousness in the land. . . .And this is the name by which He will be called: 'The Lord is our righteousness.' " Jeremiah 23:5, 6, RSV.

7. Even the birthplace of the Messiah was foretold: "Thou, Bethlehem Ephratah, though thou be little among the thousands of Judah, yet out of thee shall He come forth unto Me that is to be Ruler in Israel; whose goings forth have been from of old, from everlasting." Micah 5:2.

8. The work the Saviour was to do had been fully outlined: "To bring good tidings to the afflicted; . . . to bind up the brokenhearted, to proclaim liberty to the captives, and the opening of the prison to those who are bound; to proclaim the year of the Lord's favor, and the day of vengeance of our God; to comfort all who mourn." Isaiah 61:2, 3, RSV.

"Behold My servant, whom I uphold; Mine elect, in whom My soul delighteth; I have put My Spirit upon Him; He shall bring forth judgment to the Gentiles." "He shall not fail nor be discouraged, till He have set judgment in the earth." Isaiah 42:1, 4.

9. With convincing power Paul reasoned from the Scriptures that "it was necessary for the Christ to suffer and to rise from the dead." The Promised One, through Isaiah, had prophesied of Himself: "I gave My back to the smiters, and My cheeks to them that pulled off the hair: I hid not My face from shame and spitting." Isaiah 50:6. Through the psalmist Christ had foretold the treatment He should receive from men: "I am . . . scorned by men, and despised by the people.

All who see Me mock at Me, they make mouths at Me, they wag their heads; 'He committed His cause to the Lord; let Him deliver Him, let Him rescue Him, for He delights in Him!' " "I can count all my bones—they stare and gloat over Me; they divide My garments among them, and for My raiment they cast lots." Psalm 22:6-8, 17, 18, RSV.

10. Isaiah's prophecies of Christ's sufferings and death were unmistakably plain: "Who has believed what we have heard? And to whom has the arm of the Lord been revealed? . . . He had . . . no beauty that we should desire Him. He was despised and rejected by men; a man of sorrows, and acquainted with grief; and as one from whom men hide their faces He was despised, and we esteemed Him not. . . . But He was wounded for our transgressions, He was bruised for our iniquities; upon Him was the chastisement that made us whole, and with His stripes we are healed.

"All we like sheep have gone astray; we have turned every one to his own way; and the Lord has laid on Him the iniquity of us all. He was oppressed, and He was afflicted, yet He opened not His mouth. . . . Who considered that He was . . . stricken for the transgression of My people?" Isaiah 53:1-8, RSV.

11. Even the manner of His death had been shadowed forth. As the brazen serpent had been uplifted in the wilderness, so was the Redeemer to be "lifted up." John 3:14. If "one shall say unto Him, What are these wounds in Thine hands? then He shall answer, Those with which I was wounded in the house of My friends." Zechariah 13:6.

12. But He who was to suffer death at the hands of evil men was to rise again as a conqueror: "My flesh also shall rest in hope. For Thou wilt not leave My soul in hell [the grave]; neither wilt Thou suffer Thine Holy One to see corruption." Psalm 16:9, 10.

13. Paul showed how closely God had linked the sacrificial service with the prophecies relating to the One "brought as a lamb to the slaughter." The

Messiah was to give His life as "an offering for sin." Isaiah had testified that the Lamb of God "poured out His soul unto death: and . . . bare the sin of many, and made intercession for the transgressors." Isaiah 53:7, 10, 12.

Thus the Saviour was not to come as a temporal king to deliver the Jewish nation from earthly oppressors, but to live a life of poverty and humility and at last to be despised, rejected, and slain. The Saviour was to offer Himself as a sacrifice in behalf of the fallen race, fulfilling every requirement of the broken law. In Him the sacrificial types were to meet their antitype and His death on the cross was to lend significance to the entire Jewish economy.

Paul Relates the Story of His Conversion

Paul told the Thessalonian Jews of his wonderful experience at the gate of Damascus. Before conversion his faith had not been anchored in Christ; he had trusted in forms and ceremonies. While boasting that he was blameless in the performance of the deeds of the law, he had refused the One who made the law of value.

But at his conversion, all had been changed. The persecutor saw Jesus as the Son of God, the One who had met every specification of the Sacred Writings.

As with holy boldness Paul proclaimed the gospel at Thessalonica, a flood of light was thrown on the true meaning of the tabernacle service. He carried the minds of his hearers beyond the ministry of Christ in the heavenly sanctuary, to the time when He would come in power and great glory and establish His kingdom. Paul was a believer in the second coming. So clearly did he present the truths concerning this event that on the minds of many there was made an impression which never wore away.

For three successive Sabbaths Paul preached, reasoning from the Scriptures regarding the "Lamb slain from the foundation of the world." Revelation 13:8.

He exalted Christ, the proper understanding of whose ministry is the key that gives access to the rich treasures of the Old Testament Scriptures.

The attention of large congregations was arrested. "Some of them were persuaded, and joined Paul and Silas; as did a great many of the devout Greeks and not a few of the leading women." But as in places formerly entered, the apostles met with opposition. By uniting with "some wicked fellows of the rabble," the Jews succeeded in setting "the city in an uproar." They "attacked the house of Jason," but they could find neither Paul nor Silas. In their mad disappointment the mob "dragged Jason and some of the brethren before the city authorities, crying, 'These men who have turned the world upside down have come here also, and Jason has received them; and they are all acting against the decrees of Caesar, saying that there is another king, Jesus.' "

The magistrates put the accused believers under bonds to keep the peace. Fearing further violence, "the brethren immediately sent Paul and Silas away by night to Berea."

Those who today teach unpopular truths at times meet with no more favorable reception, even from those who claim to be Christians, than did Paul and his fellow workers. But the messengers of the cross must move forward with faith and courage, in the name of Jesus. They must exalt Christ as man's mediator in the heavenly sanctuary, the One in whom the transgressors of God's law may find peace and pardon.

23 / Paul Preaches in Berea and Athens

At Berea Paul found Jews who were willing to investigate the truth. "These Jews were more noble than those in Thessalonica, for they received the word with all eagerness, examining the Scriptures daily to see if these things were so. Many of them therefore believed, with not a few Greek women of high standing as well as men."

The Bereans studied the Bible, not from curiosity, but to learn what had been written concerning the promised Messiah. As they daily compared scripture with scripture, heavenly angels enlightened their minds.

If those to whom testing truths are proclaimed would follow the example of the Bereans, there would today be a large number loyal to God's law. But when unpopular Bible truths are presented, many manifest reluctance to study the evidences offered. Some assume that even if these doctrines are true, it matters little whether they accept the new light. Thus they become separated from heaven. Those who are sincerely seeking for truth will make a careful investigation, in the light of God's Word, of the doctrines presented to them.

The unbelieving Jews of Thessalonica, filled with hatred, followed the apostles to Berea and aroused against them the excitable passions of the lower class. Fearing violence, the brethren sent Paul to Athens, accompa-

This chapter is based on Acts 17:11-34, RSV.

nied by some Bereans who had newly accepted the faith. The enemies of Christ could not prevent the advancement of the gospel, but they made the work of the apostles exceedingly hard. Yet Paul pressed steadily forward.

On arriving in Athens, he sent the Berean brethren back with a message to Silas and Timothy to join him immediately. Timothy had come to Berea prior to Paul's departure, and with Silas had remained to instruct the new converts.

The Great City of Paganism

Athens was the metropolis of heathendom. Here Paul met with a people famous for their intelligence and culture. Everywhere statues of gods and deified heroes met the eye, while magnificent architecture and paintings represented national glory and the worship of heathen deities. The senses of the people were entranced by the splendor of art. On every hand sanctuaries and temples involving untold expense reared their massive forms. Victories of arms and deeds of celebrated men were commemorated by sculpture and shrines.

As Paul looked upon the beauty and saw the city wholly given to idolatry, his spirit was stirred, and his heart was drawn out in pity for the people who, notwithstanding their culture, were ignorant of the true God. His spiritual nature was so alive to the attraction of heavenly things that the glory of the riches which will never perish made valueless in his eyes the splendor with which he was surrounded. As he saw the magnificence of Athens, he was deeply impressed with the importance of the work before him.

While waiting for Silas and Timothy, Paul was not idle. He disputed "in the synagogue with the Jews and the devout persons, and in the market place every day with those who chanced to be there." But the apostle was soon to meet paganism in its most subtle, alluring form.

A singular teacher was setting before the people doctrines new and strange. Some of the great men of Athens sought Paul out and entered into conversation with him. Soon a crowd gathered. Some ridiculed the apostle as one far beneath them socially and intellectually, and jeered, " 'What would this babbler say?' Others said, 'He seems to be a preacher of foreign divinities.' "

The Epicurean and Stoic philosophers and others who came in contact with him soon saw that he had a store of knowledge greater than their own. His intellectual power commanded the respect of the learned, while his earnest, logical reasoning held the attention of all in the audience. He was able to meet all classes with convincing arguments. Thus the apostle stood undaunted, matching logic with logic, philosophy with philosophy.

His heathen opponents called his attention to the fate of Socrates, a setter forth of strange gods, who had been condemned to death. They counseled Paul not to endanger his life in the same way. But, satisfying themselves that he was determined to accomplish his errand among them and at all hazards to tell his story, they decided to give him a fair hearing on Mars' Hill.

Paul's Impressive Oration on Mars' Hill

This was one of the most sacred spots in Athens, regarded with a superstitious reverence. In this place matters connected with religion were often carefully considered by men who acted as judges on moral as well as civil questions. Here, away from the noise and bustle of crowded thoroughfares, the apostle could be heard without interruption. Poets, artists, philosophers—the scholars and sages of Athens—addressed him: "May we know what this new teaching is which you present? For you bring some strange things to our ears; we wish to know therefore what these things mean."

The apostle was calm and self-possessed, and his words convinced his hearers that he was no idle babbler. "Men of Athens," he said, "I perceive that in every way you are very religious. For as I passed along, and observed the objects of your worship, I found also an altar with this inscription, 'To an unknown god.' What therefore you worship as unknown, this I proclaim to you." With all their general knowledge, they were ignorant of the God who created the universe. Yet some were longing for greater light.

With hand outstretched toward the temple crowded with idols, Paul exposed the fallacies of the religion of the Athenians. His hearers were astonished. He showed himself familiar with their art, their literature, and their religion. Pointing to their statuary and idols, he declared that God could not be likened to these graven images. These images had no life, moving only when the hands of men moved them; and those who worshiped them were in every way superior to that which they worshiped.

Paul drew the minds of his hearers to the Deity whom they had styled the "Unknown God." This Being needed nothing from human hands to add to His power and glory.

The people were carried away with admiration for Paul's logical presentation of the attributes of the true God. With eloquence the apostle declared: "God who made the world and everything in it, being Lord of heaven and earth, does not live in shrines made by man, nor is He served by human hands, as though He needed anything, since He Himself gives to all men life and breath and everything."

In that age when human rights were often unrecognized, Paul declared that God "made from one every nation of men to live on all the face of the earth." All are on an equality, and to the Creator every human being owes supreme allegiance. Then the apostle showed how, through all God's dealings with man, His purpose of grace and mercy runs like a thread of gold. He "determined allotted periods and the boundaries of their habitation, that they should seek God, in the hope that they might feel after Him and find Him. Yet He is not far from each one of us."

With words borrowed from a poet of their own he pictured God as a Father, whose children they were. " 'In Him we live and move and have our being,' " he declared; "as even some of your poets have said, 'For we are indeed His offspring.' Being then God's offspring, we ought not to think that the Deity is like gold, or silver, or stone, a representation by the art and imagination of man."

The Great Philosophers Rejected the Gospel

In the ages of darkness that had preceded the advent of Christ, the divine Ruler had passed lightly over the idolatry of the heathen, but now He expected repentance, not only from the poor and humble, but from the proud philosopher and princes. "He has fixed a day on which He will judge the world in righteousness by a man whom He has appointed, and of this He has given assurance to all men by raising Him from the dead." As Paul spoke of the resurrection from the dead, "some mocked; but others said, 'We will hear you again about this.' "

Thus the Athenians, clinging to their idolatry, turned from the light. Boasting of learning and refinement, they were becoming more corrupt and more content with the vague mysteries of idolatry.

Some who listened to Paul were convicted, but they would not humble themselves to accept the plan of salvation. No eloquence, no argument, can convert the sinner. The power of God alone can apply the truth to the heart. The Greeks sought after wisdom, yet the message of the cross was to them foolishness.

In their pride of intellect may be found the reason why the gospel met with little success among the Athenians. Worldly-wise men who come to Christ as lost sinners will become wise unto salvation, but those who extol their own wisdom will fail of receiving the light and knowledge that He alone can give.

Thus Paul met the paganism of his day. His labors in Athens were not wholly in vain. Dionysius, one of the most prominent citizens, and some others accepted the gospel.

The Athenians, with all their knowledge, refinement, and art, were yet sunken in vice. God, through His servant, rebuked the sins of a proud, self-sufficient people. The words of the apostle, as traced by the pen of inspiration, bear witness of his courage in loneliness and adversity, and the victory he gained for Christianity in the very heart of paganism.

Truth to Be Taught Tactfully

Had Paul's oration been a direct attack on the gods and the great men of the city, he would have been in danger of meeting the fate of Socrates. But with a tact born of divine love, he carefully drew their minds away from heathen deities, by revealing to them the true God.

Today the truths of Scripture are to be brought before the great men of the world, that they may choose between obedience to God's law and allegiance to the prince of evil. God does not force them to accept truth, but if they turn from it, He leaves them to be filled with the fruit of their own doings.

"The preaching of the cross is to them that perish foolishness; but unto us which are saved it is the power of God." "God hath chosen the foolish things of the world to confound the wise; and God hath chosen the weak things of the world to confound the things which are mighty." 1 Corinthians 1:18, 27. Many great scholars and statesmen, the world's most eminent men, will in these last days turn from the light. Yet God's servants are to communicate the truth to these men. Some will take their place as humble learners at the feet of Jesus, the Master Teacher.

In the darkest hour there is light above. The strength of those who love and serve God will be renewed day by day. The understanding of the Infinite is placed at their service, that they may not err. The light of God's truth is to shine amid the darkness that enshrouds our world.

There is to be no despondency in God's service. God is able and willing to bestow on His servants the strength they need, and He will more than fulfill the highest expectations of those who put their trust in Him.

24 / Preaching the Power of the Cross in Corinth

Corinth was one of the leading cities of the world. Travelers from every land thronged its streets, intent on business and pleasure. It was an important place in which to establish memorials for God and His truth.

Among the Jews who had taken up residence in Corinth were Aquila and Priscilla, earnest workers for Christ. Becoming acquainted with the character of these persons, Paul stayed and worked with them.

In this thoroughfare of travel, Venus was the favorite goddess; and with the worship of Venus were connected many demoralizing rites. Even among the heathen, the Corinthians had become conspicuous for their gross immorality.

In Corinth the apostle followed a course different from his labors in Athens, where he met logic with logic, philosophy with philosophy. He realized that his teaching in Athens had been productive of but little fruit. In his efforts to arrest the attention of the careless and indifferent in Corinth he determined to avoid elaborate arguments, and "to know nothing among you except Jesus Christ and Him crucified." He would preach not "in plausible words of wisdom, but in demonstration of the Spirit and power." 1 Corinthians 2:2, 4, RSV.

Jesus, whom Paul was about to present as the Christ, was reared in a town proverbial for its wickedness. He had been rejected by His own nation and at last cruci-

This chapter is based on Acts 18:1-18, RSV.

130

fied as a malefactor. The Greeks regarded philosophy and science as the only means of attaining to true elevation and honor. Could Paul lead them to believe that faith in this obscure Jew would uplift and ennoble every power of the being?

To multitudes living at the present time, the cross of Calvary is surrounded by sacred memories. But in Paul's day the cross was regarded with horror. To uphold as the Saviour one who had met death on the cross would naturally call forth ridicule and opposition.

Paul well knew how his message would be regarded. Jewish hearers would be angered. In the estimation of the Greeks his words would be absurd. How could the cross have any connection with the elevation of the race or the salvation of mankind?

The One Object of Supreme Interest

But ever since Paul had been arrested in his career of persecution against the followers of the crucified Nazarene, he had never ceased to glory in the cross. There had been given him a revelation of the infinite love of God as revealed in the death of Christ; and a marvelous transformation had been wrought in his life, bringing all his plans and purposes into harmony with heaven. He knew by experience that when a sinner yields to the love of the Father, as seen in the sacrifice of His Son, a change of heart takes place, and Christ is all and in all.

Henceforth Paul's life was devoted to an effort to portray the love and power of the Crucified One. "I am under obligation," he declared, "both to Greeks and to barbarians, both to the wise and to the foolish." Romans 1:14, RSV. If ever his ardor flagged, one glance at the cross and the amazing love there revealed was enough to cause him to press forward in the path of self-denial.

Behold the apostle in the synagogue at Corinth, reasoning from the writings of Moses and the prophets and bringing his hearers down to the advent of the promised Messiah. Listen as he makes plain the work of the One who through the sacrifice of His own life was to make atonement for sin and then take up His ministry in the heavenly sanctuary. The Messiah for whose advent Paul's hearers had been longing, had already come; His death was the antitype of all the sacrificial offerings; His ministry in the sanctuary in heaven was the great object that cast its shadow backward and made clear the ministry of the Jewish priesthood.

From the Old Testament Scriptures Paul traced the descent of Jesus from Abraham through the royal psalmist. He read the testimony of the prophets regarding the character and work of the promised Messiah and showed that all these predictions had been fulfilled in Jesus of Nazareth.

Christ had come to offer salvation first of all to the nation that was looking for the Messiah's coming, but that nation had rejected Him and had chosen another leader, whose reign would end in death. Repentance alone could save the Jewish nation from impending ruin.

Paul related the story of his own miraculous conversion. His hearers could not but discern that with all his heart he loved the crucified and risen Saviour. They saw that his whole life was bound up with his Lord. Only those who were filled with the bitterest hatred could stand unmoved by his words.

Again the Jews Reject the Gospel

But the Jews of Corinth closed their eyes to the evidence presented by the apostle and refused to listen to his appeals. The same spirit that had led them to reject Christ filled them with fury against His servant; and had not God especially protected him, they would have put an end to his life.

''And when they opposed and reviled him, he shook out his garments and said to them, 'Your blood be upon your heads! I am innocent. From now on I will go to the Gentiles.' And he left there and went to the house of a man named Titius Justus, a worshiper of God."

Silas and Timothy had come to help Paul, and together they preached Christ as the Saviour. Avoiding complicated far-fetched reasoning, the messengers of the cross appealed to the heathen to behold the infinite sacrifice made in man's behalf. If those groping in the darkness of heathenism could see the light streaming from Calvary's cross, they would be drawn, the Saviour had declared, "to Me." John 12:32.

Clear, plain, and decided was their message. And not only in their words, but in the daily life, was the gospel revealed. Angels cooperated with them, and the grace and power of God was shown in the conversion of many. "Crispus, the ruler of the synagogue, believed in the Lord, together with all his household; and many of the Corinthians hearing Paul believed and were baptized."

Paul Bitterly Attacked

The Jews' hatred was now intensified. The baptism of Crispus exasperated these stubborn opposers. They blasphemed the gospel and the name of Jesus. No words were too bitter, no device too low, for them to use. They boldly affirmed that Paul's wonderful works were accomplished through the power of Satan.

The wickedness that Paul saw in corrupt Corinth almost disheartened him. The depravity among the Gentiles and the insult he received from the Jews caused him great anguish. He doubted the wisdom of trying to build up a church from the material he found there.

As he was planning to leave for a more promising field, the Lord appeared to him in a vision and said, "Do not be afraid, but speak and do not be silent; for I am with you. . . ; for I have many people in this city." Paul understood this to be a guarantee that the Lord would give increase to the seed sown in Corinth. Encouraged, he continued to labor there with zeal.

The apostle spent much time in house-to-house labor. He visited the sick and sorrowing, comforted the afflicted, and lifted up the oppressed. He trembled lest his teaching should bear the impress of the human rather than the divine.

"Among the mature we do impart wisdom, although it is not a wisdom of this age or of the rulers of this age, who are doomed to pass away. But we impart a secret and hidden wisdom of God, which God decreed before the ages for our glorification. None of the rulers of this age understood this; for if they had, they would not have crucified the Lord of glory." "We impart this in words not taught by human wisdom but taught by the Spirit." 1 Corinthians 2:6-8, 13, RSV.

Paul spoke of himself as "Always carrying in the body the death of Jesus, so that the life of Jesus may also be manifested in our bodies." 2 Corinthians 4:10, RSV. In the apostle's teachings, Christ was the central figure. "I live," he declared, "yet not I, but Christ liveth in me." Galatians 2:20.

Paul was an eloquent speaker. But now he set all flights of oratory aside. Instead of indulging in poetic fanciful representations which might please the senses but not touch the daily experience, he sought by simple language to bring to the heart the truths of vital importance. The present trials of struggling souls—these must be met with practical instruction in the fundamental principles of Christianity.

Many in Corinth turned from idols to serve the living God, and a large church was enrolled under the banner of Christ. Some among the most dissipated of the Gentiles became monuments of the efficacy of the blood of Christ to cleanse from sin.

Roman Proconsul Refuses to Be a Dupe of the Jews

Paul's increased success roused the unbelieving Jews to more determined opposition. They "made a united attack upon Paul, and brought him before the tribunal" of Gallio, proconsul of Achaia. With loud, angry voices they complained: "This man is persuading men to worship God contrary to the law."

The accusers of Paul thought that if they could fasten on him the charge of violating the Jewish religion, which was under the protection of the Roman power, he would probably be delivered to them for trial and sentence. But Gallio, a man of integrity, refused. Disgusted with their bigotry and self-righteousness, he would take no notice of the charge. As Paul prepared to speak in self-defense, Gallio told him it was not necessary. Then turning to the angry accusers, he said: " 'If it were a matter of wrongdoing or vicious crime, I should have reason to bear with you, O Jews; but since it is a matter of questions about words and names and your own law, see to it yourselves; I refuse to be a judge of these things.' And he drove them from the tribunal."

Gallio's immediate dismissal of the case was the signal for the Jews to retire, baffled and angry. The proconsul's decided course opened the eyes of the clamorous crowd who had been abetting the Jews. For the first time during Paul's labors in Europe, the mob turned to his side. "They all seized Sosthenes, the ruler of the synagogue, and beat him in front of the tribunal. But Gallio "paid no attention to this."

"Paul stayed many days longer" with the believers in Corinth. If the apostle had been compelled at this time to leave Corinth, the converts would have been in a perilous position. The Jews would have endeavored to follow up the advantage gained, even to the extermination of Christianity in that region.

25 / Two Important Letters to the Thessalonians

The arrival of Silas and Timothy in Corinth had greatly cheered Paul. They brought him "good news" of the "faith and love" of those who had accepted the gospel at Thessalonica. These believers in the midst of trial and adversity had remained true. He longed to visit them, but as this was not then possible, he wrote them:

"Brethren, in all our distress and affliction we have been comforted about you through your faith; for now we live, if you stand fast in the Lord. For what thanksgiving can we render to God for you, for all the joy which we feel for your sake before our God?"

Many in Thessalonica had turned from idols and had "received the word in much affliction," and their hearts were filled with "joy inspired by the Holy Spirit." In their faithfulness they were "an example to all the believers in Macedonia and in Achaia." The apostle declared: "Not only has the word of the Lord sounded forth from you in Macedonia and Achaia, but your faith in God has gone forth everywhere."

The hearts of the Thessalonian believers burned with zeal for their Saviour. A marvelous transformation had taken place in their lives, and hearts were won by the truths they presented.

In this first letter Paul declared that among the Thessalonians he had not sought to win converts through deception or guile. "For we never used either words of

This chapter is based on First and Second Thessalonians, RSV.

flattery, as you know, or a cloak for greed, as God is witness. . . . But we were gentle among you, like a nurse taking care of her children. . . . We were ready to share with you not only the gospel of God but also our own selves, because you had become very dear to us."

"You know how, like a father with his children, we exhorted each one of you and encouraged you and charged you to lead a life worthy of God, who calls you."

"What is our hope or joy or crown of boasting before our Lord Jesus at His coming? Is it not you? For you are our glory and joy."

Where Are the Dead?

Paul endeavored to instruct the Thessalonian believers regarding the true state of the dead. He spoke of those who die as being asleep—in a state of unconsciousness: "We would not have you ignorant, brethren, concerning those who are asleep, that you may not grieve as others do who have no hope. For since we believe that Jesus died and rose again, even so, through Jesus, God will bring with Him those who have fallen asleep. . . . For the Lord Himself will descend from heaven with a cry of command, with the archangel's call, and with the sound of the trumpet of God. And the dead in Christ will rise first; then we who are alive, who are left, shall be caught up together with them in the clouds to meet the Lord in the air; and so shall we always be with the Lord."

The Thessalonians had grasped the idea that Christ was coming to change the faithful who were alive and to take them to Himself. But one after another their loved ones had been taken from them, and the Thessalonians hardly dared to hope to meet them in a future life.

As Paul's letter was opened and read, great joy and consolation was brought by the words revealing the true state of the dead. Those living when Christ should come would not go to meet their Lord in advance of those who had fallen asleep in Jesus. The dead in Christ should rise first, before the touch of immortality should be given to the living. "Therefore comfort one another with these words."

The hope and joy that this assurance brought the young church at Thessalonica can scarcely be appreciated by us. They cherished the letter sent them by their father in the gospel, and their hearts went out in love to him. He had told them these things before, but at that time their minds were striving to grasp doctrines that seemed new and strange. Paul's letter gave them new hope and a deeper affection for the One who through His death had brought life and immortality to light. Their believing friends would be raised from the grave to live forever in the kingdom of God. The darkness that had enshrouded the resting place of the dead was dispelled. A new splendor crowned the Christian faith.

"God will bring with Him those who have fallen asleep," Paul wrote. Many interpret this to mean that the sleeping ones will be brought from heaven; but Paul meant that as Christ was raised from the dead, so God will call the sleeping saints from their graves.

Signs of Christ's Coming

While at Thessalonica, Paul had so fully covered the signs of the times that would occur prior to the revelation of the Son of man in the clouds of heaven, that he did not write at length regarding this subject. However, he pointedly referred to his former teachings: "As to the times and the seasons, brethren, you have no need to have anything written to you. For you yourselves know well that the day of the Lord will come like a thief in the night. When people say, 'There is peace and security,' then sudden destruction will come upon them."

Today the signs of the end are rapidly fulfilling. Paul teaches that it is sinful to be indifferent to the signs which are to precede the second coming of Christ.

Those guilty of this he calls children of darkness: "But you are not in darkness, brethren, for that day to surprise you like a thief. For you are all sons of light and sons of the day; we are not of the night or of darkness."

To those living so near the great consummation, the words of Paul should come with telling force: "Since we belong to the day, let us be sober, and put on the breastplate of faith and love, and for a helmet the hope of salvation. For God has not destined us for wrath, but to obtain salvation through our Lord Jesus Christ, who died for us so that whether we wake or sleep we might live with Him."

The watchful Christian seeks to do all in his power to advance the gospel. He has severe trials, but he does not allow affliction to sour his temper or destroy his peace of mind. He knows that trial, if well borne, will purify him and bring him into closer fellowship with Christ.

The Thessalonian believers were annoyed by men coming among them with fanatical ideas. Some were "living in idleness, mere busybodies, not doing any work." Some, self-willed and impetuous, refused to be subordinate to those who held authority in the church. They claimed the right of publicly urging their views on the church. Paul called the attention of the Thessalonians to the respect due those who had been chosen to occupy positions of authority in the church.

The apostle pleaded with them to reveal practical godliness in the daily life: "You know what instructions we gave you through the Lord Jesus. For this is the will of God, your sanctification: that you abstain from unchastity." "For God has not called us for uncleanness, but in holiness."

The apostle's desire was that they might increase in a knowledge of Jesus Christ. Often he would meet with little companies of men and women who loved Jesus, and bow with them in prayer, asking God to teach them how to maintain a living connection with Him. And often he pleaded with God to keep them from evil and help them to be earnest, active missionaries.

One of the strongest evidences of true conversion is love to God and man. "Concerning love of the brethren," the apostle wrote, "you have no need to have any one write to you, for you yourselves have been taught by God to love one another. . . . Aspire to live quietly, to mind your own affairs, and to work with your hands, as we charged you; so that you may command the respect of outsiders, and be dependent on nobody."

"And may the Lord make you increase and abound in love to one another and to all men, as we do to you, so that He may establish your hearts unblamable in holiness before our God and Father, at the coming of our Lord Jesus with all His saints."

The apostle cautioned the Thessalonians not to despise the gift of prophecy: "Do not quench the Spirit, do not despise prophesying, but test everything; hold fast what is good." He enjoined careful discrimination in distinguishing the false from the true and closed his letter with the prayer that God would sanctify them wholly, that in "spirit and soul and body" they might "be kept sound and blameless at the coming of our Lord Jesus Christ." He added, "He will do it."

Did Paul Expect to Live to See Christ Return?

Some of the Thessalonian brethren understood Paul to express the hope that he himself would live to witness the Saviour's advent. This served to increase their enthusiasm and excitement. Those who had neglected their duties became more persistent in urging their erroneous views.

In his second letter Paul sought to correct their misunderstanding. Before the coming of Christ, important developments foretold in prophecy were to take place: "We beg you, brethren, not to be quickly shaken in mind or excited, either by spirit or by word, or by letter purporting to be from us, to the effect that the day of the Lord has come. Let no one deceive you in any way; for that day will not come, unless the rebellion comes first, and the man of lawlessness [man of sin, KJV] is revealed, the son of perdition, who opposes and exalts himself against every so-called god or object of worship, so that he takes his seat in the temple of God, proclaiming himself to be God.''

It was not to be taught that Paul had warned the Thessalonians of the immediate coming of Christ. The apostle therefore cautioned the brethren to receive no such message as coming from him. He emphasized the fact that the papal power described by the prophet Daniel was yet to rise against God's people. Until this power should have performed its blasphemous work, it would be in vain for the church to look for the coming of their Lord.

Terrible were the trials that were to beset the true church. The "mystery of iniquity" had already begun to work. Future developments "by the activity of Satan will be with all power and with pretended signs and wonders, and with all wicked deceptions for those who are to perish.'' He declared of all who should deliberately reject the truth, "God sends upon them a strong delusion, to make them believe what is false.'' God withdraws His Spirit, leaving them to the deceptions they love.

Thus Paul outlined the work of that power of evil which was to continue through long centuries of darkness and persecution before the second coming of Christ. The Thessalonian believers were admonished to take up bravely the work before them and not to neglect their duties or resign themselves to idle waiting. After their glowing anticipations of immediate deliverance, the round of daily life would appear forbidding. He therefore exhorted them:

"Stand firm and hold to the traditions which you were taught by us, either by word of mouth or by letter. Now may our Lord Jesus Christ Himself, and God our Father, who loved us and gave us eternal comfort and good hope through grace, comfort your hearts and establish them in every good work and word." "May the Lord direct your hearts to the love of God and to the steadfastness of Christ."

The apostle pointed them to his own example of diligence in temporal matters while laboring in the cause of Christ. He reproved those who had given themselves up to sloth and aimless excitement, and directed that they "do their work in quietness and to earn their own living."

This letter Paul concluded with a prayer that amidst life's toils and trials the peace of God and the grace of the Lord Jesus Christ might be their consolation and support.

26 / Church Politics
at Corinth

After he left Corinth, Paul's next scene of labor was Ephesus. He was on his way to Jerusalem to attend a festival, and his stay was necessarily brief. So favorable was the impression made on the Jews in the synagogue, that they entreated him to continue among them. He promised to return, "if God wills," and left Aquila and Priscilla to carry on the work.

At this time "a Jew named Apollos, a native of Alexandria, came to Ephesus. He was an eloquent man, well versed in the Scriptures." He had heard the preaching of John the Baptist and was a living witness that the work of the prophet had not been in vain. Apollos "had been instructed in the way of the Lord; and being fervent in spirit, he spoke and taught accurately the things concerning Jesus, though he knew only the baptism of John."

In Ephesus, Apollos "began to speak boldly in the synagogue." Aquila and Priscilla, perceiving that he had not yet received the full light of the gospel, "took him and expounded to him the way of God more accurately." He became one of the ablest advocates of the Christian faith.

Apollos went to Corinth, where "he powerfully confuted the Jews . . . , showing by the Scriptures that the Christ was Jesus." Paul had planted the seed of truth; Apollos watered it. His success led some of the believers to exalt his labors above those of Paul. This

This chapter is based on Acts 18:18-28, RSV.

brought a party spirit that threatened to hinder the gospel.

During the year and a half that Paul spent in Corinth, he had purposely presented the gospel in its simplicity. "In demonstration of the Spirit and power" he had declared "the testimony of God," that their "faith should not stand in the wisdom of men, but in the power of God." 1 Corinthians 2:4, 1, 5.

"I fed you with milk, not solid food," he afterward explained, "for you were not ready for it; and even yet you are not ready." 1 Corinthians 3:2, RSV. Many Corinthian believers had been slow to learn. Their advancement in spiritual knowledge had not been proportionate to their opportunities. When they should have been able to comprehend the deeper truths, they were standing where the disciples stood when Christ said, "I have yet many things to say to you, but you cannot bear them now." John 16:12. Jealousy and evil surmising had closed the hearts of many against the full working of the Holy Spirit. They were babes in the knowledge of Christ.

Paul had instructed the Corinthians in the alphabet of faith, as those who were ignorant of divine power on the heart. Those who followed him must carry forward the work, giving spiritual light as the church was able to bear it.

How Paul Handled Sexual Immorality

The apostle knew that among his hearers in Corinth would be proud believers in human theories who would hope to find in nature theories that would contradict the Scriptures. He also knew that critics would controvert the Christian interpretation of the word and that skeptics would treat the gospel of Christ with derision.

As he endeavored to lead souls to the cross, Paul did not venture to rebuke directly those who were licentious or to show how heinous was their sin in the sight of a holy God. Rather he dwelt especially on practical godliness and the holiness to which those must attain who shall be accounted worthy of a place in God's kingdom. In the light of the gospel of Christ they might see how offensive in the sight of God were their immoral practices. Therefore the burden of his teaching was Christ and Him crucified.

The philosopher turns aside from the light because it puts his proud theories to shame; the worldling refuses it because it would separate him from his idols. Paul saw that the character of Christ must be understood before men could love Him or view the cross with the eye of faith. In the light of the cross alone can the true value of the human soul be estimated.

The refining influence of the grace of God changes the natural disposition of man. Heaven would not be desirable to the carnal-minded; and if it were possible for them to enter, they would find there nothing congenial. The propensities that control the natural heart must be subdued by the grace of Christ before man is fitted to enjoy the society of the pure, holy angels.

Paul had sought to impress his Corinthian brethren that he and the ministers with him were all engaged in the same work, alike dependent on God for success. The discussion in the church regarding the relative merits of different ministers was the result of cherishing the attributes of the natural heart. "For when one says, 'I belong to Paul,' and another, 'I belong to Apollos,' are you not merely men? . . . I planted, Apollos watered, but God gave the growth. So neither he who plants nor he who waters is anything, but only God who gives the growth." 1 Corinthians 3:4-7, RSV.

It was Paul who had first preached the gospel in Corinth and organized the church. The seed sown must be watered, and this Apollos was to do. He gave further instruction, but it was God who gave the increase. Those who plant and those who water do not cause the growth of the seed. To the Master Worker belongs the honor and glory that comes with success.

God has given to each of His messengers an individual work. All are to blend in harmony, controlled by the Holy Spirit. As they make known the gospel, the human instrumentality is hid, and Christ appears as the chiefest among ten thousand, the One altogether lovely.

"We are fellow workmen for God: you are God's field, God's building." 1 Corinthians 3:9, RSV. The apostle compares the church to a cultivated field and also to a building, which is to grow into a temple for the Lord. He gives His workmen tact and skill, and if they heed His instruction, crowns their efforts with success.

God's servants are to work together, blending in kindly, courteous order, "in honor preferring one another." Romans 12:10. There is to be no pulling to pieces of another's work; and there are to be no separate parties. Each is to do his appointed work, respected, loved, and encouraged by the others. Together they are to carry the work forward to completion.

The Letter to the Corinthians Is Timely Today

In Paul's first letter to the Corinthian church, he referred to the comparisons made between his labors and those of Apollos: "I have applied all this to myself and Apollos for your benefit, brethren, that you may learn by us to live according to scripture, that none of you may be puffed up in favor of one against another. For who sees anything different in you? What have you that you did not receive? If then you received it, why do you boast as if it were not a gift?" 1 Corinthians 4:6, 7, RSV.

Paul set before the church the hardships that he and his associates had endured. "To the present hour we hunger and thirst, we are ill-clad and buffeted and homeless, and we labor, working with our own hands. When reviled, we bless; when persecuted, we endure; when slandered, we try to conciliate; we have become, and are now, as the refuse of the world, the offscouring of all things. I do not write this to make you ashamed, but to admonish you as my beloved children. For though you have countless guides in Christ, you do not have many fathers. For I became your father in Christ Jesus through the gospel." 1 Corinthians 4:11-15, RSV.

He who sends forth gospel workers is dishonored when there is so strong an attachment to some favorite minister that there is an unwillingness to accept some other teacher. The Lord sends help to His people, not always as they may choose, but as they need; for men cannot discern what is for their highest good. It is seldom that one minister has all the qualifications necessary to perfect a church; therefore God often sends others, each possessing some qualifications in which the others were deficient.

The church should gratefully accept these servants of Christ. They should seek to derive all the benefit possible from each minister. The truths that the servants of God bring are to be accepted in humility, but no minister is to be idolized.

As God's ministers obtain the endowment of the Holy Spirit, to extend the triumphs of the cross, they will see fruit; they will accomplish a work that will withstand the assaults of Satan. Many will be turned from darkness to light, converted not to the human instrumentality but to Christ. Jesus only, the Man of Calvary, will appear. And God is just as ready to give power to His servants today as He was to Paul and Apollos, to Silas and Timothy, to Peter, James, and John.

The Peril of Trying to Go It Alone

In the apostle's day some misguided souls claimed to believe in Christ, yet refused to show respect to His ambassadors. They declared that they were taught directly by Christ without the aid of the ministers of the gospel. They were unwilling to submit to the voice of the church. Such were in danger of being deceived.

God has placed in the church men of varied talents, that through the combined wisdom of many the mind of the Spirit may be met. Men who refuse to yoke up with others who have had long experience in the work of God will be unable to discern between the false and the true. If chosen as leaders in the church, they would follow their own judgment regardless of the judgment of their brethren. It is easy for the enemy to work through them. Impressions alone are not a safe guide to duty. The enemy persuades men that God is guiding them, when in reality they are following only human impulse. But if we take counsel with our brethren, we shall be given an understanding of the Lord's will.

In the early church some refused to recognize either Paul or Apollos, but held that Peter was their leader. They affirmed that Peter had been most intimate with Christ, while Paul had been a persecutor of the believers. Bound by prejudice, they did not show the generosity, the tenderness, which reveals that Christ is abiding in the heart.

Paul was instructed by the Lord to utter words of protest. Of those who were saying, " 'I belong to Paul,' or 'I belong to Apollos,' or 'I belong to Cephas,' or 'I belong to Christ,' " he asked, "Is Christ divided? Was Paul crucified for you? Or were you baptized in the name of Paul?" "Let no one boast of men," he pleaded. "Whether Paul or Apollos or Cephas or the world or life or death or the present or the future, all are yours; and you are Christ's; and Christ is God's." 1 Corinthians 1:12, 13; 3:21-23, RSV.

Apollos grieved because of the dissension at Corinth; he did not encourage it, but hastily left the field of strife. When Paul afterward urged him to revisit Corinth, he declined until long afterward when the church had reached a better spiritual state.

27 / Witchcraft Books Burned

In the time of the apostles Ephesus was the capital of the Roman province of Asia. Its harbor was crowded with shipping, and its streets were thronged with people from every country. Like Corinth, it presented a promising field for missionary effort.

The Jews, widely dispersed in all civilized lands, were generally expecting the Messiah. When John the Baptist was preaching, many in their visits to Jerusalem had gone out to the Jordan to listen to him. There they had heard Jesus proclaimed as the Promised One, and they had carried the tidings to all parts of the world. Thus had Providence prepared the way for the apostles.

At Ephesus, Paul found twelve brethren who had been disciples of John the Baptist and who had gained some knowledge of the mission of Christ. But when asked by Paul if they had received the Holy Spirit, they answered, "No, we have never even heard that there is a Holy Spirit." "Into what then were you baptized?" Paul inquired. They said, "Into John's baptism."

Then the apostle told them of Christ's life and of His cruel death of shame, and how He had risen triumphant over death. He repeated the Saviour's commission: "All power is given unto Me in heaven and in earth. Go ye therefore, and teach all nations, baptizing them in the name of the Father, and of the Son, and of the Holy Ghost." Matthew 28:18, 19. He told them also of Christ's promise to send the Comforter and de-

This chapter is based on Acts 19:1-20, RSV.

scribed how gloriously this promise had been fulfilled on the Day of Pentecost.

With wondering joy the brethren listened. They grasped the truth of Christ's atoning sacrifice and received Him as their Redeemer. They were then baptized in the name of Jesus; and as Paul "laid his hands upon them," they received the Holy Spirit and were enabled to speak the languages of other nations and to prophesy. Thus they were qualified to proclaim the gospel in Asia Minor.

By cherishing a humble, teachable spirit, these men gained the experience that enabled them to go as workers into the harvest field. Their example presents a lesson of great value. Many make but little progress in the divine life because they are too self-sufficient. They are content with a superficial knowledge of God's Word.

If the followers of Christ were earnest seekers after wisdom, they would be led into rich fields of truth as yet wholly unknown to them. He who will give himself fully to God will be guided by the divine hand. As he treasures the lessons of divine wisdom, he will be enabled to make his life an honor to God and a blessing to the world.

The Holy Spirit Produces Fruit in the Believer

Christ calls our attention to the growth of the vegetable world as an illustration of the agency of His Spirit in sustaining spiritual life. The sap of the vine, ascending from the root, is diffused to the branches, producing fruit. So the Holy Spirit, proceeding from the Saviour, pervades the soul, renews the motives, and brings even the thoughts into obedience to the will of God, enabling the receiver to bear precious fruit.

The exact method by which spiritual life is imparted is beyond human philosophy to explain. Yet the operations of the Spirit are always in harmony with the Written Word. As the natural life is not sustained by a direct miracle, but through the use of blessings placed within our reach, so the spiritual life is sustained by the use of means that Providence has supplied. The follower of Christ must eat of the bread of life and drink of the water of salvation, in all things giving heed to the instructions of God in His Word.

There is another lesson in the experience of those Jewish converts. When they received baptism at the hand of John they did not fully comprehend the mission of Jesus as the Sin Bearer. But with clearer light, they gladly accepted Christ as their Redeemer, and as they received a purer faith, there was a corresponding change in their life. In token of this change, and as an acknowledgment of their faith in Christ, they were rebaptized in the name of Jesus.

Paul continued his work at Ephesus for three months and in the synagogue "spoke boldly, arguing and pleading about the kingdom of God." As in other fields, he was soon violently opposed. "Some were stubborn and disbelieved, speaking evil of the Way before the congregation." As they persisted in rejection of the gospel, the apostle ceased to preach in the synagogue.

Sufficient evidence had been presented to convince all who honestly desired the truth. But many refused to yield to the most conclusive evidence. Fearing that the believers would be endangered by continued association with these opposers of the truth, Paul gathered the disciples into a distinct body, continuing his public instructions in the school of Tyrannus.

The Battle Between Christ and Satan at Ephesus

Paul saw that "a great door and effectual" was opening before him, although there were "many adversaries. 1 Corinthians 16:9. Ephesus was not only the most magnificent, but the most corrupt of the cities of Asia. Superstition and sensual pleasure held sway. Under the shadow of her temples, criminals of every grade found shelter, and degrading vices flourished.

The fame of the magnificent temple of Diana of the

Ephesians extended throughout all the world. Its splendor made it the pride of the nation. The idol within the temple was declared to have fallen from the sky. Books had been written to explain the meaning of symbols inscribed in it. Among those who gave close study to these books were many magicians, who wielded a powerful influence over the superstitious worshipers of the image within the temple.

The power of God accompanied Paul's efforts at Ephesus, and many were healed of physical maladies. These manifestations of supernatural power were far more potent than had ever before been witnessed in Ephesus and could not be imitated by the skill of the juggler or the enchantments of the sorcerer. As these miracles were wrought in the name of Jesus, the people had opportunity to see that the God of heaven was more powerful than the magicians of the goddess Diana. Thus the Lord exalted His servant immeasurably above the most powerful of the magicians.

But the One to whom all the spirits of evil are subject was about to bring still greater defeat on those who despised and profaned His holy name. Sorcery had been prohibited by the Mosaic law, yet it had been secretly practiced by apostate Jews. There were in Ephesus "some of the itinerant Jewish exorcists" who, seeing the wonders wrought by Paul, "undertook to pronounce the name of the Lord Jesus over those who had evil spirits." "Seven sons of a Jewish high priest named Sceva were doing this." Finding a man possessed with a demon, they addressed him, "I adjure you by the Jesus whom Paul preaches." But "the evil spirit answered them, 'Jesus I know, and Paul I know; but who are you?' And the man in whom the evil spirit was leaped on them, mastered all of them, and overpowered them, so that they fled out of that house naked and wounded."

Thus unmistakable proof was given of the sacredness of the name of Christ and the peril of invoking it without faith in the divinity of the Saviour. "Fear fell upon them all; and the name of the Lord Jesus was extolled."

Facts previously concealed were now brought to light. To some extent some of the believers still continued the practice of magic. Now, convinced of their error, many believers "came, confessing and divulging their practices. And a number of those who practiced magic arts brought their books together and burned them in the sight of all; and they counted the value of them and found it came to fifty thousand pieces of silver. So the word of the Lord grew and prevailed mightily."

By burning their books on magic, the Ephesian converts showed that the things in which they had once delighted they now abhorred. Through magic they had especially offended God and imperiled their souls; and against magic they showed such indignation. Thus they gave evidence of true conversion.

Why the Satanic Books Were Burnt

These treatises on divination were the regulations of the worship of Satan—directions for soliciting his help and obtaining information from him. By retaining these books the disciples would have exposed themselves to temptation; by selling them they would have placed temptation in the way of others. To destroy the power of the kingdom of darkness, they did not hesitate at any sacrifice. Thus truth triumphed over their love of money. A mighty victory was gained in the very stronghold of superstition. The influence of what had taken place was more widespread than even Paul realized.

Sorcery is practiced in this age as verily as in the days of the old-time magicians. Through modern spiritualism Satan presents himself under the guise of departed friends. The Scriptures declare that "the dead know not anything." Ecclesiastes 9:5. They do not hold communion with the living. But Satan employs this device in order to gain control of minds. Through spiritualism many of the sick, the bereaved, the curious are communicating with evil spirits. All who do this are on dangerous ground.

The magicians of heathen times have their counterpart in the spiritualistic mediums and fortunetellers of today. The mystic voices at Endor and Ephesus are still by their lying words misleading the children of men. Evil angels are employing all their arts to deceive and destroy. Wherever an influence causes men to forget God, there Satan is exercising his bewitching power. When men yield to his influence, the mind is bewildered and the soul polluted. "Have no fellowship with the unfruitful works of darkness, but rather reprove them." Ephesians 5:11.

28 / The Silversmiths Riot at Ephesus

For more than three years Ephesus was the center of Paul's work. A flourishing church was raised up, and from this city the gospel spread throughout Asia among both Jews and Gentiles.

The apostle now "resolved in the Spirit to pass through Macedonia and Achaia and go to Jerusalem, saying, 'After I have been there, I must also see Rome.'" In harmony with this plan he "sent into Macedonia two of his helpers, Timothy and Erastus," but feeling that Ephesus still demanded his presence, he decided to remain until after Pentecost. An event soon occurred, however, which hastened his departure.

Once a year, special ceremonies were held at Ephesus in honor of the goddess Diana. These attracted great numbers of people. This gala season was a trying time for those who had newly come to the faith. The believers who met in the school of Tyrannus were an inharmonious note in the festive chorus, and ridicule and insult were freely heaped on them.

Paul's labors had given the heathen worship a telling blow, and there was a perceptible falling off in attendance at the national festival and in the enthusiasm of the worshipers. The influence of his teachings extended far beyond the actual converts. Many who had not accepted the new doctrines became so far enlightened as to lose all confidence in their heathen gods.

There existed also another cause of dissatisfaction.

This chapter is based on Acts 19:21-41; 20:1, RSV.

A profitable business had grown up from the sale of small shrines and images, modeled after the temple and image of Diana. Those in this industry found their gains diminishing, and all attributed the unwelcome change to Paul's labors.

Demetrius, a manufacturer of silver shrines, calling together the workmen of his craft, said: " 'Men, you know that from this business we have our wealth. And you see and hear that not only at Ephesus but almost throughout all Asia this Paul has persuaded and turned away a considerable company of people, saying that gods made with hands are not gods. And there is danger not only that this trade of ours may come into disrepute but also that the temple of the great goddess Artemis [Diana] may count for nothing, and that she may even be deposed from her magnificence.' " The excitable people "were enraged, and cried out, 'Great is Artemis [Diana] of the Ephesians!' "

A report of this speech was rapidly circulated, and "the city was filled with confusion." Search was made for Paul, but the apostle was not to be found. His brethren had hurried him from the place. Angels had been sent to guard the apostle; his time to die a martyr had not yet come.

Failing to find the object of their wrath, the mob seized "Gaius and Aristarchus, Macedonians who were Paul's companions in travel," and with these "they rushed together into the theater."

The Apostle Eager to Defend Truth Before the Multitude

Paul, not far distant, soon learned of the peril of his brethren. Forgetful of his own safety, he desired to go at once to the theater to address the rioters. But "the disciples would not let him." No serious harm to Gaius and Aristarchus was apprehended, but should the apostle's care-worn face be seen, it would arouse the worst passions of the mob, and there would not be the least human possibility of saving his life.

Paul was at last deterred by a message from the theater. Friends of his "sent to him and begged him not to venture into the theater."

The tumult there was continually increasing. "The assembly was in confusion, and most of them did not know why they had come together." The Jews, anxious to show that they were not sympathizers with Paul and his work, brought forward one of their own number to set the matter before the people. The speaker chosen was the craftsman Alexander, a coppersmith, to whom Paul afterward referred as having done him much evil. See 2 Timothy 4:14. Alexander bent all his energies to direct the wrath of the people exclusively against Paul and his companions. But the crowd, seeing that he was a Jew, thrust him aside, and "for about two hours they all with one voice cried out, 'Great is Artemis [Diana] of the Ephesians!' "

At last there was a momentary silence. Then the recorder of the city, by virtue of his office, obtained a hearing. He showed that there was no cause for the present tumult and appealed to their reason. " 'What man is there who does not know that the city of the Ephesians is temple keeper of the great Artemis, and of the sacred stone that fell from the sky? . . . You ought to be quiet and do nothing rash. . . . These men here . . . are neither sacrilegious nor blasphemers of our goddess. If therefore Demetrius and the craftsmen with him have a complaint against any one, the courts are open, and there are proconsuls; let them bring charges against one another. . . . We are in danger of being charged with rioting today, there being no cause that we can give to justify this commotion.' And when he had said this, he dismissed the assembly."

In his speech Demetrius revealed the real cause of the tumult and also much of the persecution which followed the apostles: "This trade of ours may come into disrepute." By the spread of the gospel, the business of image-making was endangered. The income of pagan priests and artisans was at stake.

The decision of the recorder and of others in the city

had set Paul before the people as innocent of any unlawful act. God had raised up a great magistrate to vindicate His apostle and hold the mob in check. Paul's
heart was filled with gratitude to God that his life had
been preserved and that Christianity had not been
brought into disrepute by the tumult at Ephesus.

"After the uproar ceased, Paul sent for the disciples
and having exhorted them took leave of them and departed for Macedonia."

Paul Endures Opposition of Enemies and Desertion of Friends

Paul's ministry in Ephesus had been one of incessant
labor, many trials, and deep anguish. He had taught the
people in public and from house to house, instructing
and warning them. Continually he had been opposed
by the Jews. And while thus battling against opposition, he was bearing on his soul a heavy burden for all
the churches. News of apostasy in some of the
churches caused his deep sorrow. Many a sleepless
night was spent in earnest prayer as he learned of the
methods employed to counteract his work.

As he had opportunity he wrote to the churches, giving reproof, counsel, admonition, and encouragement.
In these letters there were occasional glimpses of his
sufferings in the cause of Christ. Stripes and imprisonment, cold and hunger and thirst, perils by land and by
sea, in the city and in the wilderness, from his own
countrymen, from the heathen, and from false brethren—all this he endured for the gospel. He was "de-
famed," "reviled," made "the offscouring of all
things," "perplexed," "persecuted," "troubled on
every side," "in jeopardy every hour," "always delivered unto death for Jesus' sake."

The intrepid apostle almost lost heart. But he looked
to Calvary and with new ardor pressed on to spread the
knowledge of the Crucified. He was treading the
blood-stained path Christ had trodden before him. He
sought no discharge from the warfare till he should lay
off his armor at the feet of his Redeemer.

29/ Lawsuits and Sexual Looseness Challenged

For a year and a half Paul had labored among the believers in Corinth, pointing them to a crucified and risen Saviour and urging them to rely implicitly on the transforming power of His grace. Before accepting them into church fellowship he had been careful to instruct them as to the duties of the Christian believers, and he had endeavored to help them be faithful to their baptismal vows.

Paul had a keen sense of the conflict every soul must wage with the agencies of evil, and he had worked untiringly to strengthen those young in the faith. He had entreated them to make an entire surrender to God, for he knew that when the soul fails to make an entire surrender, sin is not forsaken, and temptations confuse the conscience. Every weak, doubting, struggling soul who yields fully to the Lord is placed in direct touch with agencies that enable him to overcome. He has the help of angels in every time of need.

The members of the church at Corinth were surrounded by idolatry and sensuality. While the apostle was with them, these influences had little power over them. Paul's prayers, earnest words of instruction, and godly life helped them to deny self, for Christ's sake, rather than to enjoy the pleasures of sin.

After the departure of Paul, however, little by little many became careless and allowed natural tastes and inclinations to control them. Not a few who at their

This chapter is based on First Corinthians, RSV.

conversion had put away evil habits returned to the debasing sins of heathenism. Paul had written briefly, admonishing them "not to associate" with members who should persist in profligacy; but many quibbled over his words and excused themselves for disregarding his instruction.

A letter was sent to Paul by the church, asking for counsel concerning various matters, but saying nothing of the grievous sins existing among them. The apostle was, however, impressed by the Holy Spirit that the true state of the church had been concealed.

About this time there came to Ephesus members of the household of Chloe, a Christian family in Corinth. They told Paul that the dissensions that had prevailed at the time of Apollos's visit had greatly increased. False teachers were leading the members to despise the instructions of Paul. Pride, idolatry, and sensualism were steadily increasing.

Paul saw that his worst fears were more than realized. But he did not give way to the thought that his work had been a failure. With "anguish of heart" and with "many tears" (2 Corinthians 2:4) he sought counsel from God. Gladly would he have visited Corinth at once, but he knew that in their present condition the believers would not profit by his labors; therefore he sent Titus to prepare the way for a visit from himself later on. Then the apostle wrote to the church at Corinth one of the richest, most instructive, most powerful of all his letters.

With remarkable clearness he answered questions and laid down general principles which, if heeded, would lead them to a higher spiritual plane. Faithfully he warned them of their dangers and reproved them for their sins. He reminded them of the gifts of the Holy Spirit they had received and showed them that it was their privilege to advance in the Christian life until they should attain to the purity and holiness of Christ.

Paul spoke plainly of the dissensions in the Corinthian church. "I appeal to you, brethren," he wrote, "that all of you agree and that there be no dissensions among you, but that you be united in the same mind and the same judgment." "It has been reported to me by Chloe's people that there is quarreling among you."

The Nature of a Prophet's Inspiration

Paul was an inspired apostle. The truth he taught he had received "by revelation"; yet the Lord did not directly reveal to him at all times the condition of His people. In this instance those who were interested in the church had presented the matter before the apostle, and from divine revelations he had formerly received he was prepared to judge these developments. Notwithstanding the fact that the Lord did not give him a new revelation for that special time, those who were seeking for light accepted his message as expressing the mind of Christ. As evils developed, the apostle recognized their significance. He had been set for the defense of the church. Was it not right for him to notice the reports concerning the divisions among them? Most assuredly; and the reproof he sent was as certainly written under the inspiration of the Spirit of God as were any of his other letters.

The apostle made no mention of the false teachers who were seeking to destroy the fruit of his labor. He wisely forebore to irritate them by such references. He called attention to his own work as "a skilled master builder" who had laid the foundation on which others had built. "We are God's fellow workers." He acknowledged that divine power alone had enabled him to present the truth in a manner pleasing to God. Paul had communicated lessons which were to apply at all times, in all places, and under all conditions.

One former convert had so far backslidden that his licentious course violated even the low standard of morality held by the Gentile world. The apostle pleaded with the church to put away from them this man. "Cleanse out the old leaven that you may be a new lump, as you really are unleavened."

Another grave evil was that of brethren going to law against one another. Christ Himself had given instruction as to how such matters were to be adjusted: "If your brother sins against you, go and tell him his fault, between you and him alone. If he listens to you, you have gained your brother. But if he does not listen, take one or two others along with you, that every word may be confirmed by the evidence of two or three witnesses. If he refuses to listen to them, tell it to the church." Matthew 18:15-17, RSV.

How to Handle Lawsuits Among Church Members

"When one of you," Paul asked, "has a grievance against a brother, does he dare go to law before the unrighteous instead of the saints? Do you not know that the saints will judge the world? And if the world is to be judged by you, are you incompetent to try trivial cases? Do you not know that we are to judge angels? How much more, matters pertaining to this life! . . . I say this to your shame. Can it be that there is no man among you wise enough to decide between members of the brotherhood, but brother goes to law against brother, and that before unbelievers? To have lawsuits at all with one another is defeat for you. Why not rather suffer wrong?"

Satan is constantly seeking to introduce distrust, alienation, and malice among God's people. We shall often be tempted to feel that our rights are invaded, even when there is no real cause for such feelings. Those who will place their own interests first will resort to almost any expedient to maintain them. Many are hindered by pride and self-esteem from going privately to those whom they think in error, that they may talk with them in the spirit of Christ and pray together. When they think themselves injured by their brethren, some will even go to law instead of following the Saviour's rule.

Christians should not appeal to civil tribunals to settle differences among church members. Even though injustice may have been done, the follower of the meek and lowly Jesus will suffer himself "to be defrauded" rather than open before the world the sins of his brethren in the church.

Christians who go to law with one another expose the church to the ridicule of her enemies. They are wounding Christ afresh and putting Him to open shame. By ignoring the authority of the church, they show contempt for God, who gave the church its authority.

Paul endeavored to show the Corinthians Christ's power to keep them from evil. To help them break from the thralldom of sin, Paul urged the claim of Him to whom they had dedicated their lives: "You are not your own; you were bought with a price. So glorify God in your body."

How to Live Pure Lives in an Ocean of Impurity

Paul begged them to control the lower passions and appetites. He aroused their better nature and inspired them to strive for a higher life. He knew that at every step in the Christian pathway the Corinthian believers would be opposed by Satan and that they would have to engage in conflicts daily. They would have to force back old habits and natural inclinations, ever watching unto prayer. But Paul knew also that in Christ crucified they were offered power sufficient to enable them to resist all temptations to evil.

The Corinthian believers had seen but the first rays of the early dawn of God's glory. Paul's desire for them was that they might follow on to know Him whose going forth is prepared as the morning, and learn of Him until they should come into the full noontide of a perfect gospel faith.

30/ Paul Strengthens the Church for All Time

Of all the games instituted among the Greeks and the Romans, the ancient foot races near Corinth were the most highly esteemed. They were witnessed by kings, nobles, and statesmen. Young men of rank and wealth took part and shrank from no effort or discipline necessary to obtain the prize.

The contests were governed by strict regulations, from which there was no appeal. Those who desired to enter had to undergo severe preparatory training. Harmful indulgence of appetite, or anything that would lower mental or physical vigor, was forbidden. The muscles must be strong, and the nerves well under control. The physical powers must reach the highest mark.

As the contestants made their appearance before the waiting multitude, their names were heralded, and the rules of the race were distinctly stated. Then they all started together, the fixed attention of the spectators inspiring them with determination to win. The judges were seated near the goal, that they might watch the race from beginning to end and give the prize to the true victor.

Great risks were run. Some contestants never recovered from the terrible physical strain. It was not unusual for men to fall on the course, bleeding at the mouth and nose, and sometimes a contestant would drop dead when about to seize the prize.

As the winner reached the goal, applause rent the

This chapter is based on First Corinthians, RSV.

air. The judge presented him with the emblems of victory—a laurel crown and a palm branch to carry in his hand. His praise was sung throughout the land, his parents received their share of honor, and even the city in which he lived was held in high esteem for having produced so great an athlete.

Paul referred to these races as a figure of the Christian warfare. "Every athlete," he declared, "exercises self-control in all things." The runners put aside every indulgence that would tend to weaken the physical powers. How much more important that the Christian bring appetite and passion under subjection to reason and the will of God! Never must he allow his attention to be diverted by amusements, luxuries, or ease. Reason, enlightened by God's Word and guided by His Spirit, must hold the reins of control.

In the Corinthian games the last few strides of the contestants in the race were made with agonizing effort to keep up undiminished speed. So the Christian, as he nears the goal, will press onward with even more determination than at the first of his course.

Paul contrasts the chaplet of fading laurel received in the foot races, and the crown of immortal glory that will be given to him who runs with triumph the Christian race. "They do it," he declares, "to receive a perishable wreath, but we an imperishable." The Grecian runners spared themselves no toil or discipline. How much more willing should be our sacrifice and self-denial!

"Let us lay aside every weight, and the sin which clings so closely, and let us run with perseverance the race that is set before us, looking to Jesus the pioneer and perfecter of our faith. Hebrews 12:1, 2. Envy, malice, evil-thinking, evil-speaking, covetousness—these are weights that the Christian must lay aside. Every practice that brings dishonor on Christ must be put away, whatever the sacrifice. One sin cherished is sufficient to work degradation of character and to mislead others.

The competitors in the ancient games, after they had submitted to self-denial and rigid discipline, were not even then sure of victory. "In a race all the runners compete, but only one receives the prize." One hand only could grasp the coveted garland. As some reached forth to secure the prize, another, an instant before them, might grasp the coveted treasure.

The Race Where Everyone Can Win

In the Christian warfare, not one who complies with the conditions will be disappointed at the end of the race. The weakest saint, as well as the strongest, may wear the crown of immortal glory. The principles laid down in God's Word are too often looked upon as unimportant—too trivial to demand attention. But nothing is small that will help or hinder. And the reward given to those who win will be in proportion to the energy and earnestness with which they have striven.

The apostle compared himself to a man running in a race, straining every nerve to win. "I do not run aimlessly," he says, "I do not box as one beating the air; but I pommel my body and subdue it, lest after preaching to others I myself should be disqualified." The words, "I pommel my body," literally mean to beat back by severe discipline the desires, impulses, and passions.

Paul realized that his conversation, his influence, his refusal to yield to self-gratification must show that his religion was not a profession merely, but a daily, living connection with God. One goal he ever strove earnestly to reach—"the righteousness from God that depends on faith." Philippians 3:9, RSV.

Paul realized the need of putting a strict guard on himself, that earthly desires might not overcome spiritual zeal. He continued to strive against natural inclinations. His words, his practices, his passions—all were brought under the control of the Spirit of God.

Paul knew that the Corinthian believers had before

them a life struggle from which there would be no release. He pleaded with them to lay aside every weight and press forward to the goal of perfection in Christ.

He reminded them of the miraculous way in which the Hebrews were led from Egypt—they were conducted through the Red Sea, while the Egyptians, trying to cross in like manner, were all drowned. Israel "ate the same supernatural food and all drank the same supernatural drink. For they drank from the supernatural Rock which followed them, and the Rock was Christ." The Hebrews had Christ as leader. The smitten rock typified Him, wounded for men's transgressions that the stream of salvation might flow to all.

Yet, because of the Hebrews' lust for the luxuries left behind in Egypt, and because of their rebellion, the judgments of God came on them. "Now these things are warnings," the apostle declared, "for us, not to desire evil as they did." Love of ease and pleasure had prepared the way for sins that called forth the vengeance of God. When the children of Israel sat down to eat and drink and rose up to play, they threw off the fear of God. Making a golden calf, they worshiped it. And it was after a luxurious feast connected with the worship of Baal-peor that many Hebrews fell through licentiousness. The anger of God was aroused, and 23,000 were slain by the plague in one day.

If the Corinthians should become boastful and self-confident, they would fall into grievous sin. Yet Paul gave them the assurance: "God is faithful, and He will not let you be tempted beyond your strength, but with the temptation will also provide the way of escape, that you may be able to endure it."

Paul urged his brethren to do nothing, however innocent, that would seem to sanction idolatry or offend those who might be weak in the faith. "Whether you eat or drink, or whatever you do, do all to the glory of God. Give no offense to Jews or to Greeks or to the church of God."

The apostle's words are especially applicable to our

day. By idolatry he meant not only the worship of idols, but self-serving, love of ease, the gratification of appetite and passion. A religion that sanctions self-indulgence is not the religion of Christ.

By a comparison of the church with the human body, the apostle illustrated the close relationship that should exist among all members of the church. "The body does not consist of one member but of many. If the foot should say, 'Because I am not a hand, I do not belong to the body,' that would not make it any less a part of the body. And if the ear should say, 'Because I am not an eye, I do not belong to the body,' that would not make it any less a part of the body. . . . But as it is, God arranged the organs in the body, each one of them, as He chose. . . . God has so adjusted the body, giving the greater honor to the inferior part, that there may be no discord in the body, but that the members may have the same care for one another. If one member suffers, all suffer together; if one member is honored, all rejoice together. Now you are the body of Christ and individually members of it."

Importance of Love

And then Paul set forth the importance of love: "If I speak in the tongues of men and of angels, but have not love, I am a noisy gong or a clanging cymbal. And if I have prophetic powers, and understand all mysteries and all knowledge, and if I have all faith, so as to remove mountains, but have not love, I am nothing. If I give away all I have, and if I deliver my body to be burned, but have not love, I gain nothing."

No matter how high the profession, he whose heart is not filled with love for God and his fellowmen is not a true disciple of Christ. In his zeal he might even meet a martyr's death, yet if not actuated by love, he would be a deluded enthusiast or an ambitious hypocrite.

"Love is patient and kind; love is not jealous or boastful." The noblest characters are built on the foundation of patience, love, and submission to God's will.

Love "is not arrogant or rude. Love does not insist on its own way; it is not irritable or resentful." Christ-like love places the most favorable construction on the motives and acts of others. It does not listen eagerly to unfavorable reports, but seeks to bring to mind the good qualities of others.

This love "never ends." As a precious treasure, it will be carried by its possessor through the portals of the city of God.

The Resurrection Clarifies All Scripture Truth

Among the Corinthian believers, some had gone so far as to deny the doctrine of the resurrection. Paul met this heresy with a very plain testimony regarding the unmistakable evidence of the resurrection of Christ. He was "raised on the third day," after which "He appeared to Cephas, then to the twelve. Then He appeared to more than five hundred brethren at one time, most of whom are still alive, though some have fallen asleep. Then He appeared to James, then to all the apostles. Last of all, as to one untimely born, He appeared also to me."

"If there is no resurrection of the dead," Paul argued, "then Christ has not been raised; if Christ has not been raised, then our preaching is vain and your faith is in vain. . . . For if the dead are not raised, then Christ has not been raised. If Christ has not been raised, your faith is futile and you are still in your sins. Then those also who have fallen asleep in Christ have perished. If in this life we who are in Christ have only hope, we are of all men most to be pitied."

"I tell you a mystery," he declared. "We shall not all sleep, but we shall all be changed, in a moment, in the twinkling of an eye, at the last trumpet. For the trumpet will sound, and the dead will be raised imperishable, and we shall be changed. For this perishable nature must put on the imperishable, and this mortal nature must put on immortality."

The apostle sought to set before the Corinthian believers that which uplifts from the selfish and the sensual and glorifies life with the hope of immortality. "My beloved brethren, be steadfast, immovable, always abounding in the work of the Lord, knowing that in the Lord your labor is not in vain."

Thus the apostle spoke plainly, yet in love. Light from the throne of God was shining, to reveal the hidden sins that were defiling their lives. How would it be received?

Paul dreaded a further alienation and sometimes longed to recall his words. Those who have felt responsible for churches or institutions, can appreciate his depression and self-accusing. Servants of God who bear the burden of His work for this time know something of the same experience of labor, conflict, and anxious care. Burdened by divisions in the church, realizing the peril of churches that harbored iniquity, compelled to bear a searching testimony in reproof of sin, Paul was at the same time weighed down with fear that he might have dealt with too great severity. With anxiety he waited to receive some tidings as to the reception of his message.

31 / Corinth Accepts Paul's Counsel

The "anxiety for all the churches," and particularly for the church at Corinth, rested heavily on Paul's heart. He had hoped to meet Titus at Troas and learn from him how the counsel and reproof sent to the Corinthian brethren had been received, but in this he was disappointed. "My mind could not rest," he wrote, "because I did not find my brother Titus there." He therefore left Troas and crossed over to Macedonia, where, at Philippi, he met Timothy.

At times feelings of deep sadness swept over Paul's soul, lest his admonitions to the church at Corinth might be misunderstood. He afterward wrote, "We were afflicted at every turn—fighting without and fear within. But God, who comforts the downcast, comforted us by the coming of Titus."

This faithful messenger brought the cheering news that a wonderful change had taken place among the Corinthian believers. Many had accepted the instruction in Paul's letter and had repented. Their lives were no longer a reproach to Christianity.

Filled with joy, the apostle sent another letter, expressing his gladness of heart: "Even if I made you sorry with my letter, I do not regret it (though I did regret it)." He had sometimes regretted that he had written so severely. "I rejoice," he continued, "not because you were grieved, but because you were grieved into repenting. . . . For godly grief produces a

This chapter is based on Second Corinthians, RSV.

repentance that leads to salvation and brings no regret.'' Repentance produced by divine grace will lead to confession and forsaking of sin.

Paul had been carrying a heavy burden of soul for the churches. False teachers had sought to urge their own doctrines in the place of gospel truth. The discouragements which surrounded Paul are revealed in the words, ''We were so utterly, unbearably crushed that we despaired of life itself.''

But now one cause of anxiety was removed. Paul broke forth into rejoicing: ''Blessed be the God and Father of our Lord Jesus Christ, the Father of mercies and God of all comfort, who comforts us in all our affliction, so that we may be able to comfort those who are in any affliction, with the comfort with which we ourselves are comforted by God. . . . Our hope for you is unshaken; for we know that as you share in our sufferings, you will also share in our comfort.''

Paul's Joy at Their Reconversion

Paul ascribed to God all the praise for their reconversion and transformation of heart and life: ''Thanks be to God,'' he exclaimed, ''who in Christ always leads us in triumph, and through us spreads the fragrance of the knowledge of Him everywhere. For we are the aroma of Christ to God among those who are being saved and among those who are perishing.'' A general victorious in war brought with him on his return a train of captives. Incense bearers were appointed, and as the army marched triumphantly home, the fragrant odor was to the captives appointed to die, an aroma of death, showing that they were nearing the time of their execution; but to the prisoners whose lives were to be spared, it was an aroma of life—it showed that their freedom was near.

Paul now felt that Satan was not to triumph in Corinth. He and his fellow laborers would celebrate their victory by going forth with new zeal to diffuse, like incense, the fragrance of the gospel throughout the world. To those who should accept Christ, the message would be an aroma of life, but to those who should persist in unbelief, an aroma of death.

Realizing the overwhelming magnitude of the work, Paul exclaimed, "Who is sufficient for these things?" Who is able to preach Christ in such a way that His enemies shall have no just cause to despise the messenger or the message? Faithfulness in preaching the Word, united with a pure, consistent life, can alone make the efforts of ministers acceptable to God.

There were those who had charged Paul with self-commendation in writing his former letter. "Are we beginning to commend ourselves again?" he inquired; "or do we need, as some do, letters of recommendation to you, or from you?" Believers moving to a new place often carried letters of commendation from the church, but the founders of these churches had no need of such commendation. The Corinthian believers, led from the worship of idols to the gospel, were themselves all the recommendation Paul needed. The reformation in their lives bore eloquent testimony to his labor and authority as a minister of Christ.

"You yourselves are our letter of recommendation, written on your hearts, to be known and read by all men; and you show that you are a letter from Christ delivered by us, written not with ink but with the Spirit of the living God, not on tablets of stone but on tablets of human hearts."

The Most Wonderful Career Possible

The conversion of sinners and their sanctification through the truth is the strongest proof a minister can have that God has called him. The evidence of his apostleship is written on the hearts of those converted, and is witnessed to by their renewed lives. A minister is greatly strengthened by these seals of his ministry.

Though in this age there are many preachers, there is a great scarcity of able, holy ministers, men filled with the love that dwelt in the heart of Christ. Pride, self-confidence, love of the world, fault-finding are the fruit borne by many whose lives bear sad testimony to the character of the ministerial labor under which they were "converted."

A man can have no greater honor than to be accepted by God as a minister of the gospel. But those whom the Lord blesses with power and success acknowledge their entire dependence on Him. Of themselves they have no power. With Paul they say, "Not that we are competent of ourselves to claim anything as coming from us; our competence is from God, who has made us competent to be ministers of a new covenant." A true minister realizes that he sustains to the church and to the world a relation similar to that which Christ sustained. He works untiringly to lead sinners to a nobler, higher life. He uplifts Jesus as the sinner's only hope. Those who hear him know that he has drawn near to God in fervent, effectual prayer. The Holy Spirit has rested on him. His soul has felt the vital, heavenly fire. Hearts are broken by his presentation of the love of God, and many are led to inquire, "What must I do to be saved?"

"For what we preach is not ourselves, but Jesus Christ as Lord, with ourselves as your servants for Jesus' sake. For it is the God who said, 'Let light shine out of darkness,' who has shone in our hearts to give the light of the knowledge of the glory of God in the face of Christ."

Thus the apostle magnified the grace and mercy of God. He and his brethren had been sustained in affliction and danger. They had not kept back truth in order to make their teaching attractive. And they had brought their conduct into harmony with their teaching, that truth might commend itself to every man's conscience.

"We have this treasure in earthen vessels," the apostle continued, "to show that the transcendent power belongs to God and not to us." It was not God's plan to proclaim His truth through sinless angels. The priceless treasure is placed in earthen vessels, human beings. Through them His glory is to shine forth. They are to meet the sinful and the needy and lead them to the cross.

Paul showed that in choosing the service of Christ he had not been prompted by selfish motives. "We are afflicted in every way," he wrote, "but not crushed; perplexed, but not driven to despair; persecuted, but not forsaken; struck down, but not destroyed; always carrying in the body the death of Jesus, so that the life of Jesus may also be manifested in our bodies."

As Christ's messengers he and his fellow laborers were continually in peril. "While we live," he wrote, "we are always being given up to death for Jesus' sake, so that the life of Jesus may be manifested in our mortal flesh." Through privation and toil, these ministers were conforming to Christ's death, but that which was working death in them was bringing life to the Corinthians. In view of this, the followers of Jesus were not to increase the burdens and trials of the laborers.

Nothing could induce Paul to conceal the conviction of his soul. He would not purchase wealth or pleasure by conformity to the opinions of the world. Though in constant danger of martyrdom, he was not intimidated; for he knew that He who had died and risen again would raise him from the grave and present him to the father.

The Cross Accomplishes True Conversion

Not for self-aggrandizement did the apostles preach the gospel. The hope of saving souls kept them from ceasing their efforts because of danger or suffering.

"So we do not lose heart," Paul declared. "Though our outer nature is wasting away, our inner nature is being renewed every day." Though his physical strength was declining, yet unflinchingly he declared the gospel. This hero of the cross pressed forward in the conflict. "We look not to the things that are seen but to the things that are unseen; for the things that are seen are transient, but the things that are unseen are eternal."

The apostle appealed to his Corinthian brethren to consider anew the matchless love of their Redeemer: "For you know the grace of our Lord Jesus Christ, that though He was rich, yet for your sake He became poor, so that by His poverty you might become rich." You know the height from which He stooped, the depth of humiliation to which He descended. There was no rest for Him between the throne and the cross. Point after point Paul lingered over, that those who read his letter might comprehend the condescension of the Saviour.

The apostle traced Christ's course until He had reached the depths of humiliation. Paul was convinced that if they could comprehend the amazing sacrifice made by the Majesty of heaven, all selfishness would be banished from their lives. The Son of God had humbled Himself as a servant, becoming obedient unto death, "even death on a cross" (Philippians 2:8, RSV), that He might lift fallen man from degradation.

When we study the divine character in the light of the cross, we see mercy and forgiveness blended with equity and justice. We see in the midst of the throne One bearing in hands and feet and side the marks of suffering endured to reconcile man to God. We see a Father receiving us to Himself through the merits of His Son. The cloud of vengeance that threatened misery and despair, in the light reflected from the cross reveals the writing of God: Penitent, believing soul, live! I have paid a ransom.

In the contemplation of Christ, we linger on the shore of a love that is measureless. We tell of it, but language fails us. "Herein is love, not that we loved God, but that He loved us, and sent His Son to be the propitiation for our sins." 1 John 4:10.

It was on earth that the love of God was revealed through Christ. It is on earth that His children are to reflect this love through blameless lives.

32 / The Joy of Liberal Giving

In his first letter to the Corinthian believers, Paul gave instruction regarding the support of God's work. He inquired:

"Who serves as a soldier at his own expense? Who plants a vineyard without eating any of its fruit? Who tends a flock without getting some of the milk? . . . For it is written in the law of Moses, 'You shall not muzzle an ox when it is treading out the grain.' Is it for oxen that God is concerned? Does He not speak entirely for our sake? It was written for our sake, because the plowman should plow in hope and the thresher thresh in hope of a share in the crop."

The apostle further inquired, "Do you not know that those who are employed in the temple service get their food from the temple, and those who serve at the altar share in the sacrificial offerings? In the same way, the Lord commanded that those who proclaim the gospel should get their living by the gospel." 1 Corinthians 9:7-10, 13, 14, RSV.

The priests who ministered in the temple were supported by their brethren to whom they ministered spiritual blessings. "They that are of the sons of Levi, who receive the office of the priesthood, have a commandment to take tithes of the people according to the law." Hebrews 7:5. The tribe of Levi was chosen by the Lord for the priesthood. See Deuteronomy 18:5. One tenth of all the increase was claimed by the Lord as His own, and to withhold the tithe was regarded by Him as robbery.

Paul referred to this plan for the support of the ministry when he said, "Even so hath the Lord ordained that they which preach the gospel should live of the gospel." "The laborer is worthy of his reward." 1 Timothy 5:18.

Payment of the tithe was but a part of God's plan for the support of His service. The people were taught to cherish a spirit of liberality. Numerous gifts and offerings were specified. At the harvest and the vintage, the first fruits of the field were consecrated to the Lord. The gleanings and the corners of the field were reserved for the poor. The first fruits of the wool when the sheep were shorn, and of the grain when the wheat was threshed, were set apart for God. So also were the firstborn of all animals, and a redemption price was paid for the firstborn son.

Thus the people were reminded that God was the proprietor of their fields, flocks, and herds; it was He who sent the sunshine and the rain that ripened the harvest. They were but stewards of His goods.

Should Followers of Christ Give Less?

The liberality required of the Hebrews was largely to benefit their own nation; today Christ has laid upon His followers the responsibility of giving the glad tidings of salvation to the world. Our obligations are much greater than were those of ancient Israel. As God's work extends, calls for help will come more frequently. Christians should heed the command, "Bring ye all the tithes into the storehouse, that there may be meat in Mine house." Malachi 3:10. If professing Christians would faithfully bring to God their tithes and offerings, there would be no occasion to resort to fairs, lotteries, or parties of pleasure to secure funds.

For the gratification of appetite, personal adornment, or the embellishment of their homes, many church members do not hesitate to spend extravagantly. But when asked to give to the Lord's treasury, they demur and dole out a sum far smaller than they often spend for needless indulgence. They manifest no real love for Christ's service, no earnest interest in the salvation of souls. The Christian life of such ones is a dwarfed, sickly existence!

He whose heart is aglow with the love of Christ will regard it as a pleasure to aid in the advancement of the highest, holiest work committed to man—presenting to the world the riches of truth. The spirit of liberality is the spirit of heaven. This spirit finds its highest manifestation in Christ's sacrifice on the cross. The Father gave His only-begotten Son, and Christ gave Himself, that man might be saved. The cross of Calvary should appeal to the benevolence of every follower of the Saviour. The principle there illustrated is to give, give.

The spirit of selfishness is the spirit of Satan. The principle illustrated in the lives of worldlings is to get, get. But the fruit of their sowing is misery and death.

Blessings in Gratitude Offerings

Not only should God's children render the Lord the portion that belongs to Him, they should bring also a gratitude offering, the first fruits of their bounties— their choicest possessions, their best and holiest service. Thus they will gain rich blessings. God will make their souls like a watered garden. And the sheaves that they are enabled to bring to the Master will be the recompense of their unselfish use of the talents lent them.

God's chosen messengers should never be compelled to serve at their own charges, unaided by the hearty support of their brethren. It is the part of church members to deal liberally with those who lay aside secular employment that they may give themselves to the ministry. When God's ministers are encouraged, His cause is greatly advanced.

The displeasure of God is kindled against those who allow consecrated workers to suffer for the necessities of life. These selfish ones will be called to render an account for their misuse of money, and the depression brought on His faithful servants. Those who at the call of duty give up all to engage in God's service should receive wages sufficient to support themselves and their families.

In secular labor, workmen can earn good wages. Is not the work of leading souls to Christ of more importance than any ordinary business? Are not those who faithfully engage in this work entitled to ample remuneration?

A solemn responsibility rests on ministers to keep before the churches the needs of the cause of God and to educate them to be liberal. When the churches fail to give, not only does the work of the Lord suffer, but the blessing that should come to believers is withheld.

Why the Gifts of the Poor Are Valuable

Even the very poor should bring their offerings to God. They are to be sharers of the grace of Christ by helping those whose need is more pressing than their own. The poor man's gift, the fruit of self-denial, comes up before God as fragrant incense. And every act of self-sacrifice allies him more closely to the One who was rich, yet for our sakes became poor.

Christ called the attention of the disciples to the widow who cast two mites—"all her living", (Mark 12:44)—into the treasury. He esteemed her gift of more value than the large offerings of those whose alms did not call for self-denial. The widow had deprived herself of even the necessities of life, trusting God to supply her needs. "This poor widow hath cast more in, than all they which have cast into the treasury." Verse 43. The value of the gift is estimated not by the amount, but by the proportion that is given, and the motive that actuates the giver.

The apostle Paul said, "Remember the words of the Lord Jesus, how He said, It is more blessed to give than to receive." "He which soweth sparingly shall reap also sparingly; and he which soweth bountifully shall reap also bountifully. Every man according as he purposeth in his heart, so let him give; not grudgingly, or of necessity: for God loveth a cheerful giver." Acts 20:35; 2 Corinthians 9:6, 7.

Nearly all the Macedonian believers were poor in this world's goods, but they gladly gave for the support of the gospel. The liberality of the converts in Macedonia was held up as an example to other churches: "In a severe test of affliction, their abundance of joy and their extreme poverty have overflowed in a wealth of liberality on their part." 2 Corinthians 8:2, RSV.

Moved by the Spirit of God, they "first gave their own selves to the Lord." 2 Corinthians 8:5. Then they were willing to give freely of their means for the support of the gospel. It was not necessary to urge them; rather, they rejoiced in the privilege of denying themselves even necessary things in order to supply the needs of others.

When Paul sent Titus to Corinth to strengthen the believers there, in a personal letter he added his own appeal: "Now as you excel in everything—in faith, in utterance, in knowledge, in all earnestness, and in your love for us—see that you excel in this gracious work also." "And God is able to provide you with every blessing in abundance, so that you may always have enough of everything and may provide in abundance for every good work. . . . You will be enriched in every way for great generosity, which through us will produce thanksgiving to God." 2 Corinthians 8:7; 9:8-11, RSV.

Unselfish liberality threw the early church into a transport of joy; the believers knew that their efforts were helping to send the gospel to those in darkness. Their benevolence testified that they had not received the grace of God in vain. In the eyes of believers and unbelievers such liberality was a miracle of grace.

Spiritual prosperity is closely bound up with Christian liberality. As the followers of Christ give to the Lord, they have the assurance that their treasure is going before them to the heavenly courts. Would you make your property secure? Place it in the hands that bear the marks of the crucifixion. Would you enjoy your substance? Use it to bless the needy. Would you increase your possessions? "Honour the Lord with thy substance, and with the firstfruits of all thine increase: so shall thy barns be filled with plenty, and thy presses shall burst out with new wine." Proverbs 3:9, 10. Seek to retain possessions for selfish purposes, and it will be to eternal loss. But treasure given to God bears His inscription.

"One man gives freely, yet grows all the richer; another withholds what he should give, and only suffers want." Proverbs 11:24, RSV. The sower multiplies his seed by casting it away. So those who are faithful in imparting God's gifts increase their blessings. See Luke 6:38.

33 / Working Under Great Difficulties

Among the Jews it was regarded as sin to allow youth to grow up in ignorance of physical labor. Every youth, whether his parents were rich or poor, was taught some trade. Paul had early learned the trade of tentmaking.

Before he became a disciple of Christ, he occupied a high position and was not dependent on manual labor for support. But afterward, when he had used all his means in furthering the cause of Christ, he resorted at times to his trade to gain a livelihood.

At Thessalonica Paul worked with his hands in self-supporting labor while preaching the Word. Writing to the believers there, he reminded them: "You remember our labor and toil, brethren; we worked night and day, that we might not burden any of you, while we preached to you the gospel of God." 1 Thessalonians 2:9, RSV. And again, he declared that "we did not eat any one's bread without paying." "We worked night and day," he wrote, "that we might not burden any of you. It was not because we have not that right, but to give you in our conduct an example to imitate." 2 Thessalonians 3:8, 9, RSV.

At Thessalonica Paul had met those who refused to work with their hands. "We hear that some of you are living in idleness, mere busybodies, not doing any work. Now such persons we command and exhort in the Lord Jesus Christ to do their work in quietness and to earn their own living." "Even when we were with you," he wrote, "we gave you this command: If any one will not work, let him not eat." Verses 11, 12, 10, RSV.

In every age Satan has sought to introduce fanaticism into the church. Thus it was in Paul's day, and later, during the Reformation. Wycliffe, Luther, and many others encountered overzealous, unbalanced, and unsanctified minds. Misguided souls have taught that it is a sin to work, that Christians should devote their lives wholly to spiritual things. The teaching and example of Paul rebukes such extreme views.

Paul was not wholly dependent on the labor of his hands while at Thessalonica. He wrote to the Philippian believers in acknowledgment of the gifts he had received from them, saying, "Even in Thessalonica ye sent once and again unto my necessity." Philippians 4:16. Notwithstanding the fact that he received this help, he set an example of diligence, that those who held fanatical views regarding manual labor might be given a practical rebuke.

The Greeks were keen traders, trained in sharp business practices. They had come to believe that to make money, whether by fair means or foul, was commendable. Paul would give them no occasion for saying that he preached the gospel to enrich himself. He was willing to forgo support from his Corinthian hearers lest his usefulness as a minister be injured by unjust suspicion that he was preaching for gain.

Priscilla and Aquila Encourage Paul

At Corinth Paul found "a certain Jew named Aquila, born in Pontus, lately come from Italy, with his wife Priscilla." These were "of the same craft" with himself. Aquila and Priscilla had established a business as manufacturers of tents. Learning that they feared God and were seeking to avoid the contaminating influences with which they were surrounded, "he abode with them, and wrought. . . . And he reasoned in the synagogue every Sabbath, and persuaded the Jews and the Greeks." Acts 18:2-4.

In his second letter to the believers in Corinth, Paul reviewed his manner of life among them. "And when I was with you and was in want, I did not burden any one, for my needs were supplied by the brethren who came from Macedonia. So I refrained and will refrain from burdening you in any way." 2 Corinthians 11:9, RSV.

While he had worked at tentmaking Paul had also faithfully proclaimed the gospel. He declares of his labors: "For in what were you less favored than the rest of the churches, except that I myself did not burden you? Forgive me for this wrong! Here for the third time I am ready to come to you. And I will not be a burden, for I seek not what is yours but you. . . . I will most gladly spend and be spent for your souls." 2 Corinthians 12:13-15.

During his ministry in Ephesus Paul again worked at his trade. As in Corinth, the apostle was cheered by the presence of Aquila and Priscilla, who had accompanied him to Asia at the close of his second missionary journey.

Some objected to Paul's toiling with his hands, declaring that it was inconsistent with the work of a gospel minister. Why should Paul thus connect mechanical work with the preaching of the Word? Why should he spend in making tents time that could be put to better account?

But Paul did not regard as lost the time thus spent. His mind was ever reaching out for spiritual knowledge. He gave his fellow workers instruction in spiritual things, and he also set an example of industry. He was a quick, skillful worker, diligent in business, "fervent in spirit; serving the Lord." Romans 12:11. At his trade, the apostle had access to people he could not otherwise have reached. He showed that skill in common arts is a gift from God, who provides both the gift and the wisdom to use it aright. Paul's toil-hardened hands detracted nothing from the force of his appeals as a Christian minister.

Paul sometimes worked night and day, not only for his own support, but that he might assist his fellow laborers. He even suffered hunger at times, that he might relieve the necessities of others. His was an unselfish life. On the occasion of his farewell talk to the elders at Ephesus, he could lift up his toilworn hands and say, "I have coveted no man's silver, or gold, or apparel. Yea, ye yourselves know, that these hands have ministered unto my necessities, and to them that were with me. I have showed you all things, how that so laboring ye ought to support the weak, and to remember the words of the Lord Jesus, how He said, It is more blessed to give than to receive." Acts 20:33-35.

A Suggestion for Modern Gospel Ministers

If ministers feel they are suffering hardship, let them in imagination visit Paul's workshop. Let them bear in mind that while this man of God is fashioning the canvas, he is working for bread which he has justly earned by his labors as an apostle.

Work is a blessing, not a curse. Indolence grieves the Spirit of God. A stagnant pool is offensive, but a pure, flowing stream spreads health and gladness over the land. Paul desired to teach young ministers that by exercising their muscles and sinews, they would become strong to endure the toils and privations that awaited them. His own teachings would lack vitality and force if he did not exercise.

Thousands of human beings exist only to consume the benefits which God bestows on them. They forget they are to be producers as well as consumers.

Young men who are chosen of God for the ministry will give proof of their high calling. They will endeavor to gain an experience that will fit them to plan, organize, and execute. They will, by self-discipline, become more and more like their Master, revealing His goodness, love, and truth.

Not all who feel called to preach should throw themselves and their families at once on the church for financial support. The means dedicated to the work of God should not be consumed by men who desire to preach only that they may receive support.

Although an eloquent speaker and chosen by God to do a special work, Paul was never above labor, nor did he ever weary of sacrificing for the cause he loved. "To the present hour," he wrote to the Corinthians, "we hunger and thirst, we are ill-clad and buffeted and homeless, and we labor, working with our own hands." 1 Corinthians 4:11, 12, RSV. He labored at this trade; nevertheless he ever held himself ready to lay aside his secular work in order to oppose the enemies of the gospel or to win souls to Jesus. His zeal and industry are a rebuke to indolence and desire for ease.

Paul illustrated what might be done by consecrated laymen in many places. Many can advance the cause of God, while at the same time they support themselves in daily labor. Aquila and Priscilla were used by God to show Apollos the way of truth more perfectly. While some with special talents are chosen to devote all their energies to the work of the gospel, many others are called to an important part in soul-saving.

There is a large field open before the self-supporting gospel worker. Many may gain valuable experiences in ministry while toiling a portion of the time at manual labor. By this method, strong workers may be developed for important service in needy fields.

The Heart Burden Carried by Servants of Christ

The self-sacrificing servant of God does not measure his work by hours. His wages do not influence him in his labor. From heaven he received his commission, and to heaven he looks for his recompense.

Such workers should be freed from unnecessary anxiety. While they should be careful to exercise to keep mind and body vigorous, yet they should not be compelled to spend a large part of their time at secular employment. These faithful workers are not exempt from temptation. When burdened with anxiety because of a failure of the church to give them proper financial support, some are fiercely beset by the tempter. They become depressed. Their families must have food and clothing. If they could feel released from their divine commission they would willingly labor with their hands. But they realize that their time belongs to God, and they continue to advance the cause that is dearer to them than life itself. They may, however, be forced to engage for a time in manual labor while carrying forward the ministerial work.

At times it seems impossible to do the work necessary to be done because of the lack of means. Some fear that they cannot do all that they feel it their duty to do. But if they advance in faith, prosperity will attend their efforts. He who has bidden His followers go into all the world will sustain every laborer who seeks to proclaim His message.

In the upbuilding of His work, the Lord sometimes tries the confidence of His people by bringing about circumstances which compel them to move forward in faith. Often He bids them advance when their feet seem to be touching the waters of Jordan. See Joshua 3:14-17. At such times, when prayers ascend to Him in earnest faith, God opens the way before them and brings them out into a large place. Angels will prepare the way before them, and the means necesssary for the work will be provided. Those who are enlightened will give freely to support the work. The Spirit of God will move on their hearts to sustain the Lord's cause, not only in home fields, but in the regions beyond. Thus the work of the Lord will advance in His own appointed way.

34 / The Joy of Working With Christ

God does not live for Himself. "He maketh His sun to rise on the evil and on the good, and sendeth rain on the just and on the unjust." Matthew 5:45. By His example Jesus was to teach what it means to minister. He served all, ministered to all.

Again and again He tried to establish this principle among His disciples. "Whosoever will be great among you, let him be your minister; and whosoever will be chief among you, let him be your servant: even as the Son of man came not to be ministered unto, but to minister, and to give His life a ransom for many." Matthew 20:26-28.

Since his ascension Christ has carried forward His work by chosen ambassadors, through whom He speaks to the children of men and ministers to their needs. In Christ's stead they are to beseech men and women to be reconciled to God.

Their work has been likened to that of watchmen. In ancient times sentinels were stationed on the walls of cities, where they could overlook important posts to be guarded and warn of the approach of an enemy. At stated intervals they called to one another, to make sure that all were awake and that no harm had befallen any. Each repeated the call of good cheer or of warning till it echoed round the city.

The words of the prophet Ezekiel declare the solemn responsibility of those who are appointed as guardians of the church: "So you, son of man, I have made a watchman for the house of Israel; whenever you hear a word from My mouth, you shall give them warning from Me. If I say to the wicked, O wicked man, you shall surely die, and you do not speak to warn the wicked to turn from his way, that wicked man shall die in his iniquity, but his blood I will require at your hand. But if you warn the wicked to turn from his way, . . . you will have saved your life." Ezekiel 33:7-9, RSV.

Souls are in danger of falling under temptation, and they will perish unless God's ministers are faithful. If their spiritual senses become so benumbed that they are unable to discern danger, God will require at their hands the blood of those who are lost.

Christ's Love a Greater Motivation Than Money

Watchmen on the walls of Zion may live so near to God and be so susceptible to the impressions of His Spirit that He can work through them to tell men and women of their peril and point them to safety. At no time may they relax their vigilance, and never are they to sound one wavering, uncertain note. Not for wages are they to labor, but because they realize that there is a woe upon them if they fail to preach the gospel. Chosen of God, they are to rescue men and women from destruction.

A co-worker with Christ does not study his own ease or convenience. He is forgetful of self. In his search for the lost sheep he does not realize that he himself is weary, cold, and hungry. He has but one object in view—saving the lost.

The soldier of the cross stands unshrinkingly in the forefront of the battle. As the enemy presses the attack against him, he turns to the stronghold for aid and is strengthened for the duties of the hour. The victories he gains do not lead to self-exaltation, but cause him to lean more and more heavily on the Mighty One. Relying of that Power, He is enabled to present the message of salvation so forcibly that it vibrates in other minds.

He who teaches the Word must live in hourly communion with God through prayer and study of His

Word. This will impart to his efforts a power greater than the influence of his preaching. Of this power he must not allow himself to be deprived. He must plead with God to strengthen him and touch his lips with living fire. By the power and light that God imparts they can comprehend more and accomplish more than their finite judgment had deemed possible.

Satan's craft is more successful against those who are depressed. When discouragement threatens, let the minister spread out before God his necessities. When the heavens were as brass (see Deuteronomy 28:33) over Paul, he trusted most fully in God. He knew affliction; but listen to his triumphant cry: "This slight momentary affliction is preparing for us an eternal weight of glory beyond all comparison, because we look not to the things that are seen but to the things that are unseen." 2 Corinthians 4:17, 18, RSV. By seeing Him who is invisible, strength and vigor of soul are gained.

Come Close to the People

When a minister has preached a sermon, his work has but just begun. He should visit the people in their homes and point them to the higher way. Let ministers teach the truth in families, drawing close to those for whom they labor. Christ will give them words that will sink deep into the hearts of the listeners. Paul said, "I did not shrink from declaring to you anything that was profitable, and teaching you in public and from house to house, . . . repentance to God and of faith in our Lord Jesus Christ." Acts 20:20, 21, RSV.

The Saviour went from house to house, healing the sick and speaking peace to the disconsolate. He took little children in His arms and spoke words of hope and comfort to the weary mothers. He was the servant of all. And as men and women listened to the truths that fell from His lips, hope sprang up in their hearts. There was an earnestness that sent His words home with convicting power.

God's ministers are to learn Christ's method of la-

boring. Thus only can they fulfill their trust. The same
Spirit that dwelt in Christ is to be the source of their
knowledge and the secret of their power.

Some have failed of success because they have not
given undivided interest to the Lord's work. Ministers
should have no engrossing interests aside from the
great work of leading souls to the Saviour. The fishermen whom Christ called left their nets and followed
Him. Ministers cannot work for God and at the same
time carry the burden of large personal business enterprises. The energies of the minister are all needed for
his high calling. His best powers belong to God.

The Peril of Side Businesses

"No soldier on service gets entangled in civilian pursuits, since his aim is to satisfy the one who enlisted
him." 2 Timothy 2:4, RSV. Thus the apostle emphasized the minister's need of unreserved consecration to
the Master's service. He is not striving for earthly
riches. His one desire is to bring to the indifferent and
the disloyal the realities of eternity. He may be asked
to engage in enterprises which promise large worldly
gain, but he returns the answer, "What shall it profit a
man, if he shall gain the whole world, and lose his own
soul?" Mark 8:36.

Satan presented this inducement to Christ, knowing
that if He accepted it, the world would never be ransomed. And under different guises he presents the
same temptation to God's ministers today, knowing
that those who are beguiled by it will be false to their
trust.

"The love of money is the root of all evils; it is
through this craving that some have wandered away
from the faith and pierced their hearts with many
pangs. But as for you, man of God, shun all this." By
example as well as by precept, the ambassador for
Christ is to "charge" "the rich in this world" "not to
be haughty, nor to set their hopes on uncertain riches
but on God who richly furnishes us with everything to

enjoy. They are to do good, to be rich in good deeds, liberal and generous." 1 Timothy 6:10, 11, 17, 18, RSV.

Paul's heart burned with love for sinners, and he put all his energies into the work of soul winning. The blessings he received he used in blessing others. From place to place he went, establishing churches. Wherever he could he sought to counteract wrong and to turn men and women to righteousness.

The apostle made it part of his work to educate young men for the ministry. He took them on his missionary journeys, and thus they gained experience that enabled them to fill positions of responsibility. When separated from them, he still kept in touch with their work.

Paul never forgot that if souls were lost through unfaithfulness on his part, God would hold him accountable. Christ "we proclaim, warning every man and teaching every man in all wisdom, that we may present every man mature [perfect, KJV] in Christ. For this I toil, striving with all the energy which He mightily inspires within me." Colossians 1:28, 29, RSV.

This high attainment all can reach who put themselves under the control of the great Teacher. The minister who shuts himself in with the Lord may be assured that he will receive that which will be to his hearers a savor of life unto life. Of his own work Paul has left us a picture in his letter to the Corinthian believers: "As servants of God we commend ourselves in every way: through great endurance, in afflictions, hardships, calamities, beatings, imprisonments, tumults, labors, watching, hunger, . . . in honor and dishonor, in ill repute and good repute. We are treated as impostors, and yet are true; as unknown, and yet well known; as dying, and behold we live; as punished, and yet not killed; as sorrowful, yet always rejoicing; as poor, yet making many rich." 2 Corinthians 6:4-10, RSV.

There is nothing more precious in the sight of God

than His ministers, who go forth into the waste places of the earth to sow the seeds of truth. He imparts His Spirit to them to turn souls from sin to righteousness. God is calling for men who are willing to leave their farms, their business, if need be their families to become missionaries for Him. And the call will be answered. In the past men have left home and friends, even wife and children, to go among idolaters and savages, to proclaim the message of mercy. Many in the attempt have lost their lives, but others have been raised up to carry on the work. Thus the seed sown in sorrow has yielded a bountiful harvest. The knowledge of God has been widely extended.

If Christ left the ninety and nine that He might seek and save one lost sheep, can we do less? Is not a neglect to work as Christ worked, to sacrifice as He sacrificed, a betrayal of sacred trusts?

The heart of the true minister is filled with an intense longing to save souls. Others must hear the truths that brought to his own soul such peace and joy. With his eyes fixed on the cross of Calvary, believing that the Saviour will be with him until the end, he seeks to win souls to Jesus, and in heaven he is numbered among those who are "called, and chosen, and faithful." Revelation 17:14.

35 / God's Special Plan for the Jews

After many delays, Paul reached Corinth, the scene of much labor in the past. Many of the early believers still regarded with affection the one who had first borne to them the gospel. As he saw the evidences of their fidelity he rejoiced that his work in Corinth had not been in vain. The Corinthian believers had developed strength of Christian character and were now a strong force for good in that center of heathenism and super-stition. In the society of these faithful converts, the apostle's worn and troubled spirit found rest.

At Corinth Paul's contemplated journey to Rome es-pecially occupied his thoughts. To see the Christian faith firmly established at the great center of the known world was one of his dearest hopes. The apostle de-sired the cooperation of the church already established in Rome in the work to be accomplished in Italy and other countries. To prepare the way he sent these brethren a letter announcing his purpose of visiting Rome and his hope of planting the standard of the cross in Spain.

In his letter, with clearness and power Paul pre-sented the doctrine of justification by faith in Christ. He hoped that other churches also might be helped by the instruction, but how dimly could he foresee the far-reaching influence of his words! Through all the ages, the great truth of justification by faith has stood as a mighty beacon to guide sinners into the way of life.

This chapter is based on Paul's Letter to the Romans.

This light scattered the darkness which enveloped Luther's mind and revealed to him the power of the blood of Christ to cleanse from sin. The same light has guided thousands to the true Source of pardon and peace.

Ever since his conversion, Paul had longed to help his Jewish brethren gain a clear understanding of the gospel. "My heart's desire and prayer to God for Israel is," he declared, "that they might be saved." The Israelites had failed to recognize Jesus of Nazareth as the promised Messiah. Paul assured the believers at Rome, "I could wish that myself were accursed from Christ for my brethren, my kinsmen according to the flesh." Through the Jews God had purposed to bless the entire human race. Among them many prophets had foretold the advent of a Redeemer who was to be rejected and slain by those who should have recognized Him as the Promised One.

But even though Israel rejected His Son, God did not reject them. Paul continues: "I say then, Hath God cast away His people? God forbid. For I also am an Israelite, of the seed of Abraham, of the tribe of Benjamin. God hath not cast away His people which He foreknew. . . . At this present time also there is a remnant according to the election of grace."

Those Who Fall Can Rise Again

Israel had stumbled and fallen, but this did not make it impossible for them to rise again. In answer to the question, "Have they stumbled that they should fall?" the apostle replies: "God forbid: but rather through their fall salvation is come unto the Gentiles, for to provoke them to jealousy. . . . For if the casting away of them be the reconciling of the world, what shall the receiving of them be, but life from the dead?"

It was God's purpose that His grace should be revealed among the Gentiles as well as among the Israelites. "Hath not the potter power over the clay, of the same lump to make one vessel unto honor, and another unto dishonor?'' he inquired. "What if God, willing to show His wrath, and to make His power known, endured with much long-suffering the vessels of wrath fitted to destruction: and that He might make known the riches of His glory on the vessels of mercy, which He had afore prepared unto glory, even us, whom He hath called, not of the Jews only, but also of the Gentiles?''

Notwithstanding Israel's failure as a nation, there were faithful men and women who had received with gladness the message of John the Baptist and had thus been led to study anew the prophecies concerning the Messiah. The early Christian church was composed of these faithful Jews. To this "remnant" Paul refers: "If the dough offered as first fruits is holy, so is the whole lump; and if the root is holy, so are the branches.'' Romans 11:16, RSV.

Paul compares the Gentiles to branches from a wild olive tree, grafted into the parent stock. "If some of the branches be broken off,'' he writes, "and thou, being a wild olive tree, wert grafted in among them, and with them partakest of the root and fatness of the olive tree; boast not against the branches. . . . Because of unbelief they were broken off, and thou standest by faith. Be not high-minded, but fear: for if God spared not the natural branches, take heed lest He also spare not thee.''

All Who Believe Are the True Israel

Through the rejection of Heaven's purpose for her, Israel as a nation had lost her connection with God. But God was able to reunite with the true stock of Israel the branches that had been separated from the parent stock. "If you have been cut from what is by nature a wild olive tree, and grafted, contrary to nature, into a cultivated olive tree, how much more will these natural branches be grafted back into their own olive tree. . . . A hardening has come upon part of Israel, until the full number of Gentiles come in.

"And so all Israel will be saved. . . . For the gifts and the call of God are irrevocable. Just as you were once disobedient to God but now have received mercy because of their disobedience, so they have now been disobedient in order that by the mercy shown to you they also may receive mercy. . . .

"O the depth of the riches and wisdom and knowledge of God! How unsearchable are His judgments and how inscrutable His ways!" Romans 11:24-33, RSV.

God is abundantly able to transform the hearts of Jew and Gentile alike. "For the Lord will execute His sentence upon the earth with rigor and dispatch." RSV.

When Jerusalem was destroyed and the temple laid in ruins, many Jews were sold as bondmen in heathen lands, scattered among the nations like wrecks on a desert shore. Maligned, persecuted, from century to century theirs has been a heritage of suffering.

Notwithstanding the doom pronounced upon the nation, there have lived from age to age many noble, God-fearing Jewish men and women. God has comforted their hearts in affliction and has beheld with pity their terrible situation. Some who have sought Him for a right understanding of His Word have learned to see in the lowly Nazarene the true Messiah. As their minds have grasped the significance of prophecies long obscured by tradition and misinterpretation, their hearts have been filled with gratitude to God for the unspeakable gift of Christ as a personal Saviour.

What Is Needed in Order to Awaken the Sincere Jews

Isaiah said in his prophecy, "A remnant shall be saved." From Paul's day to the present time, the Holy Spirit has been calling after the Jew as well as the Gentile. "God shows no partiality" (Galatians 2:6, RSV), declares Paul, "The gospel . . . is the power of God unto salvation to everyone that believeth; to the Jew first, and also to the Greek. For therein is the righteousness of God revealed from faith to faith: as it is written, The just shall live by faith." This gospel is equally efficacious for Jew and Gentile.

When this gospel shall be presented in its fullness to the Jews, many will accept Christ. Only a few Christian ministers feel called to labor for the Jewish people; but to those who have been often passed by, the message of Christ is to come.

In the closing proclamation of the gospel, God expects His messengers to take particular interest in the Jewish people. As many of the Jews see the Christ of the gospel in the pages of the Old Testament and percieve how the New Testament explains the Old, they will recognize Christ as the Saviour of the world. To them will be fulfilled the words, "As many as received Him, to them gave He power to become the sons of God, even to them that believe on His name." John 1:12.

Some Jews, like Saul of Tarsus, are mighty in the Scriptures, and these will proclaim with wonderful power the immutability of the law of God. The God of Israel will bring this to pass in our day. As His servants labor in faith for those who have long been neglected, His salvation will be revealed.

36 / Paul's Timeless Letter to the Galatians

Through the influence of false teachers, heresy and sensualism were gaining ground among the believers in Galatia. These false teachers were mingling Jewish traditions with the truths of the gospel. The evils introduced threatened to destroy the Galatian churches.

Paul was cut to the heart. He immediately wrote to the deluded believers, exposing the false theories that they had accepted.

"I am astonished that you are so quickly deserting Him who called you in the grace of Christ and turning to a different gospel—not that there is another gospel, but there are some who trouble you and want to pervert the gospel of Christ. But even if we, or an angel from heaven, should preach to you a gospel contrary to that which we preached to you, let him be accursed." The Holy Spirit had witnessed to his labors; therefore he warned his brethren not to listen to anything that contradicted the truths he had taught.

"O foolish Galatians!" he exclaimed, "Who has bewitched you, before whose eyes Jesus Christ was publicly portrayed as crucified?" Refusing to recognize the doctrines of the apostate teachers, the apostle endeavored to lead the converts to see that they had been grossly deceived, but that by returning to their former faith in the gospel they might yet defeat the purpose of Satan. His supreme confidence in the message he bore helped many whose faith had failed, to return to the Saviour.

This chapter is based on the Letter to the Galatians, RSV.

How different from Paul's manner of writing to the Corinthian church! The Corinthians he rebuked with tenderness; the Galatians, with words of unsparing reproof. To teach the Corinthians to distinguish the false from the true called for caution and patience. In the Galatian churches, open, unmasked error was supplanting the gospel. Christ was virtually renounced for the ceremonies of Judaism. The apostle saw that if the believers were to be saved from the dangerous influences which threatened them, decisive measures must be taken.

Why Paul Was So Abrupt

In his letter Paul briefly reviewed incidents connected with his own conversion and early Christian experience. By this he sought to show that it was through a special manifestation of divine power that he had been led to see the great truths of the gospel. Through instruction from God Himself Paul was led to admonish the Galatians in so positive a manner. With settled conviction and absolute knowledge, he clearly outlined the difference between being taught by man and receiving instruction direct from Christ.

The men who had attempted to lead the Galatians from the gospel were hypocrites, unholy in heart and corrupt in life. Through the performance of a round of ceremonies they expected to gain the favor of God. They had no desire for a gospel that called for obedience to the word, "Except a man be born again, he cannot see the kingdom of God." John 3:3. A religion based on such a doctrine required too great a sacrifice, and they clung to their errors.

To substitute external forms for holiness of heart and life is still pleasing to the unrenewed nature. It is Satan's studied effort to divert minds from the hope of salvation through faith in Christ and obedience to the law of God. The archenemy adapts his temptations to the inclinations of those whom he is seeking to deceive. In apostolic times he led the Jews to exalt the ceremonial law and reject Christ; at the present time he induces professing Christians to cast contempt on the moral law and to teach that it may be transgressed with impunity. Every servant of God must withstand firmly these perverters of the faith and expose their errors.

Success Attended the Letter

Paul ably vindicated his position as an apostle, "not from men nor through man, but through Jesus Christ and God the Father, who raised Him from the dead." From the highest Authority in heaven, he received his commission, and his position had been acknowledged by a general council at Jerusalem. Those who sought to belittle his calling and work were fighting against Christ, whose grace and power were manifested through him. The apostle was forced, by the opposition of his enemies, to take a decided stand in maintaining his authority, not to exalt self, but to magnify the grace of God.

Paul pleaded with those who had once known the power of God to return to their first love of gospel truth. He set before them their privilege of becoming free in Christ, through whose atoning grace all who make full surrender are clothed with the robe of His righteousness. Every soul who would be saved must have a genuine, personal experience in the things of God.

The apostle's earnest words were not fruitless. Many whose feet had wandered into strange paths returned to their former faith. Henceforth they were steadfast in the liberty wherewith Christ had made them free. God was glorified, and many were added to the number of believers throughout that region.

37 / Paul's Farewell Journey to Jerusalem

Paul ever cherished the hope that he might be instrumental in removing the prejudice of his unbelieving countrymen, so that they might accept the gospel. He also desired to meet the church at Jerusalem and bear to them the gifts sent by the Gentile churches. And he hoped to bring about a firmer union between Jewish and Gentile converts to the faith.

He was about to step on board ship to sail for one of the ports of Palestine when he was told of a plot by the Jews to take his life. In the past these opposers had been foiled in their efforts to end the apostle's work.

The success attending the preaching of the gospel aroused the anger of the Jews anew. Jews were released from the ceremonial law, and Gentiles were equal with Jews as children of Abraham! Paul's emphatic statement, "There is neither Greek nor Jew, circumcision nor uncircumcision" (Colossians 3:11), was regarded by his enemies as daring blasphemy, and they determined that his voice should be silenced.

Receiving warning of the plot, Paul decided to go by way of Macedonia. His plan to reach Jerusalem in time for the Passover had to be given up, but he hoped to be there at Pentecost. He had with him a large sum of money from the Gentile churches, and because of this he made arrangements for representative brethren from various contributing churches to accompany him.

At Philippi he tarried to keep the Passover. Only

This chapter is based on Acts 20:4 to 21:16.

Luke remained with him, the others passing on to Troas to await him there. The Philippians were the most loving and truehearted of the apostle's converts, and he enjoyed happy communion with them.

Sailing from Philippi, Paul and Luke reached Troas five days later and remained for seven days with the believers in that place.

The Saturday Evening Farewell Meeting

On the last evening the brethren "came together to break bread." The fact that their beloved teacher was about to depart had called together a larger company than usual. They assembled in an "upper chamber"on the third story. There, in the fervency of his solicitude for them, the apostle preached until midnight.

In one of the open windows sat a youth named Eutychus, who went to sleep and fell to the court below. The youth was taken up dead, and many gathered about him with cries and mourning. But Paul offered up earnest prayer that God would restore the dead to life. Above the sound of lamentation the apostle's voice was heard, "Trouble not yourselves; for his life is in him." With rejoicing the believers again assembled in the upper chamber. They partook of the Communion, and then Paul "talked a long while, even till break of day."

The ship was about to sail, and the brethren hastened on board. The apostle, however, chose to take the nearer route by land, meeting his companions at Assos. The difficulties connected with his visit to Jerusalem, the attitude of the church there toward him, as well as the interests of the gospel work in other fields, were subjects of anxious thought, and he took advantage of this special opportunity to seek God for strength and guidance.

As the travelers sailed south from Assos, they passed Ephesus. Paul had desired to visit the church there, but determined to hasten on, for he desired "to be at Jerusalem the day of Pentecost." At Miletus, however, about thirty miles from Ephesus, he learned that it might be possible to communicate with the church before the ship should sail. He therefore sent a message to the elders, urging them to hasten to Miletus, that he might see them.

They came, and he spoke to them touching words of admonition and farewell. "You yourselves know," he said, "how I lived among you all the time from the first day that I set foot in Asia, . . . how I did not shrink from declaring to you anything that was profitable, and teaching you in public and from house to house, testifying both to Jews and to Greeks of repentance to God and of faith in our Lord Jesus Christ."

Paul had ever exalted the divine law. He had shown that wrongdoers must repent and humble themselves before God, and exercise faith in the blood of Christ. The Son of God had died as their sacrifice and had ascended to heaven as their advocate. By repentance and faith they might be freed from condemnation, and through the grace of Christ be enabled to render obedience to the law of God.

"And now, behold," Paul continued, "I am going to Jerusalem, bound in the Spirit, not knowing what shall befall me there; except that the Holy Spirit testifies to me in every city that imprisonment and afflictions await me. . . . I know that all you among whom I have gone preaching the kingdom will see my face no more."

The Holy Spirit Moves Paul to Say Good-bye

While he was speaking, the Spirit of inspiration came on him, confirming his fears that this would be his last meeting with his Ephesian brethren.

"I have not shunned to declare unto you all the counsel of God." No fear of giving offense could lead Paul to withhold the words that God had given him for their warning or correction. If the minister of Christ today sees that any of his flock are cherishing sin, he must as a faithful shepherd give them from God's word the instruction applicable to their case. The pastor must give his people faithful instruction, showing them what they must be and do in order to stand perfect in the day of God. A faithful teacher of the truth will at the close of his work be able to say with Paul, "I am pure from the blood of all men."

"Take heed therefore unto yourselves and to all the flock, over which the Holy Ghost hath made you overseers, to feed the church of God, which He hath purchased with His own blood." Ministers are dealing with the purchase of the blood of Christ. As representatives of Christ, they are to maintain the honor of His name. By purity of life they are to prove themselves worthy of their high calling.

Dangers would assail the church at Ephesus: "I know this, that after my departing shall grievous wolves enter in among you, not sparing the flock. Also of your own selves shall men arise, speaking perverse things, to draw away disciples after them." Looking into the future, Paul saw the attacks which the church must suffer from both external and internal foes. "Therefore watch, and remember, that by the space of three years I ceased not to warn everyone night and day with tears.

"And now, brethren," he continued, "I commend you to God, and to the word of His grace, which is able to build you up, and to give you an inheritance among all them which are sanctified. I have coveted no man's silver, or gold, or apparel." Paul had never sought personal benefit from the Ephesian brethren who were wealthy. "These hands," he declared, "have ministered unto my necessities, and to them that were with me." "I have showed you . . . how that so laboring ye ought to support the weak, and to remember the words of the Lord Jesus, how He said, It is more blessed to give than to receive."

"And when he had thus spoken, he kneeled down, and prayed with them all. And they all wept sore and fell on Paul's neck, and kissed him, sorrowing most of all for the words which he spake, that they should see his face no more. And they accompanied him unto the ship.''

Fom Miletus the travelers sailed to Patara, where, "finding a ship sailing over unto Phoenicia," they "went aboard, and set forth." At Tyre, where the ship was unloaded, a few disciples were warned through the Holy Spirit of the perils awaiting Paul at Jerusalem. They urged him not to go on. But the apostle allowed no fear to turn him from his purpose.

At Caesarea Paul spent a few peaceful, happy days—the last of perfect freedom he was to enjoy for a long time. While at Caesarea "a prophet named Agabus came down from Judea. And coming to us," Luke says, "he took Paul's girdle and bound his own feet and hands, and said, 'Thus says the Holy Spirit, "So shall the Jews at Jerusalem bind the man who owns this girdle and deliver him into the hands of the Gentiles." ' " RSV.

Paul Would Not Swerve From Duty

But Paul would not swerve from the path of duty. He would follow Christ if need be to prison and to death. " 'What are you doing, weeping and breaking my heart?' " he exclaimed; "for I am ready not only to be imprisoned but even to die at Jerusalem for the name of the Lord Jesus."

The time soon came for the brief stay at Caesarea to end, and Paul and his company set out for Jerusalem, their hearts shadowed by the presentiment of coming evil.

The apostle knew he would find few friends and many enemies at Jerusalem. Remembering his own bitter prejudice against the followers of Christ, he felt the deepest pity for his deluded countrymen. And yet how little could he hope that he would be able to help them! The same blind wrath which had once burned in his own heart was now kindling the hearts of a whole nation against him.

And he could not count on the sympathy of even his own brethren in the faith. Some, even of the apostles and elders, had received the most unfavorable reports as truth, making no attempt to contradict them and manifesting no desire to harmonize with him.

Yet the apostle was not in despair. He trusted that the Voice which had spoken to his own heart would yet speak to the hearts of his countrymen and that the Master whom his fellow disciples served would yet unite their hearts with his in the work of the gospel.

38/ Paul's Brethren Give Him Bad Advice

Paul presented to the leaders at Jerusalem the contributions forwarded by the Gentile churches for the support of the poor among their Jewish brethren. The sum far exceeded the expectations of the elders at Jerusalem and represented severe privations on the part of the Gentile believers.

These freewill offerings betokened the loyalty of the Gentile converts to the organized work of God throughout the world. Yet it was apparent that some were unable to appreciate the spirit of brotherly love that had prompted the gifts.

In earlier years, some of the leading brethren at Jerusalem had not cooperated heartily with Paul. In their anxiety to preserve a few meaningless forms and ceremonies, they had lost sight of the blessing that would come through an effort to unite in one all parts of the Lord's work. They had failed to keep step with the advancing providences of God and attempted to throw about workers many unnecessary restrictions. Men unacquainted with the peculiar needs in distant fields insisted that they had the authority to direct their brethren to follow certain specified methods of labor.

Several years had passed since the brethren in Jerusalem gave careful consideration to the methods followed by those who were laboring for the Gentiles, and made recommendations concerning certain rites and ceremonies. At this general council the brethren had also united in commending Barnabas and Paul as labor-

This chapter is based on Acts 21:17 to 23:35.

ers worthy of the full confidence of every believer. At this meeting some had severely criticized the apostles upon whom rested the chief burden of carrying the gospel to the Gentile world, but during the council their views of God's purpose had broadened, and they united in making decisions which made possible the unification of the entire body of believers.

Leading Brethren Continue to Hurt Paul's Ministry

Afterward, when converts among the Gentiles were increasing rapidly, a few leading brethren at Jerusalem began to cherish anew their former prejudices against the methods of Paul. Some of the leaders determined that the work must henceforth be conducted in accordance with their own ideas. If Paul would conform to policies which they advocated, they would acknowledge and sustain his work; otherwise, they could no longer grant it their support.

These men had lost sight of the fact that God is the teacher of His people; every worker in His cause is to follow the divine Leader, not looking to man for direct guidance; His workers are to be molded after the similitude of the divine.

Paul had taught the people "not with enticing words of man's wisdom, but in demonstration of the Spirit and of power." 1 Corinthians 2:4. He had looked to God for direct guidance, yet he had been careful to labor in harmony with the decisions of the general council at Jerusalem. As a result, the churches were "established in the faith and increased in number daily." Acts 16:5. Notwithstanding the lack of sympathy shown him by some, he had encouraged in his converts a spirit of loyalty, generosity, and brotherly love, as revealed in the liberal contributions he placed before the Jewish elders.

Paul "declared particularly what things God had wrought among the Gentiles by his ministry." This brought, even to those who had been doubting, the conviction that the blessing of heaven had accompanied his labors. "When they heard it, they glorified the Lord." The methods pursued by the apostle bore the signet of Heaven. The men who had urged arbitrary control saw Paul's ministry in a new light and were convinced that their course had been wrong. They had been held in bondage by Jewish customs and traditions, and the gospel had been hindered by their failure to recognize that the wall of partition between Jew and Gentile had been broken down by the death of Christ.

This was the golden opportunity for all the leading brethren to confess frankly that God had wrought through Paul and that at times they had erred in permitting his enemies to arouse their jealousy and prejudice. But instead of doing justice to the one who had been injured, they showed that they still cherished a feeling that Paul should be held largely responsible for the existing prejudice. They did not stand nobly in his defense but sought to effect a compromise.

Advice to Compromise Leads to Disaster

"You see, brother," they said in response to his testimony, "how many thousands there are among the Jews of those who have believed; they are all zealous for the law, and they have been told about you that you teach all the Jews who are among the Gentiles to forsake Moses, telling them not to circumcise their children or observe the customs. . . . Do therefore what we tell you. We have four men who are under a vow; take these men and purify yourself along with them and pay their expenses, so that they may shave their heads. Thus all will know that there is nothing in what they have been told about you but that you yourself live in observance of the law. But as for the Gentiles who have believed, we have sent a letter with our judgment that they should abstain from what had been sacrificed to idols and from blood and from what is strangled and from unchastity." RSV.

The brethren assured Paul that the decision of the former council concerning Gentile converts and the ceremonial law still held good. But the advice now given was not consistent with that decision. The Spirit of God did not prompt this instruction; it was the fruit of cowardice.

Many of the Jews who had accepted the gospel still cherished the ceremonial law and were only too willing to make unwise concessions, hoping thus to remove prejudice and win their countrymen to faith in Christ as the world's Redeemer. Paul realized that so long as many leading members of the church at Jerusalem should continue to cherish prejudice against him, they would work constantly to counteract his influence. He felt that if by reasonable concession he could win them to the truth, he would remove a great obstacle to the success of the gospel in other places. But he was not authorized of God to concede as much as they asked.

When we think of Paul's great desire to be in harmony with his brethren, his tenderness toward the weak in faith, and his reverence for the apostles who had been with Christ, it is less surprising that he was constrained to deviate from the firm course he had hitherto followed. But his efforts for conciliation only hastened his predicted sufferings, separated him from his brethren, and deprived the church of one of its strongest pillars.

On the following day Paul began to carry out the counsel of the elders. The four men under the Nazarite vow (see Numbers 6) were taken by Paul into the temple. Those who advised Paul to take this step had not considered the great peril to which he would thus be exposed. He had visited many of the world's largest cities and was well known to thousands who had come to Jerusalem to attend the feast. Among these were men filled with bitter hatred for Paul. For him to enter the temple on a public occasion was to risk his life. For several days he was apparently unnoticed; but as he was talking with a priest concerning the sacrifices to be offered, he was recognized by some Jews from Asia.

With fury of demons they rushed upon him. "Men of

Israel, help! This is the man who is teaching men everywhere against the people and the law and this place." And as the people responded to the call for help, another accusation was added—"moreover he also brought Greeks into the temple, and he has defiled this holy place." RSV.

By Jewish law it was a crime punishable with death for an uncircumcised person to enter the inner courts of the sacred edifice. Paul had been seen in the city with Trophimus, an Ephesian, and it was conjectured that he had brought him into the temple. This he had not done; and being himself a Jew, his act in entering the temple was no violation of the law.

The Hatred Shown to Christ Repeated Against Paul

But though the charge was wholly false, it served to arouse popular prejudice. Wild excitement spread through Jerusalem. "All the city was moved, and the people ran together. They took Paul, and drew him out of the temple: and forthwith the doors were shut.

"And as they went about to kill him, tidings came unto the chief captain of the band, that all Jerusalem was in an uproar." Claudius Lysias "immediately took soldiers and centurions, and ran down unto them: and when they saw the chief captain and the soldiers, they left beating of Paul." Seeing that the rage of the multitude was directed against Paul, the Roman captain "took him, and commanded him to be bound with two chains; and demanded who he was, and what he had done." At once many voices were raised in loud and angry accusation; "and as he could not learn the facts because of the uproar, he ordered him to be brought into the barracks. . . . The mob of the people followed, crying, 'Away with him!' " RSV.

The apostle was calm and self-possessed. He knew that angels of heaven were about him. As he was about to be led into the barracks he said to the chief captain, "May I speak unto thee?" Lysias responded, "Art not thou that Egyptian, which . . . madest an uproar, and leddest out into the wilderness four thousand men that were murderers?''

In reply Paul said, ''I am . . . a Jew of Tarsus, a city in Cilicia, a citizen of no mean city: and, I beseech thee, suffer me to speak unto the people.''

The Unreasoning Malice of Paul's Enemies

The request was granted, and ''Paul stood on the stairs, and beckoned with the hand unto the people.'' His bearing commanded respect. ''And when there was made a great silence, he spake unto them in the Hebrew tongue, saying, Men, brethren, and fathers, hear ye my defense which I make now unto you.'' In the universal hush he continued:

''I am a Jew, born at Tarsus in Cilicia, but brought up in this city at the feet of Gamaliel, educated according to the strict manner of the law of our fathers, being zealous for God as you all are this day.'' RSV. The facts he referred to were well known. He then spoke of his former zeal in persecuting the disciples of Christ; and he narrated the circumstances of his conversion, telling how his proud heart had been led to bow to the crucified Nazarene. The relation of his experience seemed to soften and subdue the hearts of his opponents.

He then showed that he had desired to labor for his own nation, but in that very temple the voice of God had spoken to him, directing his course ''far hence unto the Gentiles.''

The Rage of Exclusivism

The people had listened with close attention, but when Paul reached the point where he was appointed ambassador to the Gentiles, their fury broke forth anew. They were unwilling to permit the despised Gentiles to share the privileges hitherto regarded as exclusively their own. They cried, ''Away with such a fellow from the earth: for it is not fit that he should live.''

''As they cried out, . . . the chief captain commanded him to be brought into the castle, and bade that he should be examined by scourging; that he might know whereof they cried so against him.''

"But when they had tied him up with the thongs, Paul said to the centurion who was standing by, 'Is it lawful for you to scourge a man who is a Roman citizen, and uncondemned?' When the centurion heard that, he went to the tribune and said to him, 'What are you about to do? For this man is a Roman citizen.' So the tribune came and said to him, 'Tell me, are you a Roman citizen?' And he said, 'Yes.' The tribune answered, 'I bought this citizenship for a large sum.' Paul said, 'But I was born a citizen.' So those who were about to examine him withdrew from him instantly; and the tribune also was afraid, for he realized that Paul was a Roman citizen and that he had bound him.

"But on the morrow, desiring to know the real reason why the Jews accused him, he unbound him, and commanded the chief priests and all the council to meet, and he brought Paul down and set him before them.'' Acts 22:25-30, RSV.

Paul Before the Court of Law

As he stood before the Jewish rulers, Paul's countenance revealed the peace of Christ. "Brethren, I have lived in all good conscience before God until this day. And the high priest Ananias commanded them that stood by him to smite him on the mouth.'' At this inhuman command, Paul exclaimed, "God shall smite thee, thou whited wall: for sittest thou to judge me after the law, and commandest me to be smitten contrary to the law?" "They that stood by said, Revilest thou God's high priest?" With his usual courtesy Paul answered, "I wist not, brethren, that he was the high priest: for it is written, Thou shalt not speak evil of the ruler of thy people.

"But when Paul perceived that the one part were Sadducees, and the other Pharisees, he cried out in the council, Men and brethren, I am a Pharisee, the son of a Pharisee: of the hope and resurrection of the dead I am called in question.''

The two parties began to dispute between themselves, and thus the strength of their opposition against Paul was broken. "The scribes that were of the Pharisees' party arose, and strove, saying, We find no evil in this man: but if a spirit or an angel hath spoken to him, let us not fight against God.''

The Sadducees were eagerly striving to gain possession of the apostle, that they might put him to death; and the Pharisees were as eager to protect him. "The Chief Captain, fearing lest Paul should have been pulled in pieces of them, commanded the soldiers to go down, and to take him by force from among them, and to bring him into the castle.''

Later, Paul began to fear that his course might not have been pleasing to God. Had he made a mistake in visiting Jerusalem? Had his great desire to be in union with His brethren led to this disastrous result?

How would those heathen officers look upon the Jews as God's professed people—assuming sacred office, yet giving themselves up to blind anger, seeking to destroy even their brethren who dared to differ with them in religious faith, and turning their solemn council into a scene of wild confusion? The name of God had suffered reproach in the eyes of the heathen.

And now he knew that his enemies would resort to any means to put him to death. Could it be that his work for the churches was ended and that ravening wolves were to enter in now? He thought of the perils of the scattered churches, exposed to the persecutions of such men as he had encountered in the Sanhedrin council. In distress he wept and prayed.

In this dark hour the Lord revealed Himself to His faithful witness in response to earnest prayers for guidance. "The night following the Lord stood by him, and said, Be of good cheer, Paul: for as thou hast testified of Me in Jerusalem, so must thou bear witness also at Rome.''

While the Lord encouraged His servant, Paul's enemies were plotting his destruction. Conspirators "came to the chief priests and elders, and said, We have bound ourselves under a great curse, that we will eat nothing until we have slain Paul. Now therefore ye with the council signify to the chief captain that he bring him down unto you tomorrow, as though ye would inquire something more perfectly concerning him: and we, or ever he come near, are ready to kill him."

The priests and rulers eagerly agreed. Paul had spoken the truth when he compared Ananias to a "whited wall."

Paul's Nephew Foils the Plot

But God interposed to save His servant. Paul's sister's son, hearing of the ambush of the assassins, "entered into the castle, and told Paul. Then Paul called one of the centurions unto him, and said, Bring this young man unto the chief captain: for he hath a certain thing to tell him. So he took him, and brought him to the chief captain, and said, Paul the prisoner called me unto him, and prayed me to bring this young man unto thee, who hath something to say unto thee."

Claudius Lysias received the youth kindly. "What is it that you have to tell me?" The youth replied: "The Jews have agreed to ask you to bring Paul down to the council tomorrow, as though they were going to inquire somewhat more closely about him. But do not yield to them; for more than forty of their men lie in ambush for him, having bound themselves by an oath neither to eat nor drink till they have killed him; and now they are ready, waiting for the promise from you.

"So the tribune dismissed the young man, charging him, 'Tell no one that you have informed me of this.' "

Lysias "called two of the centurions and said, 'At the third hour of the night get ready two hundred soldiers with seventy horsemen and two hundred spearmen to go as far as Caesarea. Also provide mounts for

Paul to ride and bring him safely to Felix the governor.' '' Acts 23:20-24, RSV.

No time was to be lost. "So the soldiers, according to their instructions, took Paul and brought him by night to Antipatris." RSV. The horsemen went on with the prisoner to Caesarea. The officer in charge delivered his prisoner to Felix, also presenting a letter:

"Claudius Lysias unto the most excellent governor Felix sendeth greeting. This man was taken of the Jews, and should have been killed of them: then came I with an army, and rescued him, having understood that he was a Roman. . . . And when it was told me how that the Jews laid wait for the man, I sent straightway to thee, and gave commandment to his accusers also to say before thee what they had against him."

Adding Crime to Crime

In their rage against Paul, the Jews had added another crime to the dark catalogue which marked the history of that people and had rendered their doom more certain. Christ in the synagogue at Nazareth reminded His hearers that in time past God had turned away from His chosen people because of their unbelief and rebellion, and had manifested Himself to those in heathen lands who had not rejected the light of heaven. With backsliding Israel there was no safety for the faithful messenger of God. The Jewish leaders were leading the people farther and farther from obedience to God—where He could not be their defense in the day of trouble.

The Saviour's words of reproof to the men of Nazareth applied in the case of Paul to his own brethren in the faith. Had the leaders in the church fully surrendered their bitterness toward the apostle and accepted him as one specially called of God to bear the gospel to the Gentiles, the Lord would have spared him to them. God had not ordained that Paul's labors should so soon end.

The same spirit is still depriving the church of many

a blessing. How often would the Lord have prolonged the work of some faithful minister, had his labors been appreciated. But if church members misrepresent and misinterpret the words and acts of the servant of Christ; if they allow themselves to stand in his way, the Lord sometimes removes from them the blessing which He gave.

Those whom God has chosen to accomplish a great and good work may be ready to sacrifice even life itself for the cause of Christ, yet the great deceiver will suggest to their brethren doubts concerning them which undermine confidence in their integrity and cripple their usefulness. Too often he succeeds in bringing upon them, through their own brethren, such sorrow of heart that God graciously interposes to give His persecuted servants rest. After the voice of warning and encouragement is silent, then the obdurate may see and prize the blessings they have cast from them. Their death may accomplish that which their life has failed to do.

39 / Paul's Trial at Caesarea

Five days after Paul's arrival at Caesarea, his accusers came from Jerusalem, accompanied by Tertullus, their counsel. Paul was brought before the assembly, and Tertullus "began to accuse him." The wily orator began his speech by flattering Felix: "Since through you we enjoy much peace, and since by your provision, most excellent Felix, reforms are introduced on behalf of this nation, in every way and everywhere we accept this with all gratitude."

Tertullus here desended to barefaced falsehood, for the character of Felix was contemptible. Those who heard Tertullus knew his words were untrue.

Tertullus charged Paul with high treason against the government: "We have found this man a pestilent fellow, an agitator among the Jews throughout the world, and a ringleader of the sect of the Nazarenes. He even tried to profane the temple." All the charges were vehemently supported by the Jews present, who made no effort to conceal their hatred of the prisoner.

Felix had sufficient penetration to know from what motive Paul's accusers had flattered him. He saw also that they had failed to substantiate their charges. Turning to Paul, he beckoned to him to answer for himself.

Paul wasted no words in compliments. Referring to the charges brought against him, he plainly showed that not one of them was true. He had caused no disturbance in any part of Jerusalem, nor had he profaned

This chapter is based on Acts 24, RSV.

the sanctuary. While confessing that he worshiped God "according to the Way," he asserted that He had always believed "everything laid down by the law or written in the prophets," and he held the faith of the resurrection of the dead. The ruling purpose of his life was to "always take pains to have a clear conscience toward God and toward men."

In a straightforward manner he stated the object of his visit to Jerusalem and the circumstances of his arrest and trial: "I came to bring to my nation alms and offerings. As I was doing this, they found me purified in the temple, without any crowd or tumult."

The apostle's words carried with them a weight of conviction. Claudius Lysias in his letter to Felix had borne a similar testimony in regard to Paul's conduct. Paul's plain statement of the facts enabled Felix to understand the motives by which the Jews were governed in attempting to convict the apostle of sedition and treason. The governor would not gratify them by unjustly condemning a Roman citizen; neither would he give him up to them. Yet Felix knew no higher motive than self-interest. Fear of offending the Jews held him back from doing full justice to a man whom he knew to be innocent. He therefore decided to suspend the trial until Lysias should be present.

The apostle remained a prisoner, but Felix commanded that "he should . . . have some liberty, and that none of his friends should be prevented from attending to his needs."

Felix and Drusilla Hear the Wonderful Good News

Not long after this, Felix and his wife Drusilla sent for Paul that they might hear him "speak upon faith in Christ Jesus." They were eager to listen to these new truths—truths which, if rejected, would witness against them in the day of God.

Paul knew that he stood in the presence of one who had power to put him to death or to set him free; yet he did not address Felix and Drusilla with flattery. Forgetting all selfish considerations, he sought to arouse them to a sense of their peril. The apostle realized that one day they would stand either among the holy around the great white throne, or with those to whom Christ would say, "Depart from Me, ye that work iniquity." Matthew 7:23.

Few had ever before dared even to intimate to Felix that his character and conduct were not faultless. But Paul had no fear of man. He was thus led to speak of those virtues essential to Christian character, of which the haughty pair before him were so destitute.

He held up before Felix and Drusilla God's righteousness, justice, and the nature of His law. He showed that it is man's duty to live a life of sobriety and temperance, in conformity to God's law, preserving the physical and mental powers in a healthy condition. There would surely come a day of judgment when it would be revealed that wealth, position, or titles are powerless to deliver man from the results of sin. This life is man's time of preparation for the future life. Should he neglect present opportunities he would suffer eternal loss; no new probation would be given.

Paul especially showed how God's law extends to the deep secrets of man's moral nature. The law searches his thoughts, motives, and purposes. Dark passions hidden from the sight of men, jealousy, hatred, lust, and ambition, evil deeds meditated upon yet never executed for want of opportunity—all these God's law condemns.

Paul pointed to the one great Sacrifice for sin, Christ as the only source of life and hope for fallen man. As holy men of old saw the dying agonies of the sacrificial victims, they looked across the gulf of ages to the Lamb of God that was to take away the sin of the world.

God justly claims the love and obedience of His creatures. But many forget their Maker and return enmity for love. God cannot lower the requirements of His law; neither can man, in his own power, meet the demands of the law. Only by faith in Christ can the sinner be cleansed from guilt and be enabled to render obedience to the law of his Maker.

Thus Paul the prisoner urged the claims of the divine law and presented Jesus as the Son of God, the world's Redeemer.

Felix and His Wife Reject Their Golden Opportunity

The Jewish princess understood the law she had so shamelessly transgressed, but her prejudice against the Man of Calvary steeled her heart against the word of life. But Felix, deeply agitated, felt that Paul's words were true. With terrible distinctness there came up before him the secrets of his life. He saw himself licentious, cruel, rapacious. Never before had truth been thus brought home to his heart. The thought that his career of crime was open before the eye of God and that he must be judged according to his deeds caused him to tremble.

But instead of permitting his convictions to lead him to repentance, he sought to dismiss these unwelcome reflections. "Go away for the present; when I have an opportunity I will summon you."

How wide the contrast between the course of Felix and that of the jailer of Philippi! The servants of the Lord were brought in bonds to the jailer as was Paul to Felix. The evidence they gave of being sustained by a divine power, and their spirit of forgiveness sent conviction to the jailer's heart. With trembling he confessed his sins and found pardon. Felix trembled, but did not repent. The jailer welcomed the Spirit of God; Felix bade the divine Messenger depart. One chose to become an heir of heaven; the other cast his lot with the workers of iniquity. For two years Paul remained a prisoner. Felix visited him several times and intimated that by the payment of a large sum of money Paul might secure his release. The apostle, however, was too noble to free himself by a bribe. He would not stoop to commit a wrong in order to gain freedom. He felt that he was in the hands of God, and he would not interfere with the divine purposes respecting himself.

Felix was finally summoned to Rome because of gross wrongs committed against the Jews. Before leaving Caesarea he thought to "do the Jews a favor" by allowing Paul to remain in prison. But Felix was not successful in his attempt to regain the confidence of the Jews. He was removed from office in disgrace, and Porcius Festus was appointed to succeed him.

A ray of light from heaven had shone on Felix when Paul reasoned with him "about justice and self-control and future judgment." But he said to the messenger of God, "Go away for the present; when I have an opportunity I will summon you."

Never was he to receive another call from God.

40/ Paul Appeals to Caesar

"When Festus had come into his province, after three days he went up to Jerusalem from Caesarea. And the chief priests and the principal men of the Jews informed him against Paul; and they urged him, asking as a favor to have the man sent to Jerusalem." In making this request they purposed to waylay Paul along the road and murder him.

But Festus had a high sense of responsibility, and courteously declined. He declared that it is "not the custom of the Romans to give up any one before the accused met the accusers face to face, and had opportunity to make his defense." Acts 25:16.

The Jews had not forgotten their former defeat at Caesarea. Again they urged that Paul be brought to Jerusalem for trial, but Festus held firmly to his purpose of giving Paul a fair trial at Caesarea. God controlled the decision of Festus, that the life of the apostle might be lengthened.

The Jewish leaders at once prepared to witness against Paul at the court of the procurator. Festus "took his seat on the tribunal and ordered Paul to be brought. . . . The Jews who had gone down from Jerusalem stood about him, bringing against him many serious charges which they could not prove." As the trial proceeded, the accused with calmness and candor clearly showed the falsity of their statements.

Festus discerned that there was nothing in the

This chapter is based on Acts 25:1-16, RSV.

charges against Paul that would render him subject to death or even imprisonment. Yet he saw clearly the storm of rage that would be created if Paul were not condemned or delivered into their hands. And so, "wishing to do the Jews a favor," Festus asked Paul if he was willing to go to Jerusalem under his protection, to be tried by the Sanhedrin.

The apostle knew that he would be safer among the heathen than with those who had rejected light from heaven and hardened their hearts against the gospel. He therefore decided to exercise his privilege, as a Roman citizen, of appealing to Caesar: "I am standing before Caesar's tribunal, where I ought to be tried; to the Jews I have done no wrong, as you know very well. If then I am a wrongdoer, and have committed anything for which I deserve to die, I do not seek to escape death; but if there is nothing in their charges against me, no one can give me up to them. I appeal to Caesar."

Festus knew nothing of the conspiracies of the Jews to murder Paul and was surprised at this appeal to Caesar. However, the words of the apostle put a stop to the proceedings of the court. "Festus . . . answered, 'You have appealed to Caesar; to Caesar you shall go.' "

Those Who Serve God Need Firm Courage

Once more, because of hatred, a servant of God was driven for protection to the heathen. This same hatred forced Elijah to flee to the widow of Sarepta; and it forced the heralds of the gospel to turn from the Jews to the Gentiles. And this hatred the people of God living in this age have yet to meet. Men claiming to be Christ's representatives will take a course similar to that of the priests and rulers in their treatment of Christ and the apostles. Faithful servants of God will encounter the same hardness of heart, the same cruel determination, the same unyielding hatred.

Those who are true to God will be persecuted, their

motives impugned, their best efforts misinterpreted, and their names cast out as evil. Satan will work with all his deceptive power to make evil appear good, and good evil. Fiercely will he strive to stir up against God's people the rage of those who, while claiming to be righteous, trample on the law of God. It will require the firmest trust, the most heroic purpose, to hold fast the faith once delivered to the saints.

Prepared or unprepared, God's people must all meet the soon-coming crisis; and those only who have brought their lives into conformity to the divine standard will stand firm. When secular rulers unite with ministers of religion to dictate in matters of conscience, then it will be seen who really fear and serve God. And while the enemies of truth watch the Lord's servants for evil, God will watch over them for good. He will be to them as the shadow of a great rock in a weary land.

41 / The King Who Refused the Cross

Festus could not do otherwise than send Paul to Rome. But some time passed before a suitable ship could be found. This gave Paul opportunity to present the reasons of his faith before the principal men of Caesarea and also before King Agrippa II.

"Now when some days had passed, Agrippa the king and Bernice arrived at Caesarea to welcome Festus." Festus outlined the circumstances that led to the prisoner's appeal to Caesar, telling of Paul's recent trial before him, and saying that the Jews had brought against Paul "certain points . . . about their own superstition and about one Jesus, who was dead, but whom Paul asserted to be alive."

Agrippa became interested, and said, "I should like to hear the man myself." A meeting was arranged for the following day, and "By command of Festus Paul was brought in."

Festus had sought to make this an occasion of imposing display. The rich robes of the procurator and his guests, the swords of the soldiers, and the gleaming armor of their commanders lent brilliance to the scene.

And now Paul, manacled, stood before the company. What a contrast! Agrippa and Bernice possessed power and position, but they were destitute of the character that God esteems. They were transgressors of His law, corrupt in heart and life.

The aged prisoner, chained to his guard, had in his

This chapter is based on Acts 25:13-27; 26, RSV.

appearance nothing that would lead the world to pay him homage. Yet in this man, apparently without friends, wealth, or position, all heaven was interested. Angels were his attendants. Had the glory of only one of those shining messengers flashed forth, the king and courtiers would have been stricken to the earth, as were the Roman guards at the sepulcher of Christ.

Festus presented Paul to the assembly with the words: "King Agrippa and all who are present with us, you see this man about whom the whole Jewish people petitioned me, both at Jerusalem and here, shouting that he ought not to live any longer. But I found that he had done nothing deserving death; and as he himself appealed to the emperor, I decided to send him. But I have nothing definite to write to my lord about him. . . . It seems to me unreasonable, in sending a prisoner, not to indicate the charges against him."

Paul Not Daunted by Earthly Pomp

Agrippa now gave Paul liberty to speak. The apostle was not disconcerted by the brilliant display or the high rank of his audience. Earthly pomp could not daunt his courage or rob him of his self-control.

"I think myself fortunate that it is before you, King Agrippa, I am to make my defense today against all the accusations of the Jews, because you are especially familiar with all customs and controversies of the Jews." Paul related the story of his conversion. He described the heavenly vision—a revelation of divine glory, in the midst of which sat enthroned He whom he had despised and hated, whose followers he was seeking to destroy. From that hour Paul had been a fervent believer in Jesus.

With power Paul outlined before Agrippa the leading events of the life of Christ. He testified that the Messiah had already appeared in the person of Jesus of Nazareth. The Old Testament Scriptures had declared that the Messiah was to appear as a man among men; in Jesus had been fulfilled every specification outlined by

Moses and the prophets. The Son of God had endured the cross and had ascended to heaven triumphant over death.

Once it had seemed incredible to him that Christ should rise from the dead, but how could he disbelieve what he himself had seen and heard? At the gate of Damascus he had looked upon the crucified and risen Christ. He had seen and talked with Him. The Voice had bidden him proclaim the gospel of a risen Saviour, and how could he disobey? Throughout Judea and in regions afar off he had borne witness of Jesus the Crucified, showing all classes "that they should repent and turn to God and perform deeds worthy of their repentance.

"For this reason the Jews seized me in the temple and tried to kill me. To this day I have had the help that comes from God, and so I stand here testifying both to small and great, saying nothing but what the prophets and Moses said would come to pass."

Worldly "Great" People Reject the Cross

The whole company listened spellbound. But the apostle was interrupted by Festus, who cried out, "Paul, you are mad; your great learning is turning you mad."

The apostle replied, "I am not mad, most excellent Festus, but I am speaking the sober truth. For the king knows about these things." Then, turning to Agrippa, he addressed him directly: "King Agrippa, do you believe the prophets? I know that you believe."

Agrippa for the moment lost sight of his surroundings and dignity. Seeing only the humble prisoner standing before him as God's ambassador, he answered involuntarily, "Almost thou persuadest me to be a Christian." KJV.

The apostle answered, "I would to God that not only you but also all who hear me this day might become such as I am," adding, as he raised his fettered hands, "except for these chains."

Festus, Agrippa, and Bernice, all guilty of grievous crimes, had that day heard the offer of salvation through the name of Christ. One, at least, had been almost persuaded to accept. But Agrippa refused the cross of a crucified Redeemer.

The king's curiosity was satisfied, and he signified that the interview was at an end. Though Agrippa was a Jew, he did not share the blind prejudice of the Pharisees. "This man," he said to Festus, "could have been set free if he had not appealed to Caesar."

But the case was now beyond the jurisdiction of either Festus or Agrippa.

42 / Paul Suffers Shipwreck in a Storm

At last Paul was on his way to Rome. "They delivered Paul and some other prisoners to a centurion of the Augustan Cohort, named Julius. And," Luke writes, "embarking in a ship of Adramyttium, . . . we put to sea."

In the first century traveling by sea was perilous. Mariners directed their course largely by the sun and stars; and when there were indications of storm, the owners of vessels were fearful of the open sea. During a portion of the year, safe navigation was almost impossible.

The apostle was now to endure the trying experiences of a prisoner in chains during the long voyage to Italy. From choice, Aristarchus shared Paul's bondage, that he might minister to him in his afflictions. See Colossians 4:10.

The voyage began prosperously. The following day they cast anchor in the harbor of Sidon. Here Julius "treated Paul kindly" and "gave him leave to go to his [Christian] friends and be cared for." This was appreciated by the apostle, who was in feeble health.

Leaving Sidon, the ship encountered contrary winds. At Myra the centurion found a large Alexandrian ship bound for Italy, and to this he transferred his prisoners. But the winds were still contrary. Luke writes: "We sailed slowly for a number of days. . . . Coasting along with difficulty, we came to a place called Fair Havens."

This chapter is based on Acts 27; 28:1-10, RSV.

Here they remained for some time, waiting for favoring winds. Winter was approaching rapidly, and "the voyage was already dangerous." The question now to be decided was whether to remain in Fair Havens or attempt to reach a more favorable place in which to winter.

Paul's Inspired Advice Rejected

This question was finally referred by the centurion to Paul, who had won the respect of sailors and soldiers. The apostle unhesitatingly advised remaining where they were. "I percieve that the voyage will be with injury and much loss, not only of the cargo and the ship, but also of our lives." But "the owner of the ship" and the majority of passengers and crew were unwilling to accept this counsel. They "advised to put to sea from there, on the chance that somehow they could reach Phoenix, . . . and winter there."

The centurion decided to follow the judgment of the majority. "When the south wind blew gently, . . . they weighed anchor and sailed along Crete, close inshore. But soon a tempestuous wind . . . struck down from the land." "The ship was caught and could not face the wind."

Driven by the tempest, the vessel neared the small island of Clauda, and the sailors made ready for the worst. The lifeboat, their only means of escape, was in tow and liable to be dashed in pieces any moment. Their first work was to hoist this boat on board. All possible precautions were taken to prepare the ship to withstand the tempest. The scant protection afforded by the little island did not avail long, and soon they were again exposed to the full violence of the storm.

All night the tempest raged. The vessel leaked. Night came again, but the wind did not abate. The storm-beaten ship, with shattered mast and rent sails, was tossed hither and thither. It seemed that the groaning timbers must give way as the vessel quivered under the tempest's shock. The leak increased rapidly, and passengers and crew worked continually at the pumps. Writes Luke, "When neither sun nor stars appeared for many a day, and no small tempest lay on us, all hope of our being saved was at last abandoned."

For fourteen days they drifted. The apostle, though himself suffering physically, had words of hope for the darkest hour, a helping hand in every emergency. He grasped by faith the arm of Infinite Power. He knew that God would preserve him to witness at Rome for the truth of Christ, but his heart yearned for the poor souls around him, sinful and unprepared to die. He earnestly pleaded with God to spare their lives, and his prayer was granted.

Disaster to the Ship

Taking advantage of a lull in the tempest, Paul stood on deck and said: "I now bid you take heart; for there will be no loss of life among you, but only of the ship. For this very night there stood by me an angel of the God to whom I belong and whom I worship, and he said, 'Do not be afraid, Paul; you must stand before Caesar; and lo, God has granted you all those who sail with you.' So take heart, men, for I have faith in God that it will be exactly as I have been told. But we shall have to run on some island."

At these words, passengers and crew roused from their apathy. Every effort within their power must be put forth to avert destruction.

On the fourteenth night of tossing on the heaving billows, about midnight the sailors heard the sound of breakers. "And fearing," Luke writes, "that we might run on the rocks, they let out four anchors from the stern, and prayed for day to come."

At break of day the outlines of the stormy coast were dimly visible, but so gloomy was the outlook that the heathen sailors, losing all courage, "were seeking to escape from the ship." Feigning to cast "out anchors from the bow," they had let down the lifeboat, when Paul, perceiving their base design, said to the centurion and the soldiers, "Unless these men stay in the ship, you cannot be saved." The soldiers immediately "cut away the ropes of the boat, and let it go" into the sea.

The most critical hour was still before them. The apostle again spoke words of encouragement and entreated both sailors and passengers to eat something. "Today is the fourteenth day that you have continued in suspense and without food, having taken nothing. Therefore I urge you to take some food; it will give you strength, since not a hair is to perish from the head of any of you."

"When he had said this, he took bread, and giving thanks to God in the presence of all he broke it and began to eat." Then that worn and discouraged company of 275 souls, who but for Paul would have become desperate, joined the apostle in partaking of food. "And when they had eaten enough, they lightened the ship, throwing out the wheat into the sea."

Daylight had now come. "They noticed a bay with a beach, on which they planned if possible to bring the ship ashore. So they cast off the anchors and left them in the sea, at the same time loosening the ropes that tied the rudders; then hoisting the foresail to the wind they made for the beach. But striking a shoal they ran the vessel aground; the bow stuck and remained immovable, and the stern was broken up by the surf."

The Prisoners About to Be Killed

The prisoners were now threatened by a fate more terrible than shipwreck. The soldiers saw that to reach land they would have all they could do to save themselves. Yet if any prisoners were missing, the lives of those responsible for them would be forfeited. Hence the soldiers desired to put all the prisoners to death. Roman law sanctioned this cruel policy. But Julius knew that Paul had been instrumental in saving the lives of all on board, and, convinced that the Lord was with him, he feared to do him harm. He therefore "or-

dered those who could swim to throw themselves over-
board first and make for the land, and the rest on
planks or on pieces of the ship. And so it was that all
escaped to land." When the roll was called, not one
was missing.

The barbarous people of Melita "kindled a fire,"
Luke writes, "and welcomed us all, because it had begun to rain and was cold." Having gathered "a bundle
of sticks," Paul "put them on the fire," when a viper
came forth "because of the heat and fastened on his
hand." Seeing by his chain that Paul was a prisoner,
the bystanders said, "No doubt this man is a murderer.
Though he has escaped from the sea, justice has not
allowed him to live. . . . But when they had waited a
long time and saw no misfortune come to him, they
changed their minds and said that he was a god."

During the three months that they remained at Melita, Paul improved many opportunities to preach the
gospel. The Lord wrought through him. For his sake
the entire shipwrecked company were treated with
kindness. And on leaving Melita they were provided
with everything needful for their voyage. Luke says:

"Publius . . . entertained us hospitably for three
days. It happened that the father of Publius lay sick
with fever and dysentery; and Paul visited him and
prayed, and putting his hands on him healed him. And
when this had taken place, the rest of the people on the
island who had diseases also came and were cured.
They presented many gifts to us; and when we sailed,
they put on board whatever we needed."

43 / Paul in Rome: Big-City Evangelist in Chains

With the opening of navigation, the centurion and his prisoners set out on their journey to Rome. An Alexandrian ship had wintered at Melita on her way westward, and in this the travelers embarked. The voyage safely accomplished, the ship cast anchor in the beautiful harbor of Puteoli in Italy, where a few Christians entreated the apostle to remain with them for seven days, a privilege kindly granted by the centurion.

Since receiving Paul's letter to the Romans, the Christians of Italy had eagerly looked forward to a visit from the apostle. His sufferings as a prisoner only endeared him to them the more. The seaport being only 140 miles from Rome, some of the Christians started to meet and welcome him.

On the eighth day after landing, the centurion and his prisoners set out for Rome. Julius willingly granted the apostle every favor in his power to bestow, but he could not change his condition as a prisoner. With a heavy heart Paul went forward to the world's metropolis. How was he, fettered and stigmatized, to proclaim the gospel?

At last the travelers reached Appii Forum, 40 miles from Rome. The gray-haired old man, chained with a group of hardened-looking criminals, received many a glance of scorn and was made the subject of rude jests.

Suddenly a cry of joy was heard, and a man sprang from the passing throng and fell on the prisoner's neck,

This chapter is based on Acts 28:11-31 and the Letter to Philemon, RSV.

embracing him with tears and rejoicing, as a son would welcome a long-absent father. Again and again was the scene repeated. Many discerned in the chained captive the one who at Corinth, at Philippi, at Ephesus, had spoken to them the words of life.

As the warmhearted disciples eagerly flocked around their father in the gospel, the whole company was brought to a standstill. The soldiers, impatient of delay, had not the heart to interrupt this happy meeting; for they too had learned to esteem their prisoner. In that pain-stricken face the disciples saw reflected the image of Christ. They assured Paul that they had not ceased to love him. In the ardor of their love they would bear him on their shoulders the whole way to the city, could they but have the privilege.

When Paul saw his brethren, "he thanked God and took courage." The weeping, sympathizing believers were not ashamed of his bonds. The cloud of sadness that had rested on his spirit was swept away. Bonds and afflictions awaited him, but he knew that it had been his to deliver souls from a bondage infinitely more terrible, and he rejoiced in his sufferings for Christ's sake.

Paul, in Chains, Appeals to the Jews

At Rome Julius delivered up his prisoners to the captain of the emperor's guard. The good account which he gave of Paul, with the letter from Festus, caused the apostle to be favorably regarded by the chief captain, and instead of being thrown into prison, he was permitted to live in his own hired house. Although still chained to a soldier, he was at liberty to receive his friends and to labor for the cause of Christ.

Many of the Jews previously banished from Rome had been allowed to return. To these, first of all, Paul determined to present the facts concerning himself and his work, before his enemies should have opportunity to embitter them against him. Three days after his arrival he called together their leading men, and said:

"I had done nothing against the people or the customs of our fathers, yet I was delivered prisoner from Jerusalem into the hands of the Romans. When they had examined me, they wished to set me at liberty, because there was no reason for the death penalty in my case. But when the Jews objected, I was compelled to appeal to Caesar. . . . It is because of the hope of Israel that I am bound with this chain.''

He said nothing of the repeated plots to assassinate him. He was not seeking to win sympathy, but to defend the truth and to maintain the honor of the gospel.

His hearers stated that none of the Jews who had come to Rome had accused him of any crime. They also expressed a strong desire to hear for themselves the reasons of his faith in Christ. Paul bade them set a day, and at the time appointed, many came together. "He expounded the matter to them from morning till evening, testifying to the kingdom of God and trying to convince them about Jesus both from the law of Moses and from the prophets." He related his own experience and presented arguments from the Old Testament Scriptures.

Religion Is Practical and Experiential

The apostle showed that religion is a practical, a personal experience of God's renewing power on the soul. Moses had pointed Israel to Christ as that Prophet whom they were to hear; all the prophets had testified of Him as the guiltless One who was to bear the sins of the guilty. He showed that while they maintained the ritual service with great exactness, they were rejecting Him who was the antitype of all that system.

Paul declared that he had rejected Jesus of Nazareth as an impostor because He did not fulfill his cherished conception of the Messiah to come. But now his views of Christ were more spiritual, for he had been converted. To apprehend Christ by faith, to have a spiritual knowledge of Him was more to be desired than a personal acquaintance with Him as He appeared on the earth, a mere earthly and human companion.

As Paul spoke, those who were honestly seeking for truth were convinced. Upon some minds his words made an impression that was never effaced. But others stubbornly refused to accept the testimony of the Scriptures. They could not refute Paul's arguments, but they refused to accept his conclusions.

As a Prisoner, Paul Has Stronger Influence

Many months passed by before the Jews of Jerusalem appeared to present their accusations against the prisoner. Now that Paul was to be tried before the highest tribunal of the Roman Empire, they had no desire to risk another defeat. Delay would afford them time to seek by intrigue to influence the emperor in their favor; so they waited a while before preferring their charges against the apostle.

This delay resulted in the furtherance of the gospel. Paul was permitted to dwell in a commodious house, where he could present the truth daily to those who came to hear. Thus for two years he continued his labors, "preaching the kingdom of God and teaching about the Lord Jesus Christ quite openly and unhindered."

During this time the churches he had established in many lands were not forgotten. The apostle sought to meet their needs by letters of practical instruction, and from Rome he sent consecrated workers to labor in fields that he himself had not visited. The apostle, kept informed by constant communication with them, was able to exercise a wise supervision over all.

Thus Paul exerted a wider and more lasting influence than if he had been free to travel among the churches as in former years. As a "prisoner for Jesus Christ," he had a firmer hold on the affections of his brethren, and his words commanded greater attention and respect than when he was personally with them. Heretofore the believers had largely excused themselves from responsibility and burden bearing because they lacked his wisdom, tact, and indomitable energy; but now they prized his warnings and instructions as they had not prized his personal work. And as they learned of his courage and faith during his long imprisonment they were stimulated to greater fidelity in the cause of Christ.

At Rome, Luke, "the beloved physician," who had attended him on the journey to Jerusalem, through the two years' imprisonment at Caesarea, and on his perilous voyage to Rome, was with him still. Timothy also ministered to his comfort. Tychicus stood nobly by the apostle. Demas and Mark were with him. Aristarchus and Epaphras were his "fellow prisoners." See Colossians 4:7-14.

Mark's Christian experience had deepened as he had studied more closely the life and death of Christ. Now, sharing the lot of Paul the prisoner, he understood better than ever before that it is infinite gain to win Christ, infinite loss to win the world and lose the soul. In the face of severe trial, Mark continued steadfast, a wise and beloved helper of the apostle.

Paul wrote, "Demas hath forsaken me, having loved this present world." 2 Timothy 4:10. For worldly gain, Demas bartered every high and noble consideration. Mark, choosing to suffer for Christ's sake, possessed eternal riches.

The Beautiful Story of Onesimus the Slave

Among those who gave their hearts to God in Rome was Onesimus, a pagan slave who had wronged his master, Philemon, a Christian believer in Colosse, and had escaped to Rome. In the kindness of his heart, Paul sought to relieve the distress of the wretched fugitive and then endeavored to shed the light of truth into his darkened mind. Onesimus listened, confessed his sins, and was converted to Christ.

He endeared himself to Paul by his tender care for the apostle's comfort and his zeal in promoting the gospel. Paul saw in him a useful helper in missionary labor and counseled him to return without delay to Philemon, beg his forgiveness, and plan for the future. Being about to dispatch Tychicus with letters to various churches in Asia Minor, he sent Onesimus with him to the master he had wronged. It was a severe test, but this servant had been truly converted, and he did not turn aside from duty.

Paul made Onesimus the bearer of a letter in which the apostle pleaded the cause of the repentant slave. He reminded Philemon that everything he possessed was due to the grace of Christ; this alone made him different from the perverse and the sinful. The same grace could make the debased criminal a child of God and a useful laborer in the gospel.

The apostle asked Philemon to receive the repentant slave as his own child, "no longer as a slave but more than a slave, as a beloved brother." He expressed his desire to return Onesimus as one who could minister to him in his bonds as Philemon himself would have done, though he did not desire his services unless Philemon should of his own accord set the slave free.

The apostle knew the severity which masters exercised toward their slaves. He knew also that Philemon was incensed because of the conduct of his servant. He tried to write in a way that would arouse his tenderest feelings as a Christian. Any punishment inflicted on this new convert would be regarded by Paul as inflicted on himself.

Paul volunteered to assume the debt of Onesimus in order that the guilty one might be spared the disgrace of punishment. "If you consider me your partner," he wrote to Philemon, "receive him as you would receive me. If he has wronged you at all, or owes you anything, charge that to my account. I, Paul, write this with my own hand, I will repay it."

How fitting an illustration of the love of Christ! The sinner who has robbed God of years of service has no means of canceling the debt. Jesus says, I will pay the debt. I will suffer in his stead.

Paul reminded Philemon how greatly he himself was indebted to the apostle. God had made Paul the instrument of his conversion. As he had by his liberalities refreshed the saints, so he would refresh the spirit of the apostle by granting this cause of rejoicing. "Confident of your obedience," he added, "I write to you, knowing that you will do even more than I say."

Paul's letter to Philemon shows the influence of the gospel upon the relation between master and servant. Slaveholding was an established institution throughout the Roman Empire, and masters and slaves were found in most churches for which Paul labored. In the cities where slaves often greatly outnumbered the free population, laws of terrible severity were regarded as necessary to keep slaves in subjection. A wealthy Roman often owned hundreds. With full control over the souls and bodies of these helpless beings, he could inflict on them any suffering he chose. If one in retaliation or self-defense ventured to raise a hand against his owner, the whole family of the offender might be inhumanely sacrificed.

Some masters were more humane than others, but the vast majority, given up to lust, passion, and appetite, made their slaves the wretched victims of tyranny. The whole system was hopelessly degrading.

It was not the apostle's work suddenly to overturn the established order of society. To attempt this would be to prevent the success of the gospel. But he taught principles which struck at the foundation of slavery and would surely undermine the whole system. "Where the Spirit of the Lord is, there is liberty." 2 Corinthians 3:17. When converted, the slave became a member of the body of Christ, to be loved and treated as a brother, a fellow heir with his master to the blessings of God. On the other hand, servants were to perform their duties, "not with eyeservice, as menpleasers; but as the servants of Christ, doing the will of God from the heart." Ephesians 6:6.

Master and slave, king and subject, have been washed in the same blood, quickened by the same Spirit; and they are one in Christ.

44 / Paul Wins Converts in Caesar's Palace

The gospel has ever achieved its greatest success among the humbler classes. "Not many wise men after the flesh, not many mighty, not many noble, are called." 1 Corinthians 1:26. It could not be expected that Paul, a poor, friendless prisoner, would be able to gain the attention of the wealthy classes of Roman citizens. Vice held them willing captives. But many among the toilworn, want-stricken victims of their oppression, even poor slaves, gladly listened to Paul, and in Christ found hope and peace. The apostle's work began with the lowly, but its influence extended until it reached the palace of the emperor.

Rome was the metropolis of the world. The haughty Caesars were giving laws to nearly every nation on earth. King and courtier were either ignorant of the humble Nazarene or regarded Him with hatred and derision. And yet in less than two years the gospel found its way into the imperial halls. "The word of God is not bound," said Paul. 2 Timothy 2:9.

In former years the apostle had publicly proclaimed the faith of Christ with winning power before the sages of Greece, before kings and governors. Haughty rulers trembled as if already beholding the terrors of the day of God.

Now the apostle, confined to his own dwelling, was able to proclaim the truth to those only who sought him there. Yet at this very time, when its chief advocate was cut off from public labor, a great victory was won for the gospel. From the household of the king, members were added to the church.

244

In the Roman court, Nero seemed to have obliterated from his soul the last trace of the divine, and even of the human. His courtiers, in general, were of the same character—fierce, debased, and corrupt. Yet even in Nero's household, trophies of the cross were won. From the vile attendants of the viler king were gained converts who became sons of God—Christians not ashamed of their faith.

Paul's Afflictions Do Not Hinder the Gospel

By what means was a footing gained for Christianity where it seemed impossible? Paul ascribed to his imprisonment his success in winning converts from Nero's household. He assured the Philippians, "I want you to know, brethren, that what has happened to me has really served to advance the gospel." Philippians 1:12, RSV.

When the Christian churches first learned that Paul was to visit Rome, they looked forward to a triumph of the gospel in that city. Might not this champion of the faith succeed in winning souls even in the metropolis of the world? But Paul had gone to Rome as a prisoner. How great their disappointment! Human expectations had failed, but not the purpose of God. As a captive Paul broke from many souls the bonds that held them in the slavery of sin. His cheerfulness during his long, unjust imprisonment, his courage and faith, were a continual sermon. By his example, Christians were impelled to greater energy as advocates of the cause, and when his usefulness seemed cut off, then it was that he gathered sheaves for Christ in fields from which he seemed wholly excluded.

Before the close of two years' imprisonment, Paul was able to say, "My bonds in Christ are manifest in all the palace, and in all other places." Philippians 1:13. Among those who sent greetings to the Philippians he mentions "they that are of Caesar's household." Philippians 4:22.

The Christian who manifests patience under

bereavement and suffering, who meets even death with the calmness of an unwavering faith, may accomplish for the gospel more than he could have by a long life of faithful labor. Often the mysterious providence which our shortsighted vision would lament is designed by God to accomplish a work that otherwise would never be done.

Christ's true witnesses are never laid aside. In health and sickness, in life and death, God uses them still. When through Satan's malice the servants of Christ have been persecuted, when they have been cast into prison or dragged to the scaffold, it was that truth might gain a greater triumph. Souls hitherto in doubt were convinced of the faith of Christ and took their stand for Him. From the ashes of martyrs has sprung a harvest for God.

The apostle might have argued that it would be vain to call to repentance and faith in Christ the servants of Nero, surrounded by formidable hindrances. Even should they be convinced of the truth, how could they render obedience? But in faith Paul presented the gospel to these souls, and some decided to obey at any cost. They would accept the light, and trust God to help them let it shine forth to others.

After their conversion they remained in Caesar's household. They did not feel at liberty to abandon their post of duty because their surroundings were no longer congenial. The truth had found them there, and there they remained, testifying to the transforming power of the new faith.

No Circumstances an Excuse for Not Witnessing for Christ

Consider the disciples in Caesar's household—the depravity of the emperor, the profligacy of the court. Yet they maintained their fidelity. Because of obstacles that seem insurmountable, the Christian may seek to excuse himself from obeying the truth as it is in Jesus; but no excuse will bear investigation. If he could do this he would prove God unjust in that He had made for His children conditions of salvation with which they could not comply.

Difficulties will be powerless to hinder him who seeks first the kingdom of God and His righteousness. In the strength gained by prayer and study of the Word, he will seek virtue and forsake vice. Help and grace sufficient for every circumstance are promised by Him whose word is truth. In His care we may rest safely, saying, "I will trust in Thee." Psalm 56:3.

By His own example the Saviour has shown that the Christian may stand uncontaminated in any surroundings. Not in freedom from trial, but in the midst of it, is Christian character developed. Rebuffs and opposition lead the follower of Christ to more earnest prayer to the mighty Helper. Severe trial develops patience, fortitude, and a deep trust in God. The Christian faith enables its follower to suffer and be strong; to submit, and thus to conquer; to be "killed all the day long," and yet to live; to bear the cross, and thus to win the crown of glory.

45 / The Letters Paul Wrote From Rome

Paul acknowledged that many "visions and revelations" had been given him "of the Lord." His understanding of the gospel was equal to that of "the very chiefest apostles." 2 Corinthians 12:1, 11. He had a clear comprehension of "the breadth, and length, and depth, and height" of "the love of Christ, which passeth knowledge." Ephesians 3:18, 19.

Paul could not tell all that he had seen in vision; some hearers would have misapplied his words. But that which was revealed to him molded the messages that he in later years sent to the churches. He bore a message that ever since has brought strength to the church of God. To believers today this message speaks plainly of dangers that will threaten the church.

The apostle's desire for those to whom he addressed his letters was that they should "be no more children, tossed to and fro, and carried about with every wind of doctrine," but that they should come into "the unity of the faith, and of the knowledge of the Son of God, unto a perfect man, unto the measure of the stature of the fullness of Christ." Ephesians 4:14, 13. Christ, who "loved the church, and gave Himself for it," would "present it to Himself . . . not having spot, or wrinkle, or any such thing"—a church "holy and without blemish." Ephesians 5:25, 27.

In these messages, written with a power not of man but of God, principles are laid down that should be

This chapter is based on the Letters to the Colossians and the Philippians, RSV.

followed in every church, and the way that leads to life eternal is made plain.

In his letter to "the saints" at Colosse, written while he was a prisoner in Rome, Paul mentions his joy over their steadfastness: "From the day we heard of it, we have not ceased to pray for you, asking that you may be filled with the knowledge of His will in all spiritual wisdom and understanding, to lead a life worthy of the Lord, fully pleasing to Him, bearing fruit in every good work and increasing in the knowledge of God."

There is no limit to the blessings that the children of God may receive. They may go on from strength to strength until they are made "meet to be partakers of the inheritance of the saints in light." KJV.

Christ, the Creator

The apostle exalted Christ as the One by whom God created all things. The hand that sustains the world in space is the hand that was nailed to the cross: "For in Him were all things created, in heaven and on earth, visible and invisible, . . . all things were created through Him and for Him. He is before all things, and in Him all things hold together."

The Son of God came to this earth to be "wounded for our transgressions" and "bruised for our iniquities." Isaiah 53:5. He was in all things made like unto His brethren. He became flesh, even as we are. He knew what it meant to be hungry, thirsty, and weary. He was sustained by food and refreshed by sleep. He was tempted and tried as men and women of today are tempted and tried, yet lived a life free from sin.

Surrounded by the influences of heathenism, the Colossian believers were in danger of being drawn away from the simplicity of the gospel. Paul pointed them to Christ as the only safe guide: "I say this in order that no one may delude you with beguiling speech. . . . As therefore you received Christ Jesus the Lord, so live in Him, rooted and built up in Him and established in the faith, just as you were taught. . . . See to it that no one makes a prey of you by philosophy and empty deceit, according to human tradition, according to the elemental spirits of the universe, and not according to Christ.''

Christ had foretold that deceivers would arise, through whose influence ''iniquity'' should ''abound,'' and ''the love of many'' should ''wax cold.'' Matthew 24:12. The church would be in more danger from this evil than from the persecution of her enemies. By receiving false teachers, they would open the door to errors by which the enemy would shake the confidence of those newly come to the faith. All that was not in harmony with Christ's teachings they were to reject.

As men tried in the days of the apostles by philosophy to destroy faith in the Scriptures, so today, by higher criticism, evolution, spiritualism, theosophy, and pantheism, the enemy of righteousness is seeking to lead souls into forbidden paths. To many the Bible is as a lamp without oil, because they have turned their minds into channels of speculative belief that bring confusion. The work of higher criticism, in dissecting, conjecturing, and reconstructing, is destroying faith, robbing God's Word of power to control and inspire human lives. Spiritualism teaches that desire is the highest law, that license is liberty, and that man is accountable only to himself.

The follower of Christ will meet with spiritualistic interpretations of the Scriptures, but he is not to accept them. He is to discard all ideas that are not in harmony with Christ's teaching. He is to regard the Bible as the voice of God speaking directly to him. The knowledge of God as revealed in Christ is the knowledge that all who are saved must have. This knowledge works transformation of character. This is the knowledge beside which all else is vanity and nothingness.

In every generation and in every land, the true foundation for character building has been the same—the principles contained in the Word of God. With the Word the apostles met the false theories of their day, saying, "Other foundation can no may lay than that is laid." 1 Corinthians 3:11.

In his letter, Paul entreated the Colossian believers not to forget that they must put forth constant effort: "If then you have been raised with Christ, seek the things that are above, where Christ is, seated at the right hand of God. Set your minds on things that are above, not on things that are on earth. For you have died, and your life is hid with Christ in God."

How to Break the Chains of Habit

Through the power of Christ, men and women have broken the chains of sinful habit. They have renounced selfishness. The profane have become reverent, the drunken sober, the profligate pure. This change is the miracle of miracles—"Christ in you, the hope of glory."

When the Spirit of God controls mind and heart, the converted soul breaks forth into a new song; the promise of God has been fulfilled, and the sinner's transgression has been forgiven. He has exercised repentance toward God for the violation of the divine law and faith toward Christ, who died for man's justification.

But the Christian is not to fold his hands, content with that which has been accomplished for him. He will find that all the powers and passions of unregenerate nature are arrayed against him. Each day he must renew his consecration. Old habits, hereditary tendencies to wrong, will strive for the mastery, and against these he is to strive in Christ's strength.

"Put on then, as God's chosen ones, holy and beloved, compassion, kindness, lowliness, meekness and patience, forbearing one another and, if one has a complaint against another, forgiving each other; as the Lord has forgiven you, so you also must forgive."

The power of a higher, purer life is our great need. The world has too much of our thought, and the kingdom of heaven too little. To reach God's ideal, the

Christian is to despair of nothing. Moral and spiritual perfection through the grace of Christ is promised to all. Jesus is the source of power. He brings us to His Word. He puts into our mouth a prayer through which we are brought into close contact with Himself. In our behalf He sets in operation the all-powerful agencies of heaven. At every step we touch His living power.

To the Philippians: How Perfection Is Reached

The church at Philippi had sent gifts to Paul by Epaphroditus, whom Paul calls "my brother and fellow worker." While in Rome, Epaphroditus was sick, "near to death. But God had mercy on him, and not only on him but on me also, lest I should have sorrow upon sorrow." The believers at Philippi were filled with anxiety regarding Epaphroditus, and he decided to return to them. "He has been longing for you all," Paul wrote, "and has been distressed because you heard that he was ill, . . . for he nearly died for the work of Christ, risking his life to complete your service to me."

Paul sent the Philippian believers a letter by him. Of all the churches, Philippi had been the most liberal in supplying Paul's wants. "Not that I seek the gift; but I seek the fruit which increases to your credit. I have received full payment, and more; I am filled, having received from Epaphroditus the gifts you sent."

"I thank my God in all my remembrance of you, always in every prayer of mine for you all making my prayer with joy, thankful for your partnership in the gospel from the first day until now. And I am sure that He who began a good work in you will bring it to completion at the day of Jesus Christ. . . . And it is my prayer that your love may abound more and more, with knowledge and all discernment, . . . so that you may . . . be pure and blameless for the day of Christ."

Paul's imprisonment had resulted in the furtherance of the gospel. "What has happened to me has really served to advance the gospel, so that it has become known throughout the whole praetorian guard and to all the rest."

There is a lesson for us in this experience. The Lord can bring victory out of what may seem to us defeat. When misfortune or calamity comes, we are ready to charge God with neglect or cruelty. If He sees fit to cut off our usefulness in some line, we mourn, not stopping to think that He may be working for our good. Chastisement is a part of His great plan. Under the rod of affliction the Christian may sometimes do more for the Master than when engaged in active service.

Paul pointed the Philippians to Christ, who, "though He was in the form of God, did not count equality with God a thing to be grasped, but emptied Himself, taking the form of a servant, being born in the likeness of men. And being found in human form He humbled Himself and became obedient unto death, even death on a cross."

"Therefore, my beloved," Paul continued, "God is at work in you, both to will and to work for His good pleasure. Do all things without grumbling or questioning, that you may be blameless and innocent, children of God without blemish in the midst of a crooked and perverse generation."

Paul holds up the standard of perfection and shows how it may be reached: "Work out your own salvation; . . . for God is at work in you." The work of gaining salvation is a joint operation between God and the repentant sinner. Man is to make earnest efforts to overcome, but he is wholly dependent on God for success. Without the aid of divine power human effort avails nothing. God works and man works. Resistance of temptation must come from man, who must draw his power from God.

God wishes us to have self-mastery, but He cannot help us without our consent and cooperation. The divine Spirit works through the faculties given to man. Of ourselves we are not able to bring the desires and inclinations into harmony with the will of God; but if we are "willing to be made willing," the Saviour will accomplish this for us, "casting down imaginations, . . . and bringing into captivity every thought to the obedience of Christ." 2 Corinthians 10:5.

He who would be a well-balanced Christian must give all and do all for Christ. Daily he must learn the meaning of self-surrender. He must study the Word of God, obeying its precepts. Day by day God works with him, perfecting the character that is to stand in the final test. And day by day the believer works out before men and angels a sublime experiment, showing what the gospel can do for fallen human beings.

The True Motive That Leads to Perfection

"I do not consider that I have made it my own," Paul wrote, "but one thing I do, forgetting what lies behind and straining forward to what lies ahead, I press on toward the goal for the prize of the upward call of God in Christ Jesus."

In all the busy activities of his life, Paul never lost sight of one great purpose—to press toward the prize of his high calling. To exalt the cross—this was his all-absorbing motive that inspired his words and acts.

Though he was a prisoner, Paul was not discouraged. A note of triumph rings through the letters that he wrote from Rome. "Rejoice," he wrote. "In everything by prayer and supplication with thanksgiving let your requests be made known to God. And the peace of God, which passes all understanding, will keep your hearts and your minds in Christ Jesus."

"My God will supply every need of yours according to His riches in glory in Christ Jesus."

46 / Paul Is Free Once More

Clouds were gathering that threatened not only Paul's own safety, but also the prosperity of the church. In Rome he had been placed in the charge of the captain of the imperial guards, a man of integrity, by whose clemency he was left comparatively free to pursue gospel work. But this man was replaced by an official from whom the apostle could expect no special favor.

In their efforts against Paul the Jews found an able helper in the profligate woman whom Nero had made his second wife, a Jewish proselyte. Paul could hope for little justice from Nero, debased in morals and capable of atrocious cruelty. The first year of his reign had been marked by the free poisoning of his young stepbrother, the rightful heir to the throne. Nero had then murdered his own mother and his wife. In every noble mind he inspired only abhorrence and contempt.

His abandoned wickedness created disgust, even in many who were forced to share his crimes. They were in constant fear as to what he would suggest next. Yet Nero was acknowledged as the absolute ruler of the civilized world. More than this, he was worshiped as a god.

Paul's condemnation before such a judge seemed certain. But the apostle felt that so long as he was loyal to God, he had nothing to fear. His Protector could shield him from the malice of the Jews and the power of Caesar.

And God did shield His servant. At Paul's examination the charges against him were not sustained. With a regard for justice wholly at variance with his character, Nero declared the prisoner guiltless. Paul was again a free man.

Had he been detained in Rome until the following year, he would doubtless have perished in the persecution which then took place. During Paul's imprisonment, converts had become so numerous as to arouse the enmity of the authorities. The anger of the emperor was especially excited by the conversion of members of his own household, and he soon found a pretext to make the Christians the objects of his merciless cruelty.

A terrible fire occurred in Rome; nearly half the city was burned. Nero himself, it was rumored, had caused it; but he made a pretense of great generosity by assisting the homeless and destitute. He was, however, accused of the crime. The people were enraged, and in order to clear himself, Nero turned the accusation on the Christians. Thousands of men, women, and children, were cruelly put to death.

Paul's Last Interval of Freedom

Soon after his release Paul had left Rome. Laboring among the churches, he sought to establish a firmer union between the Greek and the Eastern churches and to fortify the believers against the false doctrines creeping in to corrupt the faith.

The trials that Paul had endured had preyed upon his physical powers. He felt he was now doing his last work, and as time grew shorter, his efforts became more intense. There seemed to be no limit to his zeal. Strong in faith, he journeyed from church to church in many lands, to strengthen the believers that in the trying times on which they were entering, they might win souls and remain steadfast to the gospel, bearing faithful witness for Christ.

47 / Paul's Final Arrest and Imprisonment

Paul's work among the churches could not escape the observation of his enemies. Under Nero the Christians had everywhere been proscribed. After a time, the unbelieving Jews conceived the idea of fastening on Paul the crime of instigating the burning of Rome. Not one of them thought he was guilty, but they knew that such a charge would seal his doom. Paul was again arrested and hurried away to Rome to his final imprisonment.

He was accompanied by several companions, but he refused to permit others thus to imperil their lives. Thousands of Christians in Rome had been martyred for their faith. Many had left, and those who remained were greatly depressed.

At Rome Paul was placed in a gloomy dungeon. Accused of instigating one of the most terrible of crimes against the city and nation, he was the object of universal execration.

His few friends now began to leave, some by desertion, others on missions to various churches. Demas, dismayed by the thickening clouds of danger, forsook the persecuted apostle. Writing to Timothy, Paul said, "Only Luke is with me." 2 Timothy 4:11. Never had the apostle needed his brethren as now, enfeebled as he was by age, toil, and infirmities, and confined in the damp, dark vaults of a Roman prison. Luke, the beloved disciple and faithful friend, was a great comfort and enabled Paul to communicate with his brethren.

In this trying time Paul's heart was cheered by frequent visits from Onesiphorus. This warmhearted Ephesian spared no effort to make Paul's lot more bearable. In his last letter the apostle wrote thus: "The Lord give mercy unto the house of Onesiphorus; for he oft refreshed me, and was not ashamed of my chain: but, when he was in Rome, he sought me out very diligently, and found me. The Lord grant unto him that he may find mercy of the Lord in that day." 2 Timothy 1:16-18.

Christ longed for the sympathy of His disciples in His hour of agony in Gethsemane. And Paul yearned for sympathy and companionship at a time of loneliness and desertion. Onesiphorus brought gladness and cheer to one who had spent his life in service for others.

48 / Paul Again Before Nero

When Paul was summoned before Nero for trial, it was with the near prospect of certain death. Among the Greeks and Romans it was customary to allow an accused person an advocate who, by force of argument, impassioned eloquence, or tears, often secured a decision in favor of the prisoner, or succeeded in mitigating the severity of the sentence. But no man ventured to act as Paul's advocate. No friend was at hand even to record the charge against him or the arguments he urged in his own defense. Among the Christians at Rome, not one came forward to stand by him in that trying hour.

The only reliable record of the occasion is given by Paul himself: "At my first defense no one took my part; all deserted me. May it not be charged against them! But the Lord stood by me and gave me strength to proclaim the word fully, that all the Gentiles might hear it. So I was rescued from the lion's mouth." 2 Timothy 4:16, 17, RSV.

Nero had reached the height of earthly power, authority, and wealth, as well as the lowest depths of iniquity. There were none to question his authority. The decrees of senators and the decisions of judges were but the echo of his will. The name of Nero made the world tremble. To incur his displeasure was to lose property, liberty, life.

Without money, friends, or counsel, the aged prisoner stood before Nero—the countenance of the emperor bearing the shameful record of passions that raged within; the face of the accused telling of a heart at peace with God. Notwithstanding constant misrepresentation, reproach, and abuse, Paul had fearlessly held aloft the standard of the cross. Like his Master, he had lived to bless humanity. How could Nero understand or appreciate the character and motives of this son of God?

The vast hall was thronged by an eager crowd that pressed to the front. High and low, rich and poor, learned and ignorant, proud and humble, all alike were destitute of a true knowledge of the way of life and salvation.

The Jews brought against Paul the old charges of sedition and heresy, and both Jews and Romans accused him of instigating the burning of the city. The people and the judges looked at Paul in surprise. They had looked on many a criminal, but never had they seen a man wear a look of such holy calmness. The keen eyes of the judges searched Paul's face in vain for some evidence of guilt. When he was permitted to speak in his own behalf, all listened with eager interest.

Once more Paul uplifted before a wondering multitude the banner of the cross, his soul stirred with an intense desire for their salvation. Losing sight of the terrible fate that seemed so near, he saw only Jesus, the Intercessor, pleading in behalf of sinful men. With eloquence and power, Paul pointed to the sacrifice made for the fallen race. An infinite price had been paid for man's redemption. Provision had been made for him to share the throne of God. By angel messengers, earth is connected with heaven, and all the deeds of men, are open to the eye of Infinite Justice. Paul's words were as a shout of victory above the roar of battle. Though he might perish, the gospel would not perish.

Never had that company listened to words like these. They struck a chord that vibrated in the hearts of even the most hardened. Light shone into the minds of many who afterward gladly followed its rays. The truths spoken on that day were destined to shake nations and to live through all time, influencing men when the lips that had uttered them should be silent in a martyr's grave.

Nero Hears God's Last Call

Never had Nero heard truth as he heard it on this occasion. He trembled with terror at the thought of a tribunal before which he, the ruler of the world, would finally be arraigned. He feared the apostle's God, and he dared not pass sentence on Paul. A sense of awe restrained his bloodthirsty spirit.

For a moment, heaven was opened to the hardened Nero, and its peace and purity seemed desirable. But only for a moment was the thought of pardon welcomed. Then the command was issued that Paul be taken back to his dungeon. As the door closed upon the messenger of God, the door of repentance closed forever against the emperor of Rome. No ray of light was ever again to penetrate the darkness that enveloped him.

Not long after this, Nero sailed on his infamous expedition to Greece, where he disgraced himself and his kingdom by debasing frivolity. Returning to Rome, he engaged in scenes of revolting debauchery. In the midst of this revelry, a voice of tumult in the streets was heard. Galba, at the head of an army, was marching rapidly on Rome; insurrection had broken out in the city; the streets were filled with an enraged mob threatening death to the emperor and his supporters.

Fearful of torture at the hands of the mob, the wretched tyrant thought to end his life by his own hand, but at the critical moment his courage failed. He fled ignominiously from the city and sought shelter at a countryseat a few miles distant. But his hiding place was soon discovered, and as the pursuing horsemen drew near, he summoned a slave to his aid and inflicted on himself a mortal wound. Thus perished the tyrant Nero, at the age of thirty-two.

49 / Paul Pours Out His Heart in His Last Letter

From the judgment hall Paul returned to his cell, realizing that his enemies would not rest until they had compassed his death. But for a time truth had triumphed. To have proclaimed a crucified and risen Saviour before that vast crowd was in itself a victory. That day a work had begun which would grow and which Nero and all other enemies of Christ would seek in vain to destroy.

Sitting day after day in his gloomy cell, knowing that at a word from Nero his life might be sacrificed, Paul thought of Timothy and determined to send for him. Timothy had been left at Ephesus when Paul made his last journey to Rome. Timothy had shared Paul's labors and sufferings, and their friendship had grown deeper and more sacred until Timothy was to Paul all that a son could be to an honored father. In his loneliness, Paul longed to see him.

Under the most favorable circumstances, several months must pass before Timothy could reach Rome from Asia Minor. Paul knew that his life was uncertain, and while urging him to come without delay, he dictated the testimony that he might not be spared to utter. His soul was filled with loving solicitude for his son in the gospel and for the church under his care.

The apostle urged Timothy: "Rekindle the gift of God that is within you through the laying on of my hands; for God did not give us a spirit of timidity but a

This chapter is based on 2 Timothy, RSV.

spirit of power and love and self-control. Do not be ashamed then of testifying to our Lord, nor of me His prisoner, but share in suffering for the gospel in the power of God." "Therefore I suffer as I do. But I am not ashamed, for I know whom I have believed, and I am sure that He is able to guard until that Day what has been entrusted to me."

Through his long service Paul had never faltered in his allegiance to his Saviour. Before scowling Pharisees or Roman authorities, or the convicted sinners in the Macedonian dungeon, reasoning with panic-stricken sailors on the shipwrecked vessel, or standing alone before Nero—he had never been ashamed of the cause he was advocating. No opposition or persecution had been able to turn him aside.

"You then, my son," Paul continued, "be strong in the grace that is in Christ Jesus. . . . Take your share of suffering as a good soldier of Christ Jesus."

Grace Enlarges the Minister's Capabilities

The true minister of God will not shun hardship. From the Source that never fails, he draws strength to overcome temptation and to perform the duties God places upon him. His soul goes out in longing desire to do acceptable service. "The grace that is in Christ Jesus" enables him to be a faithful witness of the things he has heard. He commits this knowledge to faithful men, who in their turn teach others.

In this letter Paul held up before the younger worker a high ideal: "Do your best to present yourself to God as one approved, a workman who has no need to be ashamed, rightly handling the word of truth." "Shun youthful passions and aim at righteousness, faith, love, and peace, along with those who call upon the Lord from a pure heart. Have nothing to do with stupid, senseless controversies; you know that they breed quarrels." Be "an apt teacher, forbearing, correcting . . . opponents with gentleness. God may perhaps grant that they will repent and come to know the truth."

The apostle warned Timothy against false teachers who would seek entrance into the church: "Understand this, that in the last days there will come times of stress. For men will be lovers of self, lovers of money, proud, arrogant, abusive, disobedient to their parents, ungrateful, unholy, . . . holding the form of religion but denying the power of it. Avoid such people."

"But as for you, continue in what you have learned and have firmly believed, knowing from whom you learned it and how from childhood you have been acquainted with the sacred writings which are able to instruct you for salvation. . . . All scripture is inspired by God and profitable for teaching, for reproof, for correction, and for training in righteousness, that the man of God may be complete, equipped for every good work." The Bible is the armory where we may equip for the struggle. The shield of faith must be in our hand, and with the sword of the Spirit, the Word of God, we are to cut our way through the obstructions and entanglements of sin.

Timothy's Summons to Preach

Paul knew that faithful, earnest work would have to be done in the churches, and he wrote to Timothy: "Preach the word, be urgent in season and out of season, convince, rebuke, and exhort, be unfailing in patience and in teaching." Summoning Timothy before the bar of God, Paul bade him to be ready to witness for God before large congregations and private circles, by the way and at the fireside, to friends and to enemies, in safety or hardship and peril.

Fearing that Timothy's mild, yielding disposition might lead him to shun an essential part of his work, Paul exhorted him to be faithful in reproving sin. Yet he was to do this "with all long-suffering and doctrine" (KJV), explaining his reproofs by the Word.

To hate sin and at the same time show tenderness for the sinner, is difficult. We must guard against undue severity toward the wrongdoer, but we must not lose sight of the exceeding sinfulness of sin. There is danger of showing so great toleration for error that the erring one will look on himself as undeserving of reproof.

How Ministers Can Become Tools of Satan

Ministers of the gospel sometimes allow their forbearance toward the erring to degenerate into toleration of sins, and even participation in them. They excuse that which God condemns, and after a time become so blinded as to commend the ones whom God commands them to reprove. He who has blunted his spiritual perceptions by sinful leniency toward those whom God condemns, will erelong commit a greater sin by severity and harshness toward those whom God approves.

By the pride of human wisdom and by disrelish for the truths of God's Word, many who feel competent to teach others will turn away from the requirements of God. "The time is coming when people will not endure sound teaching, but having itching ears they will accumulate for themselves teachers to suit their own likings, and will turn away from listening to the truth and wander into myths."

The apostle here refers to professing Christians who make inclination their guide, and thus become enslaved by self. Such are willing to listen only to doctrines that do not rebuke sin or condemn their pleasure-loving course. They choose teachers who flatter them. And among professing ministers there are those who preach the opinions of men instead of the Word of God.

God has declared that until the close of time His holy law, unchanged in jot or tittle, is to maintain its claim on human beings. Christ came to show that it is based on the broad foundation of love to God and love to man, and that obedience to its precepts comprises the whole duty of man. In His own life He gave an example of obedience to the law of God.

But the enemy of all righteousness has led men and women to disobey the law. As Paul foresaw, multitudes have chosen teachers who present fables. Many, both ministers and people, are trampling under their feet the commandments of God. The Creator is insulted, and Satan laughs in triumph at his success.

The True Remedy for Social Evils

With contempt for God's law, there is an increasing distaste for religion, an increase of pride, love of pleasure, disobedience to parents, and self-indulgence; and thoughtful minds everywhere are anxiously inquiring, What can be done to correct these evils? The answer is, "Preach the Word." The Bible is a transcript of the will of God, an expression of divine wisdom. It will guide all who heed its precepts, keeping them from wasting their lives in misdirected effort.

After Infinite Wisdom has spoken, there can be no doubtful questions for man to settle. All that is required is obedience.

Paul was about to finish his course, and he desired Timothy to take his place, guarding the church from fables and heresies. He admonished him to shun all pursuits and entanglements that would prevent him from giving himself wholly to his work for God; to endure with cheerfulness the opposition, reproach, and persecution; to make full proof of his ministry.

Paul clung to the cross as his only guarantee of success. The love of the Saviour was the motive that upheld him in his conflicts with self and in his struggles against the unfriendliness of the world and the opposition of his enemies.

In these days of peril the church needs an army of workers who have educated themselves for usefulness and who have a deep experience in the things of God. Men are needed who will not shun trial and responsibility, who are brave and true, and who with lips touched with holy fire will "preach the Word." For want of such workers, fatal errors, like deadly poison, taint the morals and blight the hopes of a large part of the human race.

Will young men accept the holy trust? Will the apostle's charge be heeded, the call to duty be heard, amidst the incitements to selfishness and ambition?

Paul concluded his letter with the urgent request that Timothy come soon, if possible before winter. He spoke of his loneliness and stated that he had dispatched Tychicus to Ephesus. After speaking of his trial before Nero, the desertion of his brethren, and the sustaining grace of God, Paul closed by commending his beloved Timothy to the Chief Shepherd, who, though the undershepherds might be stricken down, would still care for His flock.

50 / Paul Dies for the One Who Died for Him

During Paul's final trial Nero had been so strongly impressed with the force of the apostle's words that he deferred making a decision, neither acquitting nor condemning the servant of God. But the emperor's malice soon returned. Exasperated by his inability to check the spread of the Christian religion even in the imperial household, Nero condemned Paul to a martyr's death. Inasmuch as a Roman citizen could not be subjected to torture, the apostle was sentenced to be beheaded.

Few spectators were allowed at the place of execution, for Paul's persecutors feared that converts might be won to Christianity by the scene of his death. But even the hardened soldiers listened to his words, and with amazement saw him cheerful, even joyous, in the prospect of death. More than one accepted the Saviour, and erelong fearlessly sealed their faith with their blood.

Until his latest hour the life of Paul testified to the truth of his words to the Corinthians: "For it is the God who said, 'Let light shine out of darkness,' who has shone in our hearts to give the light of the knowledge of the glory of God in the face of Christ. . . . We are afflicted in every way, but not crushed; perplexed, but not driven to despair; persecuted, but not forsaken; struck down, but not destroyed." 2 Corinthians 4:6-9, RSV.

The heaven-born peace expressed on Paul's countenance won many to the gospel. All who associated with him felt the influence of his union with Christ. His own life gave convincing power to his preaching. Herein lies the power of truth. The unstudied, unconscious influence of a holy life is the most convincing sermon that can be given in favor of Christianity. Argument may provoke only opposition; but a godly example is impossible wholly to resist.

The apostle lost sight of his own approaching sufferings in solicitude for those whom he was about to leave to cope with prejudice, hatred, and persecution. He assured the few Christians who accompanied him to the place of execution that nothing would fail of all the promises given for the Lord's tried and faithful children. For a little season they might be destitute of earthly comforts, but they could encourage their hearts with the assurance of God's faithfulness. Soon would dawn the glad morning of peace and perfect day.

Why Paul Was Not Afraid

The apostle was looking into the great beyond with joyous hope and longing expectation. As he stood at the place of martyrdom he saw not the sword of the executioner or the earth so soon to receive his blood; he looked up through the calm blue heaven of that summer day to the throne of the Eternal.

This man of faith beheld the ladder of Jacob's vision—Christ connecting earth with heaven. He called to mind how patriarchs and prophets relied upon the One who was his support, and from these holy men he heard the assurance that God is true. His fellow apostles who counted not their lives dear unto themselves that they might bear the light of the cross amidst the dark mazes of infidelity—these he heard witnessing to Jesus as the Son of God, the Saviour of the world. From the rack, the stake, the dungeon, from dens and caves of the earth, there fell on his ear the martyr's shout of triumph, declaring, "I know whom I have believed."

Ransomed by the sacrifice of Christ and clothed in

His righteousness, Paul had the witness in himself that He who conquered death is able to keep that which is committed to His trust. His mind grasped the Saviour's promise, "I will raise him up at the last day." John 6:40. His hopes centered on the second coming of his Lord. And as the sword of the executioner descended, the martyr's thought sprang forward to meet the Life-giver.

Nearly twenty centuries have passed since Paul poured out his blood for the Word of God and the testimony of Jesus. No faithful hand recorded the last scenes in the life of this holy man, but Inspiration has preserved his dying testimony. Like a trumpet peal His voice has rung out through all the ages since, nerving with courage thousands of witnesses for Christ, and wakening in sorrow-stricken hearts the echo of his own triumphant joy: "I have fought a good fight, I have finished my course, I have kept the faith: henceforth there is laid up for me a crown of righteousness, which the Lord, the righteous Judge, shall give me at that day: and not to me only, but unto all them also that love His appearing." 2 Timothy 4:7, 8.

51 / The Apostle Peter, a Faithful Undershepherd

During the busy years that followed the Day of Pentecost, the apostle Peter put forth untiring efforts to reach the Jews who came to Jerusalem at the time of the annual festivals. The talents he possessed proved of untold value to the early Christian church. Upon him had been laid a double responsibility. He bore positive witness concerning the Messiah before unbelievers, and at the same time strengthened believers in the faith in Christ.

After Peter had been led to self-renunciation and entire reliance on divine power, he received his call as an undershepherd. Christ's words to Peter before his denial, "When thou art converted, strengthen thy brethren" (Luke 22:32), were significant of the work he was to do for those who should come to the faith. For this work, Peter's experience of sin and repentance had prepared him. Not until he learned his weakness could he know the believer's need of dependence on Christ. He had come to understand that man can walk safely only as in utter self-distrust he relies on the Saviour.

At the last meeting by the sea, Peter, tested by the thrice-repeated question, "Lovest thou Me?" (John 21:15-17), was restored to his place among the Twelve. His work was appointed him: he was not only to seek those without the fold, but to be a shepherd of the sheep.

Christ mentioned only one condition of service—

This chapter is based on the First Letter of Peter, RSV.

"Lovest thou Me?" Knowledge, benevolence, eloquence, zeal—all are essential; but without the love of Christ in the heart, the Christian minister is a failure. This love is a living principle made manifest in the heart. If the character of the shepherd exemplifies the truth he advocates, the Lord will set the seal of His approval to the work.

Christ's Patience With Peter Is a Lesson

Although Peter had denied his Lord, the love Jesus bore him never faltered. And, remembering his own weakness and failure, the apostle was to deal with the sheep and lambs as tenderly as Christ had dealt with him.

Human beings are prone to deal untenderly with the erring. They cannot read the heart; they know not its struggle and pain. Of the rebuke that is love, of the warning that speaks hope, they need to learn.

Throughout his ministry Peter faithfully watched over the flock and proved himself worthy of the responsibility given him. He exalted Jesus as the Saviour and brought his own life under the discipline of the Master Worker. He sought to educate the believers for active service and inspired many young men to give themselves to the work of the ministry. His influence as an educator and leader increased. While he never lost his burden for the Jews, he bore his testimony in many lands.

In the later years of his ministry, his letters strengthened the faith of those who were enduring trial and affliction and those who were in danger of losing their hold on God. These letters bear the impress of one whose entire being had been transformed by grace and whose hope of eternal life was steadfast.

In this hope of an inheritance in the earth made new, the early Christians rejoiced even in severe affliction. "In this you rejoice," Peter wrote, "though now for a little while you may have to suffer various trials, so that the genuineness of your faith, more precious than gold which though perishable is tested by fire, may redound to praise and glory and honor at the revelation of Jesus Christ.''

The apostle's words have special significance for those who live when "the end of all things is at hand." His words of courage are needed by every soul who would maintain his faith "firm to the end." Hebrews 3:14, RSV.

The apostle sought to teach the believers to keep the mind from wandering to forbidden themes, or from spending its energies on trifling subjects. They must avoid reading, seeing, or hearing that which will suggest impure thoughts. The heart must be faithfully sentineled, or evils without will awaken evils within, and the soul will wander in darkness. "Gird up your minds," Peter wrote, "be sober, set your hope fully upon the grace that is coming to you at the revelation of Jesus Christ. . . . Do not be conformed to the passions of your former ignorance.''

"You know that you were ransomed from the futile ways inherited from your fathers, not with perishable things such as silver or gold, but with the precious blood of Christ, like that of a lamb without blemish or spot.''

Had silver and gold been sufficient to purchase salvation, how easily might it have been accomplished by Him who says, "The silver is Mine, and the gold is Mine." Haggai 2:8. But only by the blood of the Son of God could the transgressor be redeemed. And as the crowning blessing of salvation, "the gift of God is eternal life through Jesus Christ our Lord." Romans 6:23.

The Fruit Produced by the Love of Truth

Peter continued, "Love one another earnestly from the heart." The Word of God is the channel through which the Lord manifests His Spirit and power. Obedience to the Word produces fruit—"sincere love of the brethren." When truth becomes an abiding principle in the life, the soul is "born anew, not of perishable seed but of imperishable, through the living and abiding word of God." This new birth is the result of receiving Christ as the Word. When the Holy Spirit impresses divine truths on the heart, new conceptions are awakened and energies hitherto dormant are aroused to cooperate with God.

Many of the most precious lessons of the Great Teacher were spoken to those who did not then understand them. When, after His ascension, the Holy Spirit brought His teachings to their remembrance, slumbering senses awoke. The meaning of these truths flashed on their minds as a new revelation. Then the men of His appointment proclaimed the mighty truth, "The Word was made flesh, and dwelt among us, . . . full of grace and truth." "And of His fullness have all we received, and grace for grace." John 1:14, 16.

The apostle exhorted the believers to study the Scriptures. Peter realized that every soul who is finally victorious will experience perplexity and trial; but an understanding of the Scriptures will bring to mind promises that will comfort the heart and strengthen faith in the Mighty One.

Many to whom Peter addressed his letters were living in the midst of heathen, and much depended on their remaining true to their calling. "You are a chosen race, a royal priesthood, a holy nation, God's own people, that you may declare the wonderful deeds of Him who called you out of darkness into His marvelous light. . . . Beloved, I beseech you as aliens and exiles to abstain from the passions of the flesh that wage war against your soul."

Our Duty to the Government

The apostle outlined the attitude that believers should sustain toward civil authorities: "Be subject for the Lord's sake to every human institution, whether it be to the emperor as supreme, or to governors as sent by him to punish those who do wrong and to praise those who do right. For it is God's will that by doing right you should put to silence the ignorance of foolish men.''

Those who were servants were to remain subject to their masters, ''for one is approved,'' the apostle explained, ''if, mindful of God, he endures pain while suffering unjustly. For what credit is it, if when you do wrong and are beaten for it you take it patiently? But if when you do right and suffer for it you take it patiently, you have God's approval. . . . Christ also suffered for you, leaving you an example, that you should follow in His steps. He committed no sin; no guile was found on His lips. When He was reviled, He did not revile in return; when He suffered, He did not threaten; but He trusted to Him who judges justly.''

The apostle exhorted the women in the faith to be modest: ''Let not yours be the outward adorning with braiding of hair, decoration of gold, and wearing of fine clothing, but let it be that hidden person of the heart with the imperishable jewel of a gentle and quiet spirit, which in God's sight is very precious.''

The lesson applies in every age. In the life of the true Christian the outward adorning is always in harmony with the inward peace and holiness. Self-denial and sacrifice will mark the Christian's life. Evidence that the taste is converted will be seen in the dress. It is right to love beauty and desire it; but God desires us to love first the highest beauty, that which is imperishable—the ''fine linen, white and clean'' (Revelation 19:14), which all the holy ones of earth will wear. This apparel will make them beloved here and will be their badge of admission to the palace of the King.

Looking forward to the perilous times into which the church was to enter, the apostle wrote: ''Do not be surprised at the fiery ordeal which comes upon you to prove you.'' Trial is to purify God's children from the dross of earthliness. It is because God is leading His children, that trying experiences come to them. Trials and obstacles are His chosen methods of discipline and the condition of success. Some people have qualifications which, if rightly directed, could be used in His work. He brings these souls into varied positions and circumstances that they may discover the defects concealed from their own knowledge. He gives them opportunity to overcome these defects. Often He permits the fires of affliction to burn, that they may be purified.

God suffers no affliction to come upon His children but such as is essential for their present and eternal good. All that He brings in test and trial comes that they may gain deeper piety and greater strength to carry forward the triumphs of the cross.

There had been a time when Peter was unwilling to see the cross in the work of Christ. When the Saviour made known His impending sufferings and death, Peter exclaimed, "God forbid, Lord! This shall never happen to You." Matthew 16:22, RSV. It was a bitter lesson, which he learned but slowly, that the path of Christ on earth lay through agony and humiliation. Now, when his once active form was bowed with the burden of years, he could write, "Beloved, . . . rejoice in so far as you share Christ's sufferings, that you may also rejoice and be glad when His glory is revealed."

Undershepherds Are to Be Watchful

Addressing the church elders regarding their responsibilities as undershepherds of Christ's flock, the apostle wrote: "Tend the flock of God that is your charge, . . . not for shameful gain but eagerly, not as domineering over those in your charge but being examples to the flock. And when the Chief Shepherd is manifested you will obtain the unfading crown of glory."

Ministry means earnest, personal labor. Pastors are needed—faithful shepherds—who will not flatter God's people nor treat them harshly, but who will feed them with the bread of life.

The undershepherd is called to meet alienation, bitterness, and jealousy in the church, and he will need to labor in the spirit of Christ. The servant of God may be misjudged and criticized. Let him then remember that "the wisdom that is from above is first pure, then peaceable, gentle, and easy to be entreated. . . . And the fruit of righteousness is sown in peace of them that make peace." James 3:17, 18.

If the gospel minister chooses the least self-sacrificing part, leaving the work of personal ministry for someone else, his labors will not be acceptable to God. He has mistaken his calling if he is unwilling to do the personal work that the care of the flock demands.

The true shepherd loses sight of self. By personal ministry in the homes of the people, he learns their needs and comforts their distresses, relieves their soul hunger, and wins their hearts to God. In this work the minister is attended by the angels of heaven.

The apostle outlined some general principles to be followed by all in church fellowship. The younger members were to follow the example of their elders in the practice of Christlike humility: " 'God opposes the proud, but gives grace to the humble.' Humble yourselves therefore under the mighty hand of God, that in due time He may exalt you. Cast all your anxieties on Him, for He cares about you."

Thus Peter wrote at a time of peculiar trial to the church. Soon the church was to undergo terrible persecution. Within a few years many leaders were to lay down their lives for the gospel. Soon grievous "wolves" were to enter in, not sparing the flock. But with words of encouragement and cheer Peter directed the believers "to an inheritance which is imperishable, undefiled, and unfading." "The God of all grace," he fervently prayed, "after you have suffered a little while, . . . will Himself restore, establish, and strengthen you."

52 / Peter Crucified at Rome

In his second letter the apostle Peter sets forth the divine plan for developing Christian character. He writes: God "has granted to us His precious and very great promises, that through these you may escape from the corruption that is in the world because of passion, and become partakers of the divine nature."

"Make every effort to supplement your faith with virtue, and virtue with knowledge, and knowledge with self-control, and self-control with steadfastness, and steadfastness with godliness, and godliness with brotherly affection, and brotherly affection with love."

The apostle presents before the believers the ladder of Christian progress. Every step represents advancement in the knowledge of God. We are saved by climbing round after round to the height of Christ's ideal for us. God desires to see men and women reaching the highest standard; and when by faith they lay hold of Christ, when they claim His promises as their own, when they seek for the Holy Spirit, they will be made complete in Him.

Having received the faith of the gospel, the believer is to add to his character virtue, and thus prepare the mind for the knowledge of God. This knowledge is the foundation of all true service and the only real safeguard against temptation. This alone can make one like God in character. No good gift is withheld from him who sincerely desires the righteousness of God.

This chapter is based on the Second Letter of Peter, RSV.

None need fail of attaining, in his sphere, to perfection of Christian character. God places before us the example of Christ's character. In His humanity, perfected by a life of constant resistance of evil, the Saviour showed that through cooperation with Divinity, human beings may in this life attain to perfection of character. We may obtain complete victory.

Overcoming Every Fault by Grace

Before the believer there is held out the wonderful possibility of being obedient to all the principles of the law. But of himself man is unable to reach this condition. The holiness that he must have is the result of the working of divine grace as he submits to the discipline and restraining influences of the Spirit of truth. The incense of Christ's righteousness fills with divine fragrance every act of obedience. The Christian is to persevere in overcoming every fault. Constantly he is to pray the Saviour to heal the disorders of his sin-sick soul. The Lord bestows strength to overcome on those who in contrition seek Him for help.

The work of transformation from unholiness to holiness is a continuous one. Day by day God labors for man's sanctification, and man is to cooperate with Him. Our Saviour is always ready to answer the prayer of the contrite. Gladly He grants the blessings needed in their struggle against the evils that beset them.

Sad indeed is the condition of those who, becoming weary, allow the enemy of souls to rob them of the Christian graces that have been developing in their hearts and lives. "Whoever lacks these things," declares the apostle, "is blind and shortsighted and has forgotten that he was cleansed from his old sins."

Peter's faith in God's power to save had strengthened with the years. He had proved that there is no possibility of failure before the one who, advancing by faith, ascends to the topmost round of the ladder. Knowing that soon he would suffer martyrdom for his faith, Peter once more exhorted his brethren to steadfastness of purpose: "Therefore, brethren, be the more zealous to confirm your call and election, for if you do this you will never fall; so there will be richly provided for you an entrance into the eternal kingdom of our Lord and Saviour Jesus Christ."

"I think it right, as long as I am in this body, to arouse you by way of reminder, since I know that the putting off of my body will be soon, as our Lord Jesus Christ showed me. And I will see to it that after my departure you may be able at any time to recall these things."

Why Peter Was Sure of Gospel Truth

"We did not follow cleverly devised myths" about Jesus, he reminded the believers, "but we were eye-witnesses of His majesty. For when He received honor and glory from God the Father and the voice was borne to Him by the Majestic Glory, 'This is My beloved Son, with whom I am well pleased,' we heard this voice borne from heaven, for we were with Him on the holy mountain."

Yet there was another even more convincing witness. "We have," Peter declared, "the prophetic word made more sure. You will do well to pay attention to this as to a lamp shining in a dark place, until the day dawns and the morning star rises in your hearts. . . . No prophecy ever came by the impulse of man, but men moved by the Holy Spirit spoke from God."

While exalting true prophecy, the apostle solemnly warned the church against the torch of false prophecy, uplifted by "false teachers" who would bring in "destructive heresies, even denying the Master." These false teachers, accounted true by many of their brethren in the faith, the apostle compared to "waterless springs and mists driven by a storm; for them the nether gloom of darkness has been reserved. . . . It would have been better for them never to have known the way of righteousness than after knowing it to turn back from the holy commandment delivered to them."

Looking down the ages, Peter was inspired to outline conditions in the world just prior to the second coming of Christ. "Scoffers will come in the last days," he wrote, "following their own passions and saying, 'Where is the promise of His coming?' " Not all, however, would be ensnared by the enemy's devices. There would be faithful ones able to discern the signs of the times, a remnant who would endure to the end.

Peter's Faith in the Second Coming of Christ

Peter kept alive in his heart the hope of Christ's return, and he assured the church of the certain fulfillment of the Saviour's promise, "I will come again." John 14:3. The coming might seem long delayed, but the apostle assured them: "The Lord is not slow about His promise as some count slowness, but is forbearing toward you, not wishing that any should perish, but that all should reach repentance."

"Since all these things are thus to be dissolved, what sort of persons ought you to be in lives of holiness and godliness, waiting for and hastening the coming of the day of God, because of which the heavens will be kindled and dissolved, and the elements will melt with fire! But according to His promise we wait for new heavens and a new earth in which righteousness dwells."

"Beloved, knowing this beforehand, beware lest you be carried away with the error of lawless men and lose your own stability. But grow in the grace and knowledge of our Lord and Saviour Jesus Christ."

Peter closed his ministry in Rome, where his imprisonment was ordered by the emperor Nero about the time of Paul's final arrest. Thus the two apostles, for many years widely separated in their labors, were to bear their last witness for Christ in the world's metropolis, and on its soil to shed their blood as the seed of a vast harvest of saints.

Peter had braved danger and had shown a noble

courage in preaching a crucified, risen, and ascended Saviour. As he lay in his cell he called to mind the words of Christ: "When thou wast young, thou girdest thyself, and walkedst whither thou wouldst: but when thou shalt be old, thou shalt stretch forth thy hands, and another shall gird thee, and carry thee whither thou wouldest not." John 21:18. Jesus had foretold the stretching of the disciple's hands on the cross.

As a Jew and foreigner, Peter was condemned to be scourged and crucified. In prospect of this fearful death, the apostle remembered his sin in denying Jesus in the hour of His trial. Once unready to acknowledge the cross, he now counted it a joy to yield up his life for the gospel. But he felt that for him to die in the same manner as his Master died was too great an honor. He had been forgiven by Christ, but he could never forgive himself. Nothing could lessen the bitterness of his sorrow and repentance. As a last favor he entreated his executioners that he might be nailed to the cross with his head downward. This request was granted, and in this manner died the great apostle Peter.

53/ John, the Beloved Disciple

John is distinguished as "the disciple whom Jesus loved." John 21:20. He was one of the three permitted to witness Christ's glory on the mount of transfiguration and His agony in Gethsemane, and it was to his care that our Lord confided His mother in those last hours of anguish on the cross.

John clung to Christ as the vine clings to the stately pillar. He braved the dangers of the judgment hall and lingered about the cross; and at the tidings that Christ had risen, he hastened to the sepulcher, outstripping even Peter.

John did not naturally possess loveliness of character. He was proud, self-assertive, ambitious for honor, impetuous, and resentful under injury. He and his brother were called "sons of thunder" Mark 3:17. Evil temper and desire for revenge were in the beloved disciple. But beneath this the divine Teacher discerned the sincere, loving heart. Jesus rebuked his self-seeking, disappointed his ambitions, tested his faith. But He revealed to him the beauty of holiness, the transforming power of love.

The defects in John came strongly to the front on several occasions. At one time Christ sent messengers to a village of the Samaritans, requesting refreshments for Him and His disciples. But when the Saviour approached the town, instead of inviting Him to be their guest, the Samaritans withheld the courtesies they would have given a common wayfarer.

The coldness and disrespect shown to their Master filled the disciples with indignation. In their zeal James and John said, "Lord, wilt Thou that we command fire to come down from heaven, and consume them, even as Elias did?" Jesus was pained by their words. "Ye know not what manner of spirit ye are of. For the Son of man is not come to destroy men's lives, but to save them." Luke 9:54-56.

Christ Wants Only Willing Surrender

Christ does not compel men to receive Him. Satan and men actuated by his spirit seek to compel the conscience. Under a pretense of zeal for righteousness, men who are confederated with evil angels bring suffering on their fellowmen in order to "convert" them to their ideas of religion; but Christ ever seeks to win by revealing His love. He desires only the willing surrender of the heart under the constraint of love.

On another occasion James and John requested through their mother that they occupy the highest positions in Christ's kingdom. These young disciples cherished the hope that He would take His throne and kingly power in accordance with the desires of men.

But the Saviour answered, "You do not know what you are asking. Are you able to drink the cup that I drink, or to be baptized with the baptism with which I am baptized?" They answered confidently, "We are able."

"The cup that I drink you will drink; and with the baptism with which I am baptized, you will be baptized," Christ declared. Before Him was a cross instead of a throne! James and John were to share their Master's suffering—one destined to swift-coming death by the sword, the other, longest of all to follow his Master in labor, reproach, and persecution. "But to sit at My right hand or at My left," He continued, "is not Mine to grant, but it is for those for whom it has been prepared." Mark 10:38-40, RSV.

Jesus reproved the pride and ambition of the two disciples: "Whosoever will be great among you, let him be your minister; and whosoever will be chief among you, let him be your servant." Matthew 20:26, 27. In the kingdom of God, position is the result of character. The crown and the throne are tokens of self-conquest through the grace of Christ.

Long afterward, the Lord Jesus revealed to John the condition of nearness to His kingdom: "To him that overcometh will I grant to sit with Me in My throne, even as I also overcame, and am set down with My Father in His throne." Revelation 3:21. The one who stands nearest to Christ will be he who has drunk most deeply of His spirit of self-sacrificing love—love that moves the disciple to labor and sacrifice even unto death for the saving of humanity.

John Learned His Lessons Well

At another time, James and John met one who, while not an acknowledged follower of Christ, was casting out devils in His name. The disciples forbade the man to work and thought they were right. But Christ reproved them: "Do not forbid him; for no one who does a mighty work in My name will be able soon after to speak evil of Me." Mark 9:39, RSV. James and John thought they had in view Christ's honor, but they began to see they were jealous for their own. They acknowledged their error and accepted the reproof.

John treasured every lesson and sought to bring his life into harmony with the divine pattern. He had begun to discern the glory of Christ—"glory as of the Only Begotten of the Father, full of grace and truth." John 1:14.

John's affection for his Master was not the cause of Christ's love for him: it was the effect of that love. Under the transforming love of Christ he became meek and lowly. Self was hid in Jesus. Above all his companions, John yielded himself to the power of that wondrous life. His Master's lessons were graven on his soul. When he testified of the Saviour's grace, his simple language was eloquent with the love that pervaded his whole being.

The Saviour loved all the Twelve, but John's was the most receptive spirit. Younger than the others, with more of the child's confiding trust, he opened his heart to Jesus. Thus he came more into sympathy with Christ, and through him the Saviour's deepest spiritual teaching was communicated to the people. John could talk of the Father's love as no other of the disciples could. The beauty of holiness which had transformed him shone with Christlike radiance from his countenance, and fellowship with Christ became his one desire.

"Beloved, now are we the sons of God, and it doth not yet appear what we shall be: but we know that, when He shall appear, we shall be like Him; for we shall see Him as He is." 1 John 3:2.

54 / John, Faithful Witness for Christ

With the other disciples John enjoyed the outpouring of the Spirit on the Day of Pentecost, and with fresh power he continued to speak to the people the words of life. He was a powerful preacher, fervent, and deeply in earnest. In beautiful language and with a musical voice he told of Christ in a way that impressed hearts. The sublime power of the truths he uttered and the fervor that characterized his teachings, gave him access to all classes. His life was in harmony with his teachings.

Christ had bidden the disciples to love one another as He had loved them. "A new commandment I give unto you," He had said, "that ye love one another; as I have loved you, that ye also love one another." John 13:34. After they had witnessed the sufferings of Christ, and after the Holy Spirit had rested on them at Pentecost, they had a clearer concept of the nature of that love which they must have for one another. Then John could say: "By this we know love, that He laid down His life for us; and we ought to lay down our lives for the brethren."

After Pentecost, when the disciples went forth to proclaim a living Saviour, they rejoiced in the sweetness of communion with saints. They were tender, thoughtful, self-denying, revealing the love that Christ had enjoined on them. By unselfish words and deeds they strove to kindle this love in other hearts.

This chapter is based on the Letters of John, RSV.

Such love the believers were ever to cherish. Their lives were to magnify a Saviour who could justify them by His righteousness.

But gradually a change came. Dwelling upon mistakes, giving place to unkind criticism, the believers lost sight of the Saviour and His love. They became more particular about the theory than the practice of the faith. They lost brotherly love, and, saddest of all, were unconscious of their loss. They did not realize that happiness and joy were going out of their lives and that they would soon walk in darkness.

A Tragic Change Comes Into the Early Church

John realized that brotherly love was waning in the church. "Beloved, let us love one another," he writes, "for love is of God, and he who loves is born of God and knows God. He who does not love does not know God; for God is love. In this the love of God was made manifest among us, that God sent His only Son into the world, so that we might live through Him. In this is love, not that we loved God but that He loved us and sent His Son to be the expiation of our sins. Beloved, if God so loved us, we also ought to love one another."

"Any one who hates his brother is a murderer, and you know that no murderer has eternal life abiding in him. By this we know love, that He laid down His life for us; and we ought to lay down our lives for the brethren."

It is not the opposition of the world that most endangers the church. It is the evil cherished in the hearts of believers that works their most grievous disaster, and most surely retards God's cause. There is no surer way of weakening spirituality than by cherishing envy, fault-finding, and evil-surmising. The strongest witness that God has sent His Son into the world is the existence of harmony and union among people of varied dispositions who form His church. But in order to bear this witness, their characters must be conformed to Christ's character, and their wills to His will.

In the church today, many who profess to love the Saviour do not love one another. Unbelievers are watching to see if the faith of professed Christians is exerting a sanctifying influence on their lives. Let not Christians make it possible for the enemy to say, These people hate one another. Very close and tender should be the tie that binds together all the children of the same heavenly Father.

Divine love calls upon us to manifest the same compassion that Christ manifested. The true Christian will not willingly permit a soul in peril and need to go unwarned, uncared for. He will not hold himself aloof, leaving the erring to plunge farther into unhappiness and discouragement.

Those who have never experienced the tender love of Christ cannot lead others to the fountain of life. Christ's love in the heart leads men to reveal Him in conversation, in a pitiful spirit, in uplifting lives. In heaven the fitness of Christian workers is measured by their ability to love as Christ loved.

"Let us not love in word or speech," the apostle writes, "but in deed and in truth." Completeness of character is attained when the impulse to help others springs constantly from within. It is this love that makes the believer "a savor of life unto life" and enables God to bless his work. 2 Corinthians 2:16.

True Love, the Best Gift God Can Give Us

Supreme love for God and unselfish love for one another—this is the best gift our heavenly Father can bestow. This love is not an impulse, but a divine principle. Only in the heart where Jesus reigns is it found. "We love, because He first loved us." Love modifies the character, governs the impulses and passions, and ennobles the affections. This love sweetens the life and sheds a refining influence on all around.

John strove to lead the believers to understand that this love, filling the heart, would control every other motive and raise its possessors above the corrupting influences of the world. As this love became the motive power in the life, their trust and confidence in God would be complete. They could know that they would receive from Him everything needful for their present and eternal good. "In this is love perfected," John writes, "that we may have confidence for the day of judgment, because as He is so are we in this world. There is no fear in love, but perfect love casts out fear." "If we ask anything according to His will He hears us. And if we know that He hears us . . . , we know that we have obtained the requests made of Him."

"If we confess our sins, He is faithful and just, and will forgive our sins and cleanse us from all unrighteousness." The Lord does not require us to do some grievous thing in order to gain forgiveness. We need not make long, wearisome pilgrimages or perform painful penances to expiate our transgression. He that "confesseth and forsaketh" his sin "shall have mercy." Proverbs 28:13.

In the courts above, Christ is pleading for His church—those for whom He paid the redemption price of His blood. Neither life nor death can separate us from the love of God, not because we hold Him so firmly, but because He holds us so fast. If our salvation depended on our own efforts, we could not be saved; but it depends on the One who is behind all the promises. Our grasp on Him may seem feeble, but so long a we maintain our union with Him, no one can pluck us out of His hand.

As the years went by and the number of believers grew, John labored with increasing fidelity and earnestness. Satanic delusions existed everywhere. By misrepresentation and falsehood, emissaries of Satan sought to arouse opposition against the doctrines of Christ, and in consequence dissensions and heresies were imperiling the church. Some who professed Christ claimed that His love released them from obedience to the law of God. On the other hand, many taught that a mere observance of the law, without faith in the blood of Christ, was sufficient for salvation. Some held that Christ was a good man, but denied His divinity. Some, living in transgression, were bringing heresies into the church. Many were being led into skepticism and delusion.

John Saw the Dangers Threatening the Church

John was sad to see these poisonous errors creeping into the church, and he met the emergency with promptness and decision. His letters breathe the spirit of love, as if he wrote with a pen dipped in love, but when he came in contact with those who were breaking the law of God, yet claiming to live without sin, he did not hesitate to warn them of their fearful deception.

Writing to a woman of wide influence, he said: "Many deceivers have gone out into the world, men who will not acknowledge the coming of Jesus Christ in the flesh; such a one is the deceiver and the antichrist. . . . He who abides in the doctrine has both the Father and the Son. If any one comes to you and does not bring this doctrine, do not receive him into the house or give him any greeting; for he who greets him shares his wicked work."

There exist in these last days evils similar to those that threatened the early church. "You must have love," is the cry heard everywhere, especially from those who profess sanctification. But true love is too pure to cover unconfessed sin. While we are to love souls, we are to make no compromise with evil. We are not to unite with the rebellious, and call this love. God requires His people to stand for the right as unflinchingly as did John in opposition to soul-destroying errors.

The apostle teaches that we are to deal in plain terms with sin and sinners; this is not inconsistent with true love. "Every one who commits sin," he writes, "is guilty of lawlessness; sin is lawlessness. You know that He appeared to take away sins, and in Him there is no sin. No one who abides in Him sins; no one who sins has either seen Him or known Him.''

As a witness for Christ, John entered into no wearisome contention. He declared what he knew. He had been intimately associated with Christ and had witnessed His miracles. For him the darkness had passed away; the true Light was shining. Out of the abundance of a heart overflowing with love for the Saviour he spoke; and no power could stay his words.

''That which was from the beginning,'' he declared, ''which we have heard, which we have seen with our eyes, which we have looked upon and touched with our hands, concerning the word of life . . . we proclaim also to you.''

So may every true believer be able to bear witness to that which he has seen and heard and felt of the power of Christ.

55 / John's Secret of True Sanctification

In the life of John true sanctification is exemplified. During the years of his close association with Christ, he was often warned by the Saviour, and these reproofs he accepted. He saw his deficiencies and was humbled by the revelation. Day by day his heart was drawn out to Christ, until he lost sight of self in love for his Master. The strength and patience that he saw in the Son of God filled his soul with admiration. He yielded his resentful, ambitious temper to Christ, and divine love wrought transformation of character.

In striking contrast is the experience of Judas, who professed to be a disciple of Christ but possessed only a form of godliness. Often as he listened to the Saviour's words, conviction came, but he would not humble his heart or confess his sins. By resisting the divine influence, he dishonored the Master.

John warred earnestly against his faults, but Judas violated his conscience, fastening on himself more securely his habits of evil. The truth Christ taught was at variance with his desires, and he could not yield his ideas. Covetousness, revengeful passions, dark and sullen thoughts, were cherished until Satan gained full control of him.

John and Judas had the same opportunities. Both were closely associated with Jesus. Each possessed serious defects of character; each had access to divine grace. But while one was learning of Jesus, the other was a hearer only. One, daily overcoming sin, was sanctified through the truth; the other, resisting the transforming power of grace and indulging selfish desires, was brought into bondage to Satan.

Transformation as seen in John is the result of communion with Christ. There may be defects in the character, yet when one becomes a true disciple of Christ, he is changed until he is like Him whom he adores.

In his letters, John wrote, "Every man that hath this hope in him purifieth himself, even as He is pure." "He that saith he abideth in Him ought himself also so to walk, even as He walked." 1 John 3:3; 2:6. As God is holy in His sphere, so fallen man, through faith in Christ, is to be holy in his sphere.

Sanctification is God's object in all His dealings with His people. He has chosen them from eternity, that they might be holy. He gave His Son to die for them that they might be divested of all the littleness of self. God can be honored only as they are conformed to His image and controlled by His Spirit. Then they may make known what divine grace has done for them.

True sanctification comes through the working out of the principle of love. "God is love; and he that dwelleth in love dwelleth in God, and God in him." 1 John 4:16. The life of him in whose heart Christ abides will be ennobled. Pure doctrine will blend with works of righteousness.

Those who would gain the blessings of sanctification must first learn the meaning of self-sacrifice. The cross of Christ is the central pillar on which hangs the "eternal weight of glory." "If any man will come after Me," Christ says, "let him deny himself, and take up his cross, and follow Me." 2 Corinthians 4:17; Matthew 16:24. God upholds and strengthens the one who is willing to follow in Christ's way.

True Sanctification Is a Lifework

Sanctification is not the work of a moment, an hour, a day, but of a lifetime. It is not gained by a happy flight of feeling, but is the result of constantly dying to sin and constantly living for Christ. Not by intermittent efforts, but by persevering discipline and stern conflict, we shall overcome. So long as Satan reigns, we shall have self to subdue, besetting sins to overcome. So long as life shall last, there will be no point which we can reach and say, I have fully attained. Sanctification is the result of lifelong obedience.

None of the apostles or prophets ever claimed to be without sin. Men who have lived nearest to God, who would sacrifice life itself rather than knowingly commit a wrong act, have confessed the sinfulness of their nature. They have claimed no righteousness of their own, but have trusted wholly in the righteousness of Christ.

The more clearly we discern the purity of Christ's character, the more clearly shall we see the exceeding sinfulness of sin. There will be a continual confession of sin and humbling of the heart before Him. At every advance step our repentance will deepen. We shall confess: "I know that in me (that is, in my flesh,) dwelleth no good thing." "God forbid that I should glory, save in the cross of our Lord Jesus Christ." Romans 7:18; Galatians 6:14. Let not God be dishonored by the declaration from human lips, "I am sinless; I am holy." Sanctified lips will never give utterance to such presumptuous words.

Let those who feel inclined to make a high profession of holiness look into the mirror of God's law. As they understand its work as a discerner of the thoughts and intents of the heart, they will not boast of sinlessness. "If," says John, "we say we have no sin, we deceive ourselves, and the truth is not in us." "If we say that we have not sinned, we make Him a liar." "If we confess our sins, He is faithful and just to forgive us our sins, and to cleanse us from all unrighteousness." 1 John 1:8, 10, 9.

There are those who profess holiness, who claim a right to the promises of God, while refusing to obey His commandments. But this is presumption. True love for God will be revealed in obedience to all His commandments: "He that saith, I know Him, and keepeth not His commandments is a liar, and the truth is not in him." "He that keepeth His commandments dwelleth in Him, and He in him." 1 John 2:4; 3:24.

John did not teach that salvation is to be earned by obedience; but obedience is the fruit of faith and love. "Ye know that He was manifested to take away our sins; and in Him is no sin. Whosoever abideth in Him sinneth not: whosoever sinneth hath not seen Him, neither known Him." 1 John 3:5, 6. If we abide in Christ, our feelings, our thoughts, our actions, will be in harmony with the will of God. The sanctified heart is in harmony with the precepts of God's law.

Faith Is the Key to Overcoming

Many, though striving to obey God's commandments, have little peace or joy. Such do not correctly represent sanctification. The Lord would have all His sons and daughters happy, peaceful, and obedient. Through faith the believer possesses these blessings. Through faith, every deficiency of character may be supplied, every defilement cleansed, every fault corrected, every excellence developed.

Prayer is heaven's ordained means of success in the development of character. For pardon of sin, for the Holy Spirit, for a Christlike temper, for wisdom and strength to do His work, for any gift He has promised, we may ask; and the promise is, "Ye shall receive."

It is in the secret place of communion that we are to contemplate God's glorious ideal for humanity. In all ages, through the medium of communion with heaven, God has worked out His purpose for His children by unfolding to their minds gradually the doctrines of grace.

True sanctification means perfect love, perfect obedience, perfect conformity to the will of God. We are to be sanctified through obedience to the truth. It is our privilege to cut away from the entanglements of self and sin and advance to perfection.

Many interpret the will of God to be what they will to

do. These have no conflicts with self. Others for a time sincerely struggle against their selfish desire for pleasure and ease, but grow weary of daily death, of ceaseless turmoil. Death to self seems repulsive, and they fall under the power of temptation instead of resisting it.

The Word of God leaves no room for compromise with evil. At whatever sacrifice of ease or selfish indulgence, of labor or suffering, Christ's followers must maintain a constant battle with self.

The greatest praise we can bring to God is to become consecrated channels through whom He can work. Let us not refuse God that which, though it cannot be given with merit, cannot be denied without ruin. He asks for a whole heart; give it. It is His, both by creation and redemption. He asks for your intellect; give it. It is His. He asks for your money; give it. It is His. "Ye are not your own. For ye are bought with a price." 1 Corinthians 6:19, 20. God holds up before us the highest ideal—perfection. He asks us to be absolutely and completely for Him in this world as He is for us in the presence of God.

"This is the will of God" concerning you, "even your sanctification." 1 Thessalonians 4:3. Is it your will also? If you humble your heart and confess your sins, trusting in the merits of Jesus, He will forgive and cleanse you. God demands entire conformity to His law. Let your heart be filled with an intense longing for His righteousness.

As you contemplate the unsearchable riches of God's grace you will come into possession of them and will reveal the merits of the Saviour's sacrifice, the protection of His righteousness, and His power to present you before the Father "without spot, and blameless." 2 Peter 3:14.

56/ John Is Exiled to Lonely Patmos

After more than half a century the enemies of the gospel succeeded in enlisting the power of the Roman emperor against the Christians. In the terrible persecution that followed, the apostle John did much to help his brethren meet with courage the trials that came upon them. The old, tried servant of Jesus repeated with power and eloquence the story of the crucified and risen Saviour. From his lips came the same glad message: "That which was from the beginning, which we have heard, which we have seen with our eyes, which we have looked upon, and our hands have handled, of the Word of life; . . . that which we have seen and heard declare we unto you." 1 John 1:1-3.

John lived to be very old. He witnessed the destruction of Jerusalem and the temple. The last survivor of the disciples who had been intimately connected with the Saviour, his message had great influence. Through his teachings many were led to turn from unbelief.

The Jews were filled with bitter hatred against him. They declared that their efforts would avail nothing so long as John's testimony kept ringing in the ears of the people. In order that the miracles and teachings of Jesus might be forgotten, the voice of the bold witness must be silenced. Accordingly John was summoned to Rome. His enemies hoped to bring about his death by accusations of teaching seditious heresies.

John answered for himself in a clear, convincing manner. But the more convincing his testimony, the deeper was the hatred of his opposers. The emperor

Domitian was filled with rage. He could not dispute the reasoning of Christ's faithful advocate, yet he determined to silence his voice.

John was cast into a caldron of boiling oil; but the Lord preserved His faithful servant as He preserved the three Hebrews in the fiery furnace. As the words were spoken, Thus perish all who believe in that deceiver, Jesus Christ, John declared, My Master gave His life to save the world. I am honored to suffer for His sake. I am a weak, sinful man. Christ was holy, harmless, undefiled.

Saved From the Boiling Oil

These words had their influence, and John was removed from the caldron by the very men who had cast him in.

Again by the emperor's decree, John was banished to the Isle of Patmos "for the word of God, and for the testimony of Jesus." Revelation 1:9. Here, his enemies thought, he must die of hardship and distress. Patmos, a barren island in the Aegean Sea, was a place of banishment for criminals; but to the servant of God this gloomy abode became the gate of heaven. Shut away from the active labors of former years, he had the companionship of God and heavenly angels. The events that would take place in the closing scenes of earth's history were outlined before him; and there he wrote out the visions he received from God. The messages given him on that barren coast were to declare the sure purpose of the Lord concerning every nation on earth.

Among the cliffs and rocks of Patmos, John held communion with his Maker. Peace filled his heart. He could say in faith, "We know that we have passed from death unto life." 1 John 3:14.

In his isolated home John was able to study more closely the book of nature. He was surrounded by scenes that to many would appear gloomy and uninteresting. But to John it was otherwise. While his surroundings might be desolate, the blue heavens above were as beautiful as the skies above his beloved Jerusalem. In the wild, rugged rocks, in the mysteries of the deep, in the glories of the firmament, he read important lessons of God's power and glory.

John Was Happy in His Exile

Around him the apostle beheld witnesses to the Flood that had deluged the earth—rocks thrown up from the great deep and from the earth by the breaking forth of the waters. The mighty waves in commotion, restrained by an invisible hand, spoke of the control of an infinite Power. And in contrast he realized the weakness and folly of mortals who glory in their supposed wisdom and strength, and set their hearts against the Ruler of the universe. From the exiled apostle there went up the most ardent longing of soul after God, the most fervent prayers.

The history of John illustrates the way God can use aged workers. Many thought him to be past service, an old and broken reed, ready to fall at any time. But the Lord saw fit to use him still. In Patmos he made friends and converts. His was a message of joy, proclaiming a risen Saviour interceding for His people until He should return to take them to Himself. After John had grown old in the service of his Lord he received more communications from heaven than during all the former years of his life.

Aged workers whose life interest has been bound up with the work of God may have infirmities, but they still possess talents that qualify them to stand in their place in God's cause. From their failures they have learned to avoid errors and dangers, and therefore are competent to give wise counsel. Though they have lost some of their vigor, the Lord does not lay them aside. He gives them special grace and wisdom.

Those who endured poverty and remained faithful when there were few to stand for truth are to be honored and respected. The Lord desires younger laborers to gain wisdom and maturity by association with these faithful men. Let the younger men give them an honored place in their councils. God desires the old and tried laborers to do their part to save men and women from being swept downward by the mighty current of evil. He desires them to keep the armor on till He bids them lay it down.

Trials Are Worth the Pain They Cost

In the experience of the apostle John there is a lesson of wonderful strength and comfort. God causes the plottings of wicked men to work for good to those who maintain their faith and loyalty amid storms of persecution, bitter opposition, and unjust reproach. God brings His children near to Him that He may teach them to lean on Him. Thus He prepares them to fill positions of trust and to accomplish the great purpose for which their powers were given them.

In all ages God's witnesses have exposed themselves to reproach and persecution. Joseph was maligned and persecuted because he preserved his virtue and integrity. David was hunted like a beast of prey by his enemies. Daniel was cast into a den of lions. Job was so afflicted in body that he was abhorred by his relatives and friends. Jeremiah's testimony so enraged the king and princes that he was cast into a loathsome pit. Stephen was stoned. Paul was imprisoned, beaten, stoned, and finally put to death. And John was banished to Patmos.

These examples of human steadfastness bear witness to God's abiding presence and sustaining grace. They testify to the power of faith to withstand the powers of the world. In the darkest hour our Father is at the helm.

Jesus calls on His people to follow Him in the path of self-denial and reproach. He was opposed by evil men and evil angels in an unpitying confederacy. His unlikeness to the world provoked the bitterest hostility. So it will be with all who are imbued with the Spirit of Christ. The character of the persecution changes with the times, but the spirit that underlies it is the same that has slain the chosen of the Lord ever since the days of Abel.

Satan has tortured and put to death the people of God, but in dying they bore witness to the power of One mightier than Satan. Wicked men cannot touch the life that is hid with Christ in God. Prison walls cannot bind the spirit.

Believers in Christ, persecuted by the world, are educated and disciplined in the school of Christ. On earth they follow Christ through sore conflicts; they endure self-denial and bitter disappointments; but thus they learn the woe of sin, and they look on it with abhorrence. Being partakers of Christ's sufferings, they look beyond the gloom to the glory, saying, "I consider that the sufferings of this present time are not worth comparing with the glory that is to be revealed to us." Romans 8:18, RSV.

57/ John Sees the Visions of the Revelation

So untiringly did the Christians in the days of the apostles labor that notwithstanding fierce opposition, in a short time the gospel was sounded to all the inhabited earth. Their zeal has been recorded for the encouragement of believers in every age. The Lord Jesus used the church at Ephesus as a symbol of the church in the apostolic age:

"I know your works, your toil and your patient endurance, and how you cannot bear evil men but have tested those who call themselves apostles but are not, and found them to be false; I know you are enduring patiently and bearing up for My name's sake, and you have not grown weary." Revelation 2:2, 3, RSV.

At first the believers sought to obey every word of God. Filled with love for their Redeemer, their highest aim was to win souls. They did not think of hoarding the precious treasure of the grace of Christ. Weighted with the message, "Peace on earth, good will toward men," they burned with desire to carry the glad tidings to earth's remotest bounds. Sinful men, repentant, pardoned, cleansed and sanctified, were brought into partnership with God. In every city the work was carried forward. Souls were converted who, in their turn, felt they could not rest till the light was shining on others. Inspired personal appeals were made to the erring, to the outcast.

But after a time the believers' zeal and love for God and for one another grew less. One by one the old stan-

dard-bearers fell at their post. Some of the younger
workers who might have shared the burdens of these
pioneers, and thus have been prepared for wise leadership, became weary of oft-repeated truths. In their desire for something novel and startling, they attempted
to introduce doctrine not in harmony with the fundamental principles of the gospel. In their spiritual blindness they failed to discern that these sophistries would
cause many to question the experiences of the past,
and thus would lead to confusion and unbelief.

The Revelation Comes When Needed

As false doctrines were urged, differences sprang
up. The discussion of unimportant points occupied
time that should have been spent in proclaiming the
gospel. The masses were left unwarned. Piety was rapidly waning, and Satan seemed about to gain the ascen-
dancy. At this critical time John was sentenced to banishment. Nearly all his former associates had suffered
martyrdom. To all outward appearance the day was
not far distant when the enemies of the church would
triumph.

But the Lord's hand was moving unseen in the darkness. John was placed where Christ could give him a
wonderful revelation of Himself and divine truth for
the churches. The exiled disciple received a message
the influence of which was to strengthen the church till
the end of time. Those who banished John became in-
struments in the hand of God to carry out Heaven's
purpose; and the very effort to extinguish the light
placed the truth in bold relief.

It was on the Sabbath that the Lord of glory appeared to the exiled apostle. The Sabbath was as sa-
credly observed by John on Patmos as when he was in
Judea. He claimed the precious promises given regarding that day. "I was in the Spirit on the Lord's day, and
heard behind me a great voice, as of a trumpet. . . .
And I turned to see the voice that spake with me. And
being turned, I saw seven golden candlesticks; and in

the midst of the seven candlesticks one like unto the Son of man." Revelation 1:10-13.

This beloved disciple had seen his Master in Gethsemane, His face marked with the blood drops of agony, His "visage . . . marred more than any man, and His form more than the sons of men." Isaiah 52:14. He had seen Him hanging on the cross, the object of mockery and abuse. Now John once more beholds his Lord. But He is no longer a man of sorrows, humiliated by men. He is clothed in a garment of heavenly brightness, "His eyes were as a flame of fire." Revelation 1:14. Out of His mouth issues a sharp two-edged sword, an emblem of the power of His word.

Then before John's wondering vision were opened the glories of heaven. He was permitted to see the throne of God, and looking beyond the conflicts of earth, to behold the white-robed throng of the redeemed. He heard the music of angels and the triumphant songs of those who had overcome by the blood of the Lamb. There was unfolded scene after scene of thrilling interest to the close of time. In figures and symbols, subjects of vast importance were presented, that the people of God in his age and in future ages might have guidance and comfort and an intelligent understanding of the perils and conflicts before them.

Sincere Students Can Understand Revelation

Religious teachers have declared that Revelation is a sealed book and its secrets cannot be explained. But God does not wish His people to regard the book thus. It is "the revelation of Jesus Christ, which God gave unto Him, to show unto His servants things which must shortly come to pass." "Blessed is he that readeth, and they that hear the words of this prophecy, and keep those things which are written therein: for the time is at hand." Verses 1, 3. "He which testifieth these things saith, Surely I come quickly." Revelation 22:20.

The very name given to its inspired pages, "the Revelation," contradicts the statement that this is a sealed book. A revelation is something revealed. Its truths are addressed to those living in the last days, as well as to those living in the days of John. Some of the scenes depicted are in the past, some are now taking place; some bring to view the close of the great conflict, and some reveal the joys of the redeemed in the earth made new.

Let none think it is useless for them to search this book to know the meaning of the truth it contains. Those whose hearts are open to truth will be enabled to understand its teachings.

In the Revelation all the books of the Bible meet and end. Here is the complement of the book of Daniel. One is a prophecy, the other a revelation. The book that was sealed is not the Revelation; the angel commanded, "But thou, O Daniel, shut up the words, and seal the book, even to the time of the end." Daniel 12:4.

"What thou seest, write in a book," Christ commanded John, "and send it unto the seven churches." "Write . . . the things which are, and the things which shall be hereafter. . . . The seven stars are the angels of the seven churches: and the seven candlesticks which thou sawest are the seven churches." Revelation 1:11, 19, 20.

The names of the seven churches are symbolic of the condition of the church in different periods of history. The number—seven—indicates completeness; the messages extend to the end of time.

Christ walks in the midst of the golden candlesticks. Thus is symbolized His constant communication with His people. He knows their true state, their order, their devotion. Although He is High Priest in the sanctuary above, He is represented as walking in the midst of His churches on earth. With unremitting vigilance He watches. If the candlesticks were left to mere human care, the flickering flame would languish and die, but He is the true warden. His continued care and sustaining grace are the source of life and light.

"These things saith He that holdeth the seven stars in His right hand." Revelation 2:1. These words are spoken to the teachers in the church—those entrusted with weighty responsibilities. The stars of heaven are under God's control. He fills them with light. He guides their movements. If He did not do this, they would become fallen stars. So with His ministers. Through them His light is to shine forth. If they will look to the Saviour as He looked to the Father, He will give them His brightness to reflect to the world.

Christ Preserves His Church Today

Early in the history of the church the mystery of iniquity foretold by Paul began its baleful work, and many were ensnared by false doctrines. At the time John was given this revelation, many had lost their first love of gospel truth. "Remember," God pleaded, "from whence thou art fallen, and repent, and do the first works." Verse 5.

The church needed stern reproof and chastisement. But always the rebuke that God sends is spoken in tender love, and with the promise of peace to every penitent believer. "If any man hear My voice, and open the door, I will come in to him, and will sup with him and he with Me." Revelation 3:20. The believers were admonished, "Be watchful, and strengthen the things which remain, that are ready to die." "I come quickly: hold that fast which thou hast, that no man take thy crown." Verses 2, 11.

Looking down through long centuries of darkness, the aged exile saw multitudes suffering martyrdom. But he saw also that He who sustained His early witnesses would not forsake His faithful followers during the centuries that must pass before the close of time. "Fear none of those things which thou shalt suffer," the Lord declared; "behold, the devil shall cast some of you into prison, that ye may be tried; and ye shall have tribulation: . . . be thou faithful unto death, and I will give thee a crown of life." Revelation 2:10.

John heard the promises: "To him that overcometh will I give to eat of the tree of life." "I will not blot out his name out of the book of life, but I will confess his name before My Father, and before His angels." I will "grant [him] to sit with Me in My throne." Revelation 2:7; 3:5, 21. John saw sinners finding a Father in Him of whom their sins had made them afraid.

The Saviour was presented before John under the symbols of "the Lion of the tribe of Judah," and of "a Lamb as it had been slain." Revelation 5:5, 6. These symbols represent the union of omnipotent power and self-sacrificing love. The Lion of Judah, terrible to the rejectors of God's grace, will be the Lamb of God to the faithful. The pillar of fire that speaks terror and wrath to the transgressor of God's law is a token of mercy and deliverance to those who have kept His commandments. God's angels "shall gather together His elect . . . , from one end of heaven to the other." Matthew 24:31.

When God's People Will Be the Majority

In comparison with the billions of the world, God's people will be a little flock; but God will be their refuge. When the sound of the last trump shall penetrate the prison house of the dead, and the righteous shall come forth, standing then with the loyal and true of all ages, the children of God will be far in the majority.

Christ's true disciples follow Him through self-denial and bitter disappointment; but this teaches them to look upon the guilt and woe of sin with abhorrence. Partakers of Christ's sufferings, they are destined to be partakers of His glory. In holy vision the prophet saw the ultimate triumph of God's remnant church.

"I saw as it were a sea of glass mingled with fire: and them that had gotten the victory . . . stand on the sea of glass, having the harps of God." Revelation 15:2.

"And I looked, and, lo, a Lamb stood on the Mount Sion, and with Him a hundred forty and four thousand, having His Father's name written in their foreheads."

Revelation 14:1. In this world they served God with the intellect and with the heart; and now He can place His name "in their foreheads." Christ welcomes them as His children, saying, "Enter thou into the joy of thy Lord." Matthew 25:21.

"These are they which follow the Lamb whithersoever He goeth." Revelation 14:4. But all who follow the Lamb in heaven must first follow Him on earth, not fretfully or capriciously, but in loving, willing obedience, as the flock follows the shepherd. "In their mouth was found no guile: for they are without fault before the throne of God." Verse 5.

"And I John saw the Holy City, New Jerusalem, coming down from God out of heaven, prepared as a bride adorned for her husband." Revelation 21:2.

"Blessed are they that do His commandments, that they may have right to the tree of life, and may enter in through the gates into the city." Revelation 22:14.

58/ A Glorious Future Is Before Us

More than eighteen centuries have passed since the apostles rested from their labors, but the history of their sacrifices for Christ is till among the most precious treasures of the church. As these messengers of the cross went forth to proclaim the gospel, there was such a revelation of the glory of God as had never before been witnessed. To every nation was the gospel carried in a single generation.

At the beginning, some of the apostles were unlearned men, but under the instruction of their Master they gained a preparation for the great work committed to them. Grace and truth reigned in their hearts, and self was lost sight of.

How closely they stood by the side of God and bound their personal honor to His throne! Any attack made on the gospel was as if cutting deep into their souls, and with every power they battled for the cause of Christ. They expected much, and they attempted much. Their understanding of truth and their power to withstand opposition were proportionate to their conformity to God's will. Jesus was the theme of every discourse. As they proclaimed Christ their words moved hearts, and multitudes who had reviled the Saviour's name now confessed themselves disciples of the Crucified.

The apostles encountered hardship, grief, calumny, and persecution; but they rejoiced that they were called to suffer for Christ. They were willing to spend and be spent, and the grace of heaven was revealed in the conquests they achieved for Christ.

On the foundation that Christ had laid, the apostles built the church. Peter says, "Come to Him, to that living stone, rejected by men but in God's sight chosen and precious; and like living stones be yourselves built into a spiritual house, to be a holy priesthood, to offer spiritual sacrifices acceptable to God through Jesus Christ." 1 Peter 2:4, 5, RSV.

In the quarry of the Jewish and the Gentile world the apostles labored, bringing out "stones" to lay on the foundation. Paul said, "You are . . . built upon the foundation of the apostles and prophets, Christ Jesus Himself being the cornerstone, in whom the whole structure is joined together and grows into a holy temple in the Lord." Ephesians 2:19-21, RSV.

"I laid a foundation, and another man is building upon it. Let each man take care how he builds upon it. For no other foundation can anyone lay than that which is laid, which is Jesus Christ." 1 Corinthians 3:10, 11, RSV.

The apostles built upon the Rock of Ages. To this foundation they brought the stones that they quarried from the world. Their work was made exceedingly difficult by the enemies of Christ. They had to contend against bigotry, prejudice, and hatred. Kings and governors, priests and rulers, sought to destroy the temple of God. But faithful men carried the work forward; and the structure grew, beautiful and symmetrical. At times the workmen were almost blinded by the mists of superstition around them or were almost overpowered by the violence of their opponents. But with faith and courage they pressed on.

One after another the builders fell. Stephen was stoned; James was slain by the sword; Paul was beheaded; Peter was crucified; John was exiled. Yet the church grew. New workers took the place of those who fell, and stone after stone was added to the building.

Centuries of fierce persecution followed, but always

there were men who counted the building of God's temple dearer than life itself. The enemy left nothing undone to stop the work committed to the Lord's builders. But God raised up workers who ably defended the faith. Like the apostles, many fell at their post, but the building of the temple went steadily forward.

The Waldenses, John Wycliffe, Huss and Jerome, Martin Luther and Zwingli, Cranmer, Latimer, Knox, the Huguenots, John and Charles Wesley, and a host of others, brought to the foundation material that will endure throughout eternity. And those who have so nobly promoted the circulation of God's Word and in heathen lands have prepared the way for the last great message—these also have helped to rear the structure.

We may look back through the centuries and see the living stones of which God's temple is composed gleaming like jets of light through the darkness. Throughout eternity these precious jewels will shine with increasing luster, revealing the contrast between the gold of truth and the dross of error.

How We Help the Building

Paul, the other apostles, and all the righteous since them, have acted their part in building the temple. But the structure is not yet complete. We who are living in this age are to bring to the foundation material that will stand the test of fire—gold, silver, and precious stones. To those who thus build for God, Paul speaks words of encouragement: "If the work which any man has built on the foundation survives, he will receive a reward. If any man's work is burned up, he will suffer loss, though he himself will be saved, but only as through fire." 1 Corinthians 3:14, 15, RSV. The Christian who faithfully presents the word of life is bringing to the foundation material that will endure, and in the kingdom he will be honored as a wise builder.

As Christ sent forth His disciples, so today He sends the members of His church. If they will make God their strength, they shall not labor in vain. God said to Jeremiah, "Do not say, 'I am only a youth'; for to all to whom I send you you shall go." Then the Lord touched His servant's mouth, saying, "Behold, I have put My words in your mouth." Jeremiah 1:7, 9, RSV. And He bids us go forth to speak the words He gives us, feeling His holy touch on our lips. There is nothing that the Saviour desires so much as agents who will represent to the world His Spirit and His character.

The church is God's agency for the proclamation of truth, and if she is loyal to Him, obedient to all His commandments, there is no power that can stand against her.

Zeal for God and His cause moved the disciples to witness to the gospel with mighty power. Should not a like zeal fire our hearts with a determination to tell the story of Christ and Him crucified? It is the privilege of every Christian, not only to look for, but to hasten the coming of the Saviour.

Nothing Can Stop the Triumph of Truth

If the church will put on the robe of Christ's righteousness, withdrawing from all allegiance with the world, there is before her the dawn of a glorious day. Truth, passing by those who reject it, will triumph. When the message of God meets opposition, He gives it additional force. Endowed with divine energy it will cut its way through the strongest barriers and triumph over every obstacle.

What sustained the Son of God during His life of toil and sacrifice? Looking into eternity, He beheld the happiness of those who through His humiliation had received pardon and everlasting life.

We may have a vision of the future, the blessedness of heaven. By faith we may stand on the threshold of the eternal city and hear the gracious welcome given those who in this life cooperate with Christ. As the words are spoken, "Come, ye blessed of My Father," they cast their crowns at the feet of the Redeemer, exclaiming, "Worthy is the Lamb that was slain to receive power, and riches, and wisdom, and strength, and honor, and glory, and blessing!" Matthew 25:34; Revelation 5:12.

Then the redeemed greet those who led them to the Saviour, and all unite in praising Him who died that human beings might have the life that measures with the life of God. The conflict is over. Songs of victory fill all heaven.

"These are they who have come out of the great tribulation; they have washed their robes and made them white in the blood of the Lamb. Therefore are they before the throne of God, and serve Him day and night within His temple; and He who sits upon the throne will shelter them with His presence. . . . The Lamb in the midst of the throne will be their Shepherd, and He will guide them to springs of living water; and God will wipe away every tear from their eyes." Revelation 7:14-17, RSV.

Something for you . . .

☐ Send me a free copy of *Signs of the Times*, the international prophetic monthly.

☐ Enroll me in one of your free Bible courses.

☐ I want information about the Five-Day Plan to Stop Smoking.

☐ I would like more information about the Bible prophecies of Daniel and Revelation.

☐ Send me the address of the nearest Adventist Church.

☐ I would like to know more about Seventh-day Adventists and what they believe.

Complete the coupon below, and mail to

Pacific Press Publishing Association
P.O. Box 7000, Boise, ID 83707

Name

Street or Box

City   State   Zip

For faster service call:
Alaska or Hawaii
   call toll free: 800-253-3002
Michigan call collect: 616-471-3522
Others call toll free: 800-253-7077

Something for you . . .

☐ Send me a free copy of *Signs of the Times*, the international prophetic monthly.

☐ Enroll me in one of your free Bible courses.

☐ I want information about the Five-Day Plan to Stop Smoking.

☐ I would like more information about the Bible prophecies of Daniel and Revelation.

☐ Send me the address of the nearest Adventist Church.

☐ I would like to know more about Seventh-day Adventists and what they believe.

Complete the coupon below, and mail to

Pacific Press Publishing Association
P.O. Box 7000, Boise, ID 83707

Name

Street or Box

City   State   Zip

For faster service call:
Alaska or Hawaii
  call toll free: 800-253-3002
Michigan call collect: 616-471-3522
Others call toll free: 800-253-7077

Something for you . . .